Star Wars:
The Essential Guide to
Vehicles and Vessels

Star Wars:
The Essential Guide to Vehicles and Vessels

by Bill Smith

Original Illustrations by Doug Chiang
Schematics by Troy Vigil

A Del Rey® Book
Ballantine Books • New York

A Del Rey® Book
Published by Ballantine Books

ISBN 0-345-39299-X (pbk.)

Interior and cover design by Michaelis/Carpelis Design Associates, Inc.
Cover art by Doug Chiang
Edited by Allan Kausch (Lucasfilm) and Steve Saffel (Del Rey)

Manufactured in the United States of America

Table of Contents

Acknowledgments

This book is a compilation of the ideas of many individuals whose visions have expanded a wonderful universe. Of course, it all began with George Lucas and the creative teams he assembled for each movie. Thanks also go out to (by category):

Novelists Timothy Zahn, Brian Daley, Kevin J. Anderson, Kathy Tyers, Dave Wolverton, Roger MacBride Allen, Steven Perry, Alan Dean Foster, and L. Neil Smith.

Comics creators (both past and current) Al Williamson, Archie Goodwin, Tom Veitch, Cam Kennedy, Chris Gossett, David Michelinie, Tom Palmer, Walter Simonson, and Jo Duffy.

My predecessors and coworkers for West End's roleplaying products, including Bill Slavicsek, Curtis Smith, Stephen Crane, Peter Schweighofer, Paul Sudlow, Eric Trautmann, Matt Hong, John Paul Lona, Allen Nunis, Michael Allen Horne, Greg Gorden, Paul Murphy, Douglas Kaufman, Grant Boucher, and Michael Stern.

The computer game creators in the LucasArts Design Team, including Lawrence Holland, Edward Kilham, Peter Lincroft, David Maxwell, David Wessman, Martin Cameron, Jim McLeod, Jon Knoles, Dave Bengel, John Bell, and Wade Lady. Thanks also go out to Rusel DeMaria and Ocean Quigley.

Starlog Technical Journal author Shane Johnson.

A personal round of thanks goes out to Allan Kausch, Sue Rostoni, and Lucy Autrey Wilson of Lucasfilm Licensing; Steve Saffel and Fred Dodnick of Del Rey Books; Daniel Scott Palter and Richard Hawran of West End Games; Timothy Zahn; and finally, Amy and my family for boundless support and encouragement.

—Bill Smith

Introduction

"Do you remember when you first saw *Star Wars*?"

Anyone who grew up in the late 1970s knows the answer to that question and it invariably evokes images of the cantina scene, Luke Skywalker gazing out at Tatooine's twin suns, and the dramatic space battle above the Death Star. However, the very *first* moment that grabbed us all was the scene when the Imperial Star Destroyer *Devastator*, seemingly *miles* long, rumbled overhead, turbolasers blasting away.

While the *Star Wars* movies form an epic myth about people and the challenges they must overcome, the starships and vehicles are virtually characters in their own right. George Lucas created a universe so vibrant that even the objects in it have a life of their own. The *Millennium Falcon*, "the fastest hunk of junk in the galaxy," is more than just an anonymous ship; it is a character with a personality, as are the droids Artoo-Detoo and See-Threepio. The Rebel Alliance's sleek X-wing and Y-wing fighters are breathtaking. The Rebel snowspeeder and AT-AT walkers are still stunning a decade and a half after the release of *The Empire Strikes Back*. And who can forget the spectacular battle aboard Jabba's sail barge in *Return of the Jedi*?

Star Wars: The Essential Guide to Vehicles and Vessels is a handbook for people who are fascinated by this technology. One of the most successful elements of the *Star Wars* movies is the illusion of reality—the sense that, if the camera were looking in a different direction, we would find other equally interesting characters, situations, and, of course, more ships and vehicles.

Through the various novels, comics, roleplaying games, computer games, and other sources, we've been introduced to many new vessels, each uniquely a part of the *Star Wars* universe. This book describes one hundred such vehicles—only a fraction of those so far created—in an effort to provide an overview of these amazing wonders.

From Luke Skywalker's landspeeder to the Death Star, from the opening credits of *Star Wars IV: A New Hope* to the final pages of the latest novels, games, and comics, these entries describe the vehicles and vessels from the most popular science fiction movie series in history . . . and perhaps they offer a few tantalizing glimpses of what is yet to come.

Enjoy, and may the Force be with you. (I just *had* to say it.)

Bill Smith
September 14, 1995

Timeline

This book includes many references to important events in *Star Wars* history. This timeline notes many of those events for easy referral. The common reference point is the Battle of Yavin, where Luke Skywalker destroyed the first Death Star, labeled here as "SW4" for *Star Wars IV: A New Hope*.

BSW4 = Before *Star Wars IV: A New Hope*
ASW4 = After *Star Wars IV: A New Hope*

25,000 years BSW4: The Old Republic is formed. Jedi Knights appear.

4,000 years BSW4: The Great Sith War. (Depicted in *Tales of the Jedi, Dark Lords of the Sith,* and *The Sith War.*)

29 years BSW4: Han Solo born in the Corellian star system.

Fall of the Republic: A dark period of corruption and social injustice sweeps through the Republic, paving the way for Senator Palpatine's rise to power.

18 years BSW4: Luke Skywalker and Leia Organa born and placed in hiding; Anakin Skywalker becomes Darth Vader; Jedi Knights hunted and killed; Palpatine becomes Emperor; Empire formed; first stirrings of rebellion begin.

1-5+ years BSW4: Han Solo and Chewbacca operate as smugglers. Their travels take them to the Corporate Sector, the Hutt-owned worlds of Nar Shaddaa and Nal Hutta, and other sections of the galaxy. (Depicted in *Han Solo at Stars' End, Han Solo's Revenge, Han Solo and the Lost Legacy, Dark Empire,* and *Tales from the Mos Eisley Cantina.*)

SW4: The Battle of Yavin. Luke Skywalker destroys the first Death Star. (Depicted in *Star Wars IV: A New Hope.*)

3 years ASW4: The Battle of Hoth. The main Rebel base is destroyed. Boba Fett captures Han Solo, while Luke Skywalker confronts Darth Vader. (Depicted in *Star Wars V: The Empire Strikes Back.*)

3-4 years ASW4: Galactic criminal leader Prince Xizor plots the death of Luke Skywalker. Leia Organa, Luke, and Lando Calrissian track Boba Fett, hoping to save Han Solo. (Depicted in *Shadows of the Empire.*)

4 years ASW4: Luke and Leia free Han Solo; Jabba the Hutt dies. Lando Calrissian and Admiral Ackbar lead the attack that destroys the second Death Star. Luke Skywalker confronts the Emperor and Darth Vader; Palpatine dies when Vader redeems himself and turns on his former master.

Luke Skywalker leads a Rebel fleet to Bakura, devastating an advance Ssi-ruuvi invasion force.

The New Republic created by declaration of Mon Mothma; the fledgling government begins the work of reuniting the galaxy.

(Depicted in *Star Wars VI: Return of the Jedi, The Truce at Bakura,* and the *Heir to the Empire Sourcebook.*)

8 years ASW4: The New Republic continues to unite the worlds of the galaxy under its rule. Hapan Prince Isolder seeks the hand of Princess Leia Organa in marriage. Warlord Zsinj killed over the planet Dathomir. Han Solo weds Leia Organa. (Depicted in *The Courtship of Princess Leia.*)

9 years ASW4: Grand Admiral Thrawn's campaign nearly succeeds in toppling the New Republic. Luke Skywalker confronts the mad Jedi Joruus C'Baoth. Smuggling leader Talon Karrde allies with the New Republic. Jacen and Jaina Solo born to Han Solo and Leia Organa Solo. (Depicted in *Heir to the Empire, Dark Force Rising,* and *The Last Command.*)

10 years ASW4: The remnants of the Empire, under the direction of a reincarnated Emperor Palpatine, reduces the New Republic's sphere of influence to less than half of the galaxy. Despite the introduction of many new weapons, such as World Devastators and tank droids, the Empire is defeated. (Depicted in *Dark Empire, Dark Empire II,* and *Empire's End.*)

11 years ASW4: Imperial forces from the secret Maw Installation, under the command of Admiral Daala, attack the New Republic using an experimental weapon named the Sun Crusher. The Imperial fleet is devastated and the Sun Crusher is destroyed, although Daala escapes. Luke Skywalker establishes his Jedi Praxeum (Academy) on Yavin Four. (Depicted in *Jedi Search, Dark Apprentice,* and *Champions of the Force.*)

A Layman's Guide to Technology

To primitive civilizations, the technology of the Old Republic, and of the later Empire and New Republic, might seem wondrous, even magical. The scientists of these early civilizations might decry the wonders of hyperdrive and repulsorlift drive as "impossible," obviously not realizing that, just because something is not understood, it is not impossible.

In the galaxy of the Empire and the New Republic, faster-than-light drives, antigravity vehicles, and energy weapons are more than just possible; they are taken for granted, and as predictable as gravity and the changing of the seasons.

Starships and vehicles are tools that are used every day. They get dinged and dented. Many of them need a new coat of paint. Pilots and mechanics make repairs as best they can, often using replacement parts and jury-rigged engineering that *might* make it through three or four more hyperspace jumps. Manufacturers produce "after-market kits" so ship owners can install shield generators and more powerful weapons. It's a common saying among freighter pilots that "There's no such thing as a 'stock' light freighter."

Of course, any specialized field is bound to have unique jargon. Here are some of the terms used in hangar bays around the galaxy.

CLASSES OF SHIPS

Capital Ship

The term "capital ship" refers to any military starship 100 meters or more in length. These ships tend to have large crews (Imperial Star Destroyers have maintained over 37,000 crewers aboard), with multiple turbolaser and laser cannons for deep-space battles. They are heavily armored, with powerful deflector shields and immense power generators. Many capital ships carry squadrons of starfighters within their hangars.

One of the smaller capital ships in this book is the Rebel Blockade Runner *Tantive IV*, which is a Corellian corvette. Medium-size capital ships in this book include the Carrack Cruiser, the Lancer Frigate, and the Nebulon-B Frigate. The Empire's Imperial Star Destroyers, Super Star Destroyers, and *Eclipse* Star Destroyer are among the largest capital ships.

Speeders

"Speeders" are high-speed ground vehicles which hover above a planet's surface. Luke Skywalker's landspeeder and the Rebel snowspeeder are two such examples.

Speeders and other levitating vehicles—such as skiffs and sail barges—all use a form of antigravity drive called "repulsorlift" to hover and fly. Many speeders also have ion-drive afterburners for high speed flight.

Starfighter

"Starfighters" are among the most glamorous starships in the *Star Wars* universe. The Rebel Alliance's X-wings, Y-wings, and A-wings, and the Empire's TIE fighters, are just a few of the many types of starfighters. Blindingly fast and heavily armed, starfighters do much of the fighting in space.

Transport

Any nonmilitary starship used to carry cargo or passengers is classified as a "transport." Transports range from small light freighters (like the Corellian YT-1300, of which the *Millennium Falcon* is one) to massive bulk transports and container ships, which can carry thousands of tons of cargo.

Most transports travel regular routes among several star systems. These ships form a vital link in the galactic economy. Transports are slow at both sublight and hyperdrive speeds and most have no weaponry or shielding to speak of. However, some transports are heavily modified with weapons, high-performance drives, and military-grade shield generators: again, the *Millennium Falcon* is one such ship. Pirates, smugglers, and Rebel sympathizers often modify their transports for combat.

COMMON TECHNOLOGIES

Hyperdrive

"Hyperdrive" is the miraculous technology which allows starships to enter the alternate dimension known as hyperspace and travel faster than the speed of light. Hyperdrive allows travel between the millions of settled worlds in the Empire.

Traveling in hyperspace can be quite dangerous—objects in our universe, or "realspace," produce "mass shadows" in hyperspace. Any ship striking a mass shadow in hyperspace is instantly destroyed. Starships have navigational "nav computers" (also nicknamed "navicomputers") to calculate safe travel routes through hyperspace, taking the ship around stars, planets, stray asteroids, and other stellar hazards. Once a ship has entered hyperspace, it cannot change course.

Hyperdrives are rated by "classes"; the lower the class, the faster the hyperdrive. Class Three and higher hyperdrives are common on civilian ships. Most military ships have Class Two or Class One hyperdrives. Some exceptional ships, such as the *Millennium Falcon* or Dash Rendar's *Outrider*, have exceptionally fast Class 0.75 or Class 0.5 hyperdrives.

Sublight Drives

Starships fly at slower-than-light speeds using "sublight drives." Sublight drives are used to propel a starship from a planetary surface into orbit, and from there into open space, where a ship can engage its hyperdrive. All starship battles take place at sublight speeds.

The most common sublight drive is the Hoersch-Kessel ion drive. This type of ion drive draws from power cells or generators to create a controlled fusion reaction. The reaction releases charged particles, which blast from the engines to provide thrust. Most ships rely on power cells, although the Hoersch-Kessel drive can be converted to use heavy metals, liquid reactants, or virtually any substance as fuel.

Repulsorlift Drives

"Repulsorlift drives" are the most common form of antigravity drive. Landspeeders, snowspeeders, sail barges, and cloud cars use repulsorlifts. Most starships also have repulsorlift drives for planetary landings and atmospheric flight.

Repulsorlifts use power supplied by a fusion generator to create an antigravity field which repels against a planet's gravity. The resulting field allows repulsorlift vehicles to hover and fly above a planet. Depending upon the drive, a vehicle's hovering altitude can range from a few centimeters above ground level to low orbit. The most powerful repulsorlift units can propel vehicles to speeds over 1,000 kilometers per hour, although many vehicles use ion afterburners to increase speeds. Repulsorlift drives do not work in space.

Weaponry

There are several common weapons used throughout the galaxy. With the continuing threat of pirates and the ongoing civil war between the forces of the Empire and the New Republic (formerly the Rebel Alliance), weapons are a virtual necessity for any starship.

Laser and Blaster Cannons

These are the most common weapons; blaster cannons are less powerful laser cannons and are used on vehicles. Laser cannons fire coherent packs of intense light energy which cause physical damage.

X-wings, TIE fighters, Rebel snowspeeders, AT-AT walkers, the *Millennium Falcon,* and most other vehicles and small starships have onboard laser or blaster cannons.

Turbolasers

Turbolasers are much more powerful versions of laser cannons; they are used by capital ships. Turbolasers require multiperson crews and large generators for power, but they can cut through the shields and armament of enemy capital ships.

The Death Star, Imperial Star Destroyers, Mon Calamari Star Cruisers, and most other capital ships have turbolasers.

Ion Cannons

Ion cannons are specialized versions of laser cannons. They penetrate shields, making them valuable weapons against heavily shielded vessels. Ion cannon blasts consist of high-energy ionized particles which disable electronic systems without causing physical damage. Ion cannons disable enemy ships so they can be captured intact.

Imperial Star Destroyers, Mon Calamari Star Cruisers, and many other starships have ion cannons.

Proton and Concussion Weapons

Proton torpedoes, concussion missiles, and bombs are weapons used by fighters, transports, and capital ships. These weapons are physical weapons, rather than blasts of energy. They can be used aboard any vehicle or vessel.

Luke Skywalker fired proton torpedoes down the Death Star's exhaust vent.

Tractor Beams

Tractor-beam projectors create powerful beams which can capture, stop, and reel in enemy starships. Since tractor beams are bulky, it is difficult to hit a ship with a tractor beam, but once a target ship is struck, escape is almost impossible.

The Imperial Star Destroyer *Devastator* captured Princess Leia's Rebel Blockade Runner *Tantive IV* with a tractor beam. Additionally, the Death Star captured the *Millennium Falcon* with a tractor beam.

Shields

There are two common types of shields: particle shields and ray/energy shields. Shield generators shroud starships and vehicles in fields of energy, absorbing energy blasts and physical attacks. Shields can absorb only a limited amount of energy before they burn out, but they provide significant protection while they last. Shields are found on almost all starships; vehicle shields are much weaker.

Particle shielding protects against physical objects, such as missiles, proton torpedoes, and space debris. Particle shields must be turned off to allow a vessel to fire its own missiles, or to launch or receive other vehicles.

Energy/ray shielding protects only against laser, blaster, and turbolaser attacks. Energy shields require significantly more power to maintain than particle shields and are normally raised only in combat.

Major Manufacturers

Thousands of companies manufacture starships, vehicles, replacement parts, or after-market upgrade kits. These companies range from sprawling supercorporations like Corellian Engineering Corporation to small, local companies like Pantolomin Shipwrights.

Ship entries in this book include the manufacturer wherever possible. If the entry is keyed to a specific vessel (such as the *Millennium Falcon* or *Slave I*) or uses a nickname, the ship type's formal name is listed in parentheses. Vehicles manufactured by a government—such as the Death Star and Imperial walkers—are not discussed here.

Alderaan Royal Engineers

- *Hosk Station* (*Delaya*-Class Space Station)

Alderaan Royal Engineers was a prominent starship manufacturing concern during much of the Old Republic's history. While the company had several successful designs in the fighter and capital warship markets, Alderaan Royal Engineers was most famous for its luxury yachts, deep-space stations, and exotic vessels. The company's once-grand luster faded in the latter years of the Old Republic as more aggressive companies like Kuat Drive Yards and Sienar Fleet Systems rose to prominence. The company was secretly part of the Royal House of Alderaan's rearmament program, but the company ceased operations after Alderaan's destruction.

Arakyd Industries

- Tank Droid (XR-85 Tank Droid)
- Probot (Viper Probe Droid)

Arakyd Industries is a major droid, heavy weapons, and starship manufacturer. The company developed its reputation through several high-profile military contracts with the Empire. Arakyd pioneered advances in artificial intelligence during the reign of the Emperor, its most noteworthy achievement being the Viper Probe Droid model, which the Empire used to discover the hidden Rebel base on the planet Hoth. The company designs starship components and complete designs, including the Helix starfighter. Despite the death of Emperor Palpatine, Arakyd remains a loyal Imperial company. With assistance from top Imperial Army advisers, Arakyd developed the XR-85 Tank Droid, which saw extensive use during the battle to retake Coruscant.

Aratech Repulsor Company

- Speeder Bike (74-Z Military Speeder Bike)

Aratech is a company made famous for its speeder-bike designs, particularly the Yellow Demon line and the 74-Z military speeder bike. Despite being a decade-old design, the 74-Z speeder bike remains a popular choice among both Imperial and New Republic forces due to its speed, maneuverability, and durability.

Bespin Motors

- Twin Pod Cloud Car (Storm IV)

Bespin Motors was formed specifically for the construction of Cloud City on Bespin. The company was founded as a subsidiary of Incom Corporation, but Bespin executives rigged a self-buyout shortly after the parent company was nationalized by the Empire. Bespin Motors pioneered the development of high-altitude cloud cars. While other companies now produce competing cloud car designs, Bespin Motors remains the dominant manufacturer.

Byblos Drive Yards

- *Marauder Starjacker* (E-2 Asteroid Miner)

Byblos Drive Yards (BDY) is a regional starship manufacturer based in the Colonies region of the galaxy. BDY's most successful product lines are its transports, freighters, and industrial mining and construction vessels. A BDY subsidiary, Byblos RepulsorDrive, provides Combat Cloud Cars and airspeeders for Imperial, New Republic, and planetary police forces.

Core Galaxy Systems

- *Enforcer One* (Dreadnaught)

Core Galaxy Systems was one of the famed "founding shipwrights" of the Old Republic. Like Alderaan Royal Engineers and Rendili StarDrive, the company's history dates back over twenty millennia. Core Galaxy Systems fell on hard times five centuries prior to the Battle of Yavin and the company was bought out by Kuat Drive Yards, at which time the Core Galaxy Systems name was retired.

Corellia StarDrive

- *Nebulon Ranger* (*Coruscant*-Class Heavy Courier)

Corellia StarDrive was a company with a brief but spectacular history. Founded by a former executive of Corellian Engineering Corporation (CEC) one millennia prior to the Great Sith War, Corellia StarDrive developed several exceptionally successful ship designs in both the civilian and military markets. Corellia StarDrive warships carried the flag of the Old Republic Navy, much to the chagrin of CEC. However, the good times did not last forever—the company's entire senior design team was killed in a freak shuttle crash. It was a loss from which Corellia StarDrive was never able to recover and roughly two millennia after its founding, the company folded and was bought by CEC.

Corellian Engineering Corporation

- Dash Rendar's *Outrider* (YT-2400 Freighter)
- Escape Pod (Class-6 Escape Pod)
- *Hound's Tooth* (YV-666 Light Freighter)
- *Millennium Falcon* (YT-1300 Transport)
- Rebel Blockade Runner (Corvette)
- *Wild Karrde* (Action VI Transport)

Famous for fast, heavily armed, and easily modified starships, Corellian Engineering Corporation (CEC) is one of the galaxy's three largest starship manufacturers. (The other two are Kuat Drive Yards [KDY] and Sienar Fleet Systems [SFS].) CEC, however, has the distinction of owing its success to civilian sales, unlike KDY and SFS, both of which rely on Imperial military contracts.

Part of CEC's success can be attributed to geography—the Corellian worlds tend to produce some of the galaxy's top starship engineers and CEC has little trouble recruiting talented designers and engineers. The company's YT- and YV-freighters and Action transports are some of the most successful civilian designs in the galaxy. CEC's few military designs, particularly the corvette and gunship, are also quite successful.

Cygnus Spaceworks

- Imperial Landing Craft (*Sentinel*-Class landing craft; manufactured with Sienar Fleet Systems)

Cygnus Spaceworks is an important military starship manufacturer with strong ties to both Sienar Fleet Systems and the Imperial Navy. The company builds shuttle and landing-craft variants based on the Sienar Fleet Systems *Lambda*-Class shuttle. Cygnus also builds the *Alpha*-Class Xg-1 Star Wing assault gunboat and *Delta*-Class JV-7 "Escort Shuttle." Cygnus remains an Imperial-allied corporation and produces many cutting-edge designs for the Imperial Navy.

Damorian Manufacturing Corporation

- Carrack Cruiser

Damorian Manufacturing Corporation is a small starship company based on the planet Esseles, on the edge of the Core Worlds. Damorian's main claim to fame is the Carrack light cruiser, which has proven more successful as a marketing tool than a means of securing military contracts. Damorian has successful freighter, bulk transport, and starfighter lines.

FreiTek, Inc.

- E-wing Fighter

FreiTek, Inc. is a pro–New Republic military starship manufacturer founded by the design team that created the X-wing fighter. These designers, former Incom Corporation employees who defected to the Rebel Alliance before the Battle of Yavin, started the company to fill the New Republic's need for superior starfighters. The company's first design was the E-wing fighter, which was introduced during Grand Admiral Thrawn's campaign against the New Republic. With the success of the E-wing, FreiTek increased the size of its design department and continues to work on new fighter designs for the New Republic.

Gallofree Yards, Inc.

- Rebel Transport (Medium Transport)

Gallofree Yards, Inc. was a small starship manufacturer that tried to compete in the crowded transport and freighter markets. Despite repeated product overhauls and slick marketing, the company seldom turned a profit. Gallofree went bankrupt several years prior to the Battle of Yavin; many of the company's remaining transports found their way into the Rebel Alliance's fleet.

Hapan Consortium

- *Hapes Nova*–Class Battle Cruiser

The Hapan Consortium is a privately owned company controlled by the Hapan Royal Family. Originating in the isolationist Hapan Cluster, the company's products are seldom seen in New Republic or Imperial space. The Consortium's designs have adequate hull integrity and shielding, but underpowered fusion generators combined with antiquated weapon designs make the Consortium's vessels vulnerable against comparable Imperial and New Republic ships.

Hoersch-Kessel Drive, Inc.

- *SunGem* (Master Arca's ship, *Delaya*-Class Courier)

Hoersch-Kessel Drive, Inc. (HKD) was once one of the most successful starship design firms in the Old Republic, and had the distinction of being wholly owned by Duros investors. When the company fell on hard times, HKD was sold off to a Nimbanese clan, which dismantled many of the company's less profitable divisions. However, the quest to develop a leaner bottom line destroyed morale, driving many designers to work for other starship firms. Hoersch-Kessel remains in business despite a succession of owners over the past few centuries, although the company is a shadow of its former self. HKD now specializes in constructing supertransports and container vessels, producing fewer than one hundred ships per standard year.

Incom Corporation

- I-7 Howlrunner
- Rebel Snowspeeder (T-47 "Snowspeeder")
- T-16 Skyhopper
- X-wing Fighter
- Y-4 "Raptor" Transport
- Z-95 Headhunter (manufactured with Subpro)

Incom Corporation has been a leading starship designer for nearly two millennia. The company counts the Z-95 Headhunter (jointly designed with Subpro Corporation), the T-16 Skyhopper, and the T-47 Airspeeder as being among the most successful of many profitable starship and vehicle designs. However, despite commercial success, Incom chose to ignore the changing political winds as the Old Republic became the Empire. Incom's designers, infuriated by the increasingly oppressive Imperial rule, defected to the Rebel Alliance, bringing with them the then-new T-65 fighter, dubbed the "X-wing." Incom Corporation was nationalized by direct order of the Emperor. Since that time, Incom has produced few new designs, instead concentrating on aftermarket modifications of existing designs and specialty products for the Imperial Navy. Incom reentered the starfighter market with the release of the I-7 Howlrunner shortly after Grand Admiral Thrawn's campaign, but the company's onetime Rebel sympathies have not endeared "The New Incom" to skeptical Imperial commanders.

Koensayr

- Y-wing Fighter

Koensayr has long been a components manufacturer recognized for its excellent engine, weapon, shield, and sensor designs. The company can boast of having equipment in nearly one-fifth of all starships in production. The company has produced a few starships and vehicles over the years, including the famous Y-wing fighter and the *Sigma*-Class shuttle. Koensayr continues to manufacture vehicles and ships for recreational and military markets, although parts sales constitute nearly 72 percent of the company's profits.

Kuat Drive Yards

- A-9 Vigilance
- Eclipse Star Destroyer
- *Executor* (Super Star Destroyer)
- Imperial Star Destroyer
- Juggernaut (HAVw A5 Juggernaut)
- Lancer Frigate
- Rebel Cruiser (Nebulon-B Frigate)

Kuat Drive Yards (KDY) ranks with Corellian Engineering Corporation and Sienar Fleet Systems as one of the "top three" starship manufacturers in the Empire. The company's designs include the Imperial Star Destroyer and the Super Star Destroyer, the two starships most indicative of the Empire's incredible military might. Even with the rise of the New Republic, Kuat remains allied with the many Imperial factions, producing the Eclipse Star Destroyer and the A-9 Vigilance starfighter.

Kuat Systems Engineering

- CloakShape Fighter
- *Slave I* (*Firespray*-Class Patrol and Attack Ship)

Kuat Systems Engineering was a short-lived subsidiary of Kuat Drive Yards (KDY) during the waning days of the Old Republic. Despite several critically successful designs, including the CloakShape fighter and the Firespray patrol and attack ship, the company's lack of commercial success led to its being reorganized back under the KDY banner and dedicated to after-market starship upgrade kits. Shortly before the death of the Emperor at Endor, Kuat Systems Engineering was sold to a group of investors thought to be Imperial loyalists. Only years later was it revealed that the buyers were Vaathkree merchants with strong Rebel sympathies. The new Kuat Systems Engineering is a pro–New Republic company, although its Vaathkree owners demand top prices.

MandalMotors

- Prince Xizor's *Virago* (StarViper)
- *Slave II* (Pursuer Enforcement Ship)

With a rich legacy of exceptional starships, MandalMotors is a Mandalorian company with an outstanding reputation for its military designs. Only after an Imperial "adviser" was placed on MandalMotors' executive board was the company allowed to conduct normal business in the Empire. After the death of the Emperor, MandalMotors installed a new pro–New Republic executive board and the company is developing into a valuable military supplier for New Republic worlds.

Mobquet Swoops and Speeders

- *Starlight Intruder* (Medium Transport)
- Swoop (Flare-S Swoop)

A subdivision of the immensely powerful Tagge Company (TaggeCo.), Mobquet manufactures landspeeders, airspeeders, and many other repulsorlift vehicles. Mobquet's many swoop models, from the powerful Nebulon-Q racer to the advanced Flare-S, rank among the most popular swoops for sale. Mobquet's success in Core swoop-racing leagues enhances the company's reputation.

Mon Calamari

- Mon Cal Cruiser (MC80 Star Cruiser)
- *Mon Remonda* (MC80B Star Cruiser)

The Mon Calamari design and build their own starships in shipyards orbiting their homeworld of Calamari. Over the past decade, Mon Calamari Star Cruisers have been the cornerstone of the Rebel Alliance and New Republic fleets. The Mon Calamari also produce their own transports and freighters.

Olanjii/Charubah

- Hapan Battle Dragon

One of the primary military starship designers in the Hapan Cluster, Olanjii/Charubah produces vehicles and vessels for the Hapan Royal Family, as well as other Hapan interests. Olanjii/Charubah is so favored by the Royal Family that the company was granted the contract for the main cruisers in the Hapan fleet, the famed Hapan Battle Dragons.

Pantolomin Shipwrights

- *Coral Vanda* (Cruiser)

Pantolomin Shipwrights is a small, family-owned ship construction firm based in the space station Panto Prime. The company produces oceanic and surface luxury cruisers custom-built to exacting specifications. Pantolomin Shipwrights vessels feature a level of craftsmanship rarely found in mass-produced vessels and the company produces less than a dozen craft per standard year.

Rendili StarDrive

- Dreadnaught
- Victory Star Destroyer

Rendili StarDrive is a company whose origins date back to the founding of the Old Republic. The company reached its zenith in the past century, laying claim to such designs as the Victory Star Destroyer, the Dreadnaught, and the Mandalorian Dungeon Ships. While Rendili hasn't won a major military starship contract in over

a decade, it has spent a great deal of capital developing new ship designs, intriguing both New Republic and Imperial military strategists.

Republic Engineering Corporation

- Shieldship

Republic Engineering Corporation was founded in the years following the death of the Emperor. The company was financed by several of the New Republic's key corporate supporters, and the company's first product—the shieldships for the Nomad City mining colony on Nkllon—was commissioned by Lando Calrissian, hero of the Battle of Endor. Following the success of the shieldship design, Republic Engineering Corporation is now concentrating on specialty designs and its lines of short-range fighters and high-altitude combat speeders.

Republic Fleet Systems

- *Chu'unthor*

Republic Fleet Systems played a large role in Old Republic starship design for over fifteen millennia. The company was founded to design warships to counter the threat of Sith-backed uprisings in distant corners of the Old Republic. In time, the company expanded its operations to design exploration, transport, passenger, and colony vessels. In the final days of the Old Republic, Republic Fleet Systems was formally disbanded by decree of the Senate and most of the company's resources were absorbed by the Republic's Navy.

Republic Sienar Systems

- Marauder Corvette

The predecessor of Sienar Fleet Systems, Republic Sienar Systems was one of the most successful starship manufacturers in the Old Republic. Republic Sienar produced the first TIE fighter. Improvements in this design led to the TIE and TIE/ln fighters. Republic Sienar Systems was renamed Sienar Fleet Systems after the collapse of the Old Republic.

Santhe/Sienar Technologies, Sienar Army Systems

- TIE Crawler (Century Tank)

Formerly known as Sienar Technologies, Santhe/Sienar Technologies is the parent corporation of Sienar Fleet Systems. Prior to the Battle of Endor, Santhe/Sienar concentrated on civilian starship manufacturing and replacement components, although it also had a large stake in the military market through Sienar Fleet Systems. As the market for new military hardware grew during the prolonged warfare after the Battle of Endor, Santhe/Sienar finally entered the military market using the brand name Sienar Army

Systems. The company's first major military success was the TIE Crawler, which saw extensive use during the Empire's campaign to retake Coruscant from the New Republic.

SedriMotors Ltd.

- Amphibion

SedriMotors Ltd. is a New Republic–allied company founded by the Sedrians, an aquatic species native to the planet Sedri, who were saved from extinction by a small Rebel strike team. The Sedrians joined the Rebel Alliance, adopting galactic-standard technology. SedriMotors is the most successful Sedrian company and it specializes in aquatic and oceanic vehicles, including combat repulsorcraft and deep-water combat pods. SedriMotors uses many unusual drive systems, including hydro-jets and hover propulsion drives.

Sienar Fleet Systems

- Darth Vadar's TIE Fighter (TIE Advanced x1 Prototype)
- Imperial Landing Craft (Sentinel-Class Landing Craft; manufactured with Cygnus Spaceworks)
- Interdictor Cruiser (Immobilizer 418)
- Lambda-Class Shuttle
- Scimitar Assault Bomber
- Skipray Blastboat (GAT-12h)
- TIE Bomber
- TIE Defender
- TIE/D Fighter
- TIE Fighter (TIE/In)
- TIE Interceptor

Sienar Fleet Systems (SFS) is a prime military contractor and the manufacturer of the Empire's TIE fighters. A subsidiary of Santhe/Sienar Technologies, SFS is acknowledged as one of the dominant fighter manufacturers in the galaxy, although the success of the Skipray Blastboat and the Interdictor Cruiser makes the company a major player in the capital ship market, as well. Sienar's most recent design is the Scimitar Assault Bomber, yet another stunning success for the company.

Slayn & Korpil

- B-wing Fighter
- Expanded B-wing (B-wing/E2 Assault Fighter)
- V-wing Airspeeder

Slayn & Korpil is a Verpine Hive colony company based in the Roche Asteroid Field, home system of the insectoid Verpine species. Slayn & Korpil has been allied with the Rebel cause since the days following the Battle of Yavin, and the company worked closely with then-Commander Ackbar to develop the B-wing fighter. Slayn & Korpil produces at least three standard B-wings (the B-wing, the B-wing/E, and the B-wing/E2) in addition to several limited-production B-wing units. The company's other main military vehicle used by the New Republic is the V-wing combat airspeeder, which played a key role in the Battle of Calamari.

SoroSuub

- Flurry (Quasar Fire–Class Bulk Cruiser)
- Lady Luck (Personal Luxury Yacht 3000)
- Lars Family Landspeeder (V-35 Courier)
- Luke Skywalker's Landspeeder (X-34)
- XP-38 Sport Landspeeder

SoroSuub is a prominent corporation based on the Outer Rim Territories world of Sullust. SoroSuub produces an incredible variety of goods, including foodstuffs, droids, and weapons, in addition to its many starship and vehicle designs. SoroSuub also has valuable interests in mining and mineral processing. When the Empire cracked down on rebellious worlds shortly after the Battle of Yavin, SoroSuub's board of directors took control of Sullust, although the company and the Sullustan people allied with the Rebel Alliance shortly before the Battle of Endor. As the Empire crumbled following Emperor Palpatine's death, SoroSuub became an important ally of the New Republic government.

Ssi-ruuvi

- Battle Droid (Swarm-Class Battle Droid)
- Picket Ship (Fw'Sen-Class Picket Ship)
- Sh'ner Planetary Assault Carrier
- Shriwirr (Shree Battle Cruiser)

Ssi-ruuvi starships are manufactured by the mysterious Ssi-ruuk aliens, who inhabit a remote stellar cluster beyond the boundaries of the Empire. The Ssi-ruuk rely on primitive fusion drives to power their starships. To supplement their energy resources, they use the unusual and disturbing entchment process to draw life energies from captured enemies. As a result, they favor ion cannons and tractor beams so they can capture enemy starships and imprison and entech their crews.

Subpro Corporation

- Z-95 Headhunter (manufactured with Incom Corporation)

Subpro Corporation is a large starship manufacturer based in the Inner Rim. While its designs, including the famed Z-95 Headhunter, are of good quality, its location, far from the Core Worlds, has virtually assured the company "second-class" status in the eyes of most military and civilian purchasers. However, the company's designs, from its nimble sublight fighters to its large and medium combat cruisers, are "undiscovered gems" which offer excellent performance at a competitive price. While its freighters lag behind those produced by Corellian Engineering

Corporation, Subpro's designs are favored by the notoriously independent captains who fly the starlanes in the galaxy's backwaters.

SURRONIAN

- Guri's *Stinger* (Conqueror Assault Ship)

Starships of Surronian design are more than mere vehicles—they are artifacts. Every Surronian vessel is built by a hive's crafts-guild with technology developed solely by the Surronians. These ships are bequeathed to the favored offspring of a guildmember so that the young guild-apprentice may acquire knowledge and artifacts to merit the child's acceptance into a Surronian guild. Outsiders are never sold these vessels, although the ships may be given in thanks for rare and valuable gifts.

TAGGECO. (THE TAGGE COMPANY)

- Swoop (Air-2 Swoop)

The Tagge Company (TaggeCo.) is one of the most powerful and diverse corporations in the galaxy. Owned by the influential House of Tagge, TaggeCo. has subsidiaries in virtually every segment of the galactic economy. With close ties to the Imperial military through the late General Tagge—who served aboard the first Death Star—TaggeCo. is a company with tremendous clout. While TaggeCo. also owns Mobquet Speeders and Swoops, Tagge Industries, and Trast Heavy Transports, the parent company produces several vehicle lines under the TaggeCo. brand name.

TENLOSS SYNDICATE

- Hornet Interceptor

The Tenloss Syndicate is a powerful criminal organization with the industrial resources to design and build its own starfighters and heavy-combat vehicles. The Syndicate is based in the lawless Bajic sector, but its operations extend to over sixty different star systems in the Outer Rim Territories. Tenloss controls at least a dozen front companies in fields as diverse as entertainment, cargo hauling, and business management. Tenloss also has close ties to the powerful Hutt crime clans.

TRANSGALMEG INDUSTRIES, INC.

- *Hyperspace Marauder* (*Xiytiar*-Class Transport)

TransGalMeg Industries, Inc., commonly known as TGM, is similar to TaggeCo. in that it has many different types of product lines. TGM has strong colonization, mining, and agricultural interests. Its starship and vehicle product divisions were originally founded to design products for TGM's own internal use—only after the product lines were proven reliable were they sold to the general public.

TRILON, INC.

- *IG-2000* (Aggressor Assault Fighter)

Trilon, Inc. is just one of many small companies that produce fewer than a dozen different designs. Due to the very limited production runs, buyers can specify custom modifications to a degree not offered by most larger companies. While Trilon's starship hulls are self-designed, the company purchases most of its components from large suppliers like Kuat Drive Yards, Arakyd, and Santhe/Sienar Technologies. As a result, buyers can "mix and match" ship systems, including engines, weapons, and sensors, to optimize performance.

UBRIKKIAN

- Combat Cloud Car (Talon I Combat Cloud Car)
- Desert Skiff (Bantha II Cargo Skiff)
- Hutt Caravel (Seltiss-2 Caravel)
- Jabba the Hutt's Sail Barge (Luxury Sail Barge)
- Jabba the Hutt's Space Cruiser (Luxury Space Yacht)

Ubrikkian is one of the larger manufacturers in the speeder market, with best-selling designs in the skiff, sail barge, land-speeder, cloud car, and speeder bike markets. The company also offers several military vehicles, including the infamous Floating Fortress combat landspeeder favored by the Empire for urban operations.

UULSHOS MANUFACTURING

- Chariot LAV (LAVr QH-7 Chariot)

Uulshos Manufacturing is a military and civilian vehicle manufacturer best known for its Chariot LAV military speeder and the Storm Skimmer patrol sled. Currently Uulshos designs cheap, unexceptional vehicles that are affordable for militias and defense forces on poor backwater worlds. The company has a limited line of transports which can be outfitted for cargo hauling, scouting, or passenger-liner duty.

Star Wars:
The Essential Guide to
Vehicles and Vessels

STAR WARS

AT-AT WALKER

IMPERIAL ALL TERRAIN ARMORED TRANSPORT WALKER

Among the most awesome vehicles in the Empire's ground combat forces, All Terrain Armored Transports (AT-ATs) were unmatched by anything in the Alliance's arsenal. At twenty meters long and over fifteen meters tall, these four-legged monsters towered over the galaxy's battlefields and resembled ancient beasts of war.

Walkers were designed to fill the need for a nonrepulsorlift heavy assault vehicle for armored platoons. While the Empire had countless repulsorlift vehicles, drive systems could be foiled by gravity fluctuations, unusual planetary magnetic fields, and other special conditions; the Empire needed a vehicle which could be used on any terrain on millions of different worlds. Designers turned to ancient technology, which had received limited use in older vehicles, such as the Old Republic's All Terrain Personal Transport (AT-PT), but had never been applied on such a large scale for combat vehicles.

The finished AT-AT walkers surpassed Imperial expectations. Almost unstoppable as weapons platforms, they proved potent psychological weapons.

AT-ATs were virtually impervious to all but heavy artillery weapons. Walkers formed the core of many Imperial heavy ground assaults, often the first vehicles to leave their transport shuttle barges or drop ships and enter a combat zone. AT-AT walkers were used to crush and demoralize enemy forces. They also acted as transports for Imperial ground troops and light vehicles.

A walker's movable "head" section contains the command cockpit, with room for the commander, pilot, and gunner. It also houses all the walker's weapons. Holographic targeting systems assist the gunners with a 360-degree view of their position.

The AT-AT's main weapons are two heavy laser cannons mounted on the "chin." Two medium blasters are mounted on each side of the head. They can be independently rotated for different targets. The head can rotate as much as ninety degrees right or left and thirty degrees up or down for a large field of fire.

AT-AT walkers have an immense armored body section that carries five speeder bikes and up to forty troops (normally stormtroopers or Imperial Army assault troopers). To unload troops, AT-AT walkers kneel to three meters above

ground level and sliding ramps on the main body section extend to the ground for exiting. Instead of troops and bikes, an AT-AT walker may be loaded with two AT-ST (All Terrain Scout Transport) walkers.

Beneath the main body section are the AT-AT's two immense drive motors. Four massive legs propel the walker at a top ground speed of up to sixty kilometers per hour, although this is possible only on flat, stable terrain. While their immense size gives the illusion that they are slow, plodding vehicles, Rebel troops reported that "walkers are upon you before you know it."

Imperial AT-ATs draw components from a number of different corporations but are assembled under strict Imperial military supervision at Kuat Drive Yards factories. Known AT-AT factories are on Kuat, Carida, and Belderone; several more are suspected to exist.

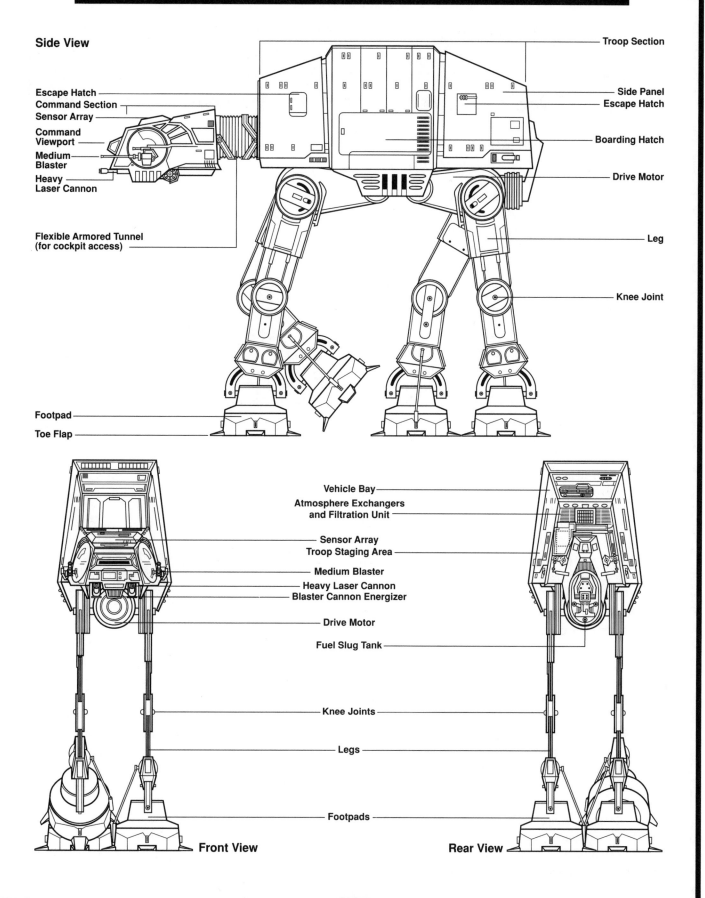

Side View

Escape Hatch
Command Section
Sensor Array
Command Viewport
Medium Blaster
Heavy Laser Cannon

Flexible Armored Tunnel (for cockpit access)

Footpad
Toe Flap

Troop Section
Side Panel
Escape Hatch
Boarding Hatch
Drive Motor
Leg
Knee Joint

Vehicle Bay
Atmosphere Exchangers and Filtration Unit
Sensor Array
Troop Staging Area
Medium Blaster
Heavy Laser Cannon
Blaster Cannon Energizer
Drive Motor
Fuel Slug Tank
Knee Joints
Legs
Footpads

Front View

Rear View

AT-PT TRANSPORT

IMPERIAL ALL TERRAIN PERSONAL TRANSPORT

The All Terrain Personal Transport (AT-PT) was an experimental one-man walker originally designed by the *Old* Republic. This two-legged walker stands nearly three meters tall and was designed to turn a single soldier into an armed force that could stop a full squad of opponents. Ultimately, the AT-PT project was canceled, although Imperial engineers later used many of its concepts when they created the All Terrain Armored Transport (AT-AT) and the All Terrain Scout Transport (AT-ST).

The AT-PT was intended to be a major component of the Republic's ground forces. AT-PTs cannot match the speed of repulsorcraft, but they can be devastating against conventional ground forces. Project designers developed the vehicle to be suitable for open ground, shallow water, jungle, mountain terrain, and urban areas. The independently adjusting leg suspension system allows the walker to scramble over inclines and obstacles that block repulsorlift and treaded vehicles.

The AT-PT features a central command pod and two side-mounted legs. The legs can be fully extended upward for high-speed movement or to give the driver a better observation position. In cramped conditions the AT-PT moves in a "half crouch," with the command pod lowered to be even with the legs' drive joints. This drive system gives the light walker superior balance compared with the larger AT-ST. The AT-PT can reach a top speed of sixty kilometers per hour in open terrain, and its drive unit can handle up to forty-five-degree inclines.

The command pod is heavily armored, giving the driver outstanding protection. Entered from small side hatches, the cramped cockpit is designed for a single driver, but in an emergency an extra passenger can be carried. When sealed, the craft is virtually impenetrable by small-arms fire. The pod has a primitive sensor system for navigation. In addition to the cramped pilot compartment, the command pod holds the weapon systems and the main drive unit. Standard weaponry for an AT-PT includes a twin blaster cannon and a concussion-grenade launcher.

The Republic planned to assign platoons of soldiers to AT-PTs, thus giving a single platoon the firepower of nearly a company of ground soldiers: AT-PT platoons were to be equivalent to light mechanized infantry units, but at a sub-

stantially reduced price. And, with the speed of the AT-PTs, plus their extended comlink ranges, the platoon could patrol a far larger area than could comparable ground forces.

AT-PTs were never given the thorough battlefield testing they deserved. The majority of the Republic's AT-PTs were stored aboard the *Katana* Dreadnaughts: when those ships disappeared, momentum for furthering the AT-PT project vanished. AT-PTs were rediscovered when New Republic forces found the lost *Katana* fleet. While aboard one of those Dreadnaughts, Luke Skywalker and Han Solo used an AT-PT to fend off Grand Admiral Thrawn's clone stormtroopers, thus beginning a new chapter in the history of the All Terrain Personal Transport.

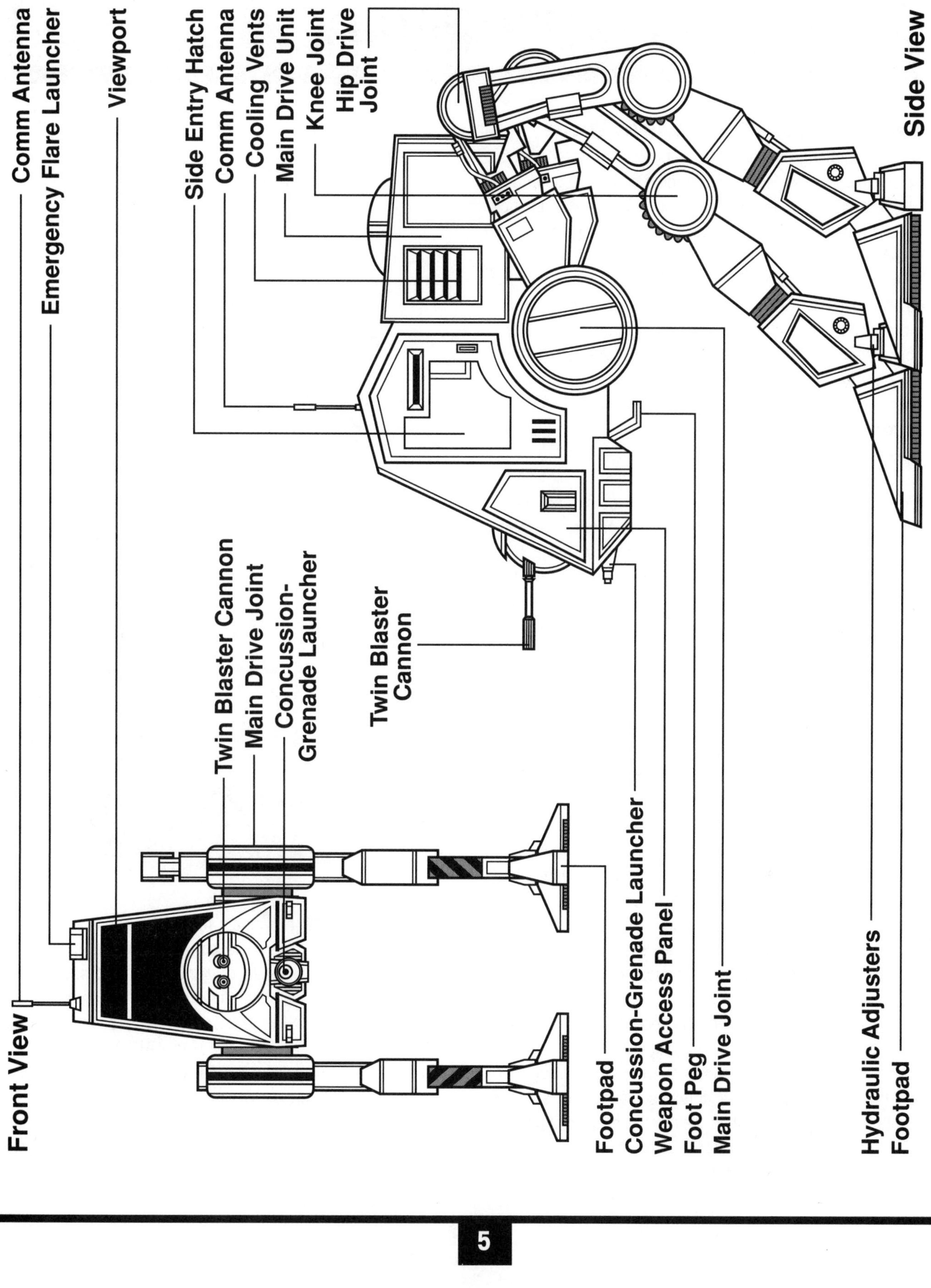

Front View

- Comm Antenna
- Emergency Flare Launcher
- Viewport
- Twin Blaster Cannon
- Main Drive Joint
- Concussion-Grenade Launcher
- Twin Blaster Cannon

Side View

- Side Entry Hatch
- Comm Antenna
- Cooling Vents
- Main Drive Unit
- Knee Joint
- Hip Drive Joint

- Footpad
- Concussion-Grenade Launcher
- Weapon Access Panel
- Foot Peg
- Main Drive Joint

- Hydraulic Adjusters
- Footpad

AT-ST WALKER

IMPERIAL ALL TERRAIN SCOUT TRANSPORT WALKER

Light scouting and perimeter vehicles that were used by the Empire, the two-legged All Terrain Scout Transports (AT-STs) are small, agile walkers. Their primary uses include scouting, perimeter defense, and support for Imperial troops and AT-AT walkers.

AT-STs rely on agility rather than heavy armor for defense. Their two-legged drive system means that they are more easily unbalanced than AT-ATs, but they are considerably faster, with a top speed of ninety kilometers per hour. They are devastating in combat, especially against infantry troops and light repulsorcraft. While smaller than four-legged AT-AT walkers, AT-STs are still intimidating at 8.6 meters tall.

AT-STs have a crew of only two persons: a pilot and a gunner. Armor plating protects the entire command cabin, with closable viewports for both pilot and gunner. As in the AT-AT, a holographic targeting system provides a 360-degree view of the battlefield as well as range and targeting information.

The head can turn independently of the drive and leg mechanism to fire in all directions. The primary weapons are chin-mounted twin blaster cannons with a maximum range of two kilometers. Twin light blasters are mounted on the port side, while a concussion-grenade launcher is located on the starboard side of the vehicle: both weapons are particularly useful against ground troops. Cutting claws on each leg can slice through fences and other obstacles.

AT-ST walkers have a single drive system to power their legs. An advanced gyro system maintains balance, although the unit is susceptible to damage or collapse. While the AT-ST is excellent on open ground, it can be slowed or even dangerously unbalanced by dense foliage, uneven terrain, or hidden traps. The drive system is entirely exposed to enemy fire if troops are able to get close enough for pinpoint targeting.

AT-STs are excellent patrol vehicles and often are deployed alone for scouting and reconnaissance duties. They can provide covering fire for advancing ground-troops, and the drive unit allows them to work through terrain that would stop traditional repulsorlift vehicles such as combat landspeeders. When they are used in conjunction with AT-AT walkers, their maneuverability allows them to cover the larger walkers' flanks.

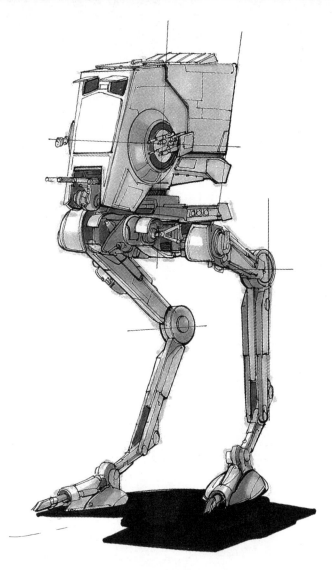

Access is through a single hatch at the top of the command cabin. Crew members can climb up the side of the walker by using a series of handholds, but specialized loading platforms are generally used at military bases.

A number of AT-ST walker variants have been produced. Most notable are the medium All Terrain Scout Transport/Assault walkers (AT-ST/As). They are significantly larger than standard AT-STs and are over ten meters tall. They carry a single heavy blaster cannon as the main weapon. They also have reinforced leg braces and a more advanced gyro balance system.

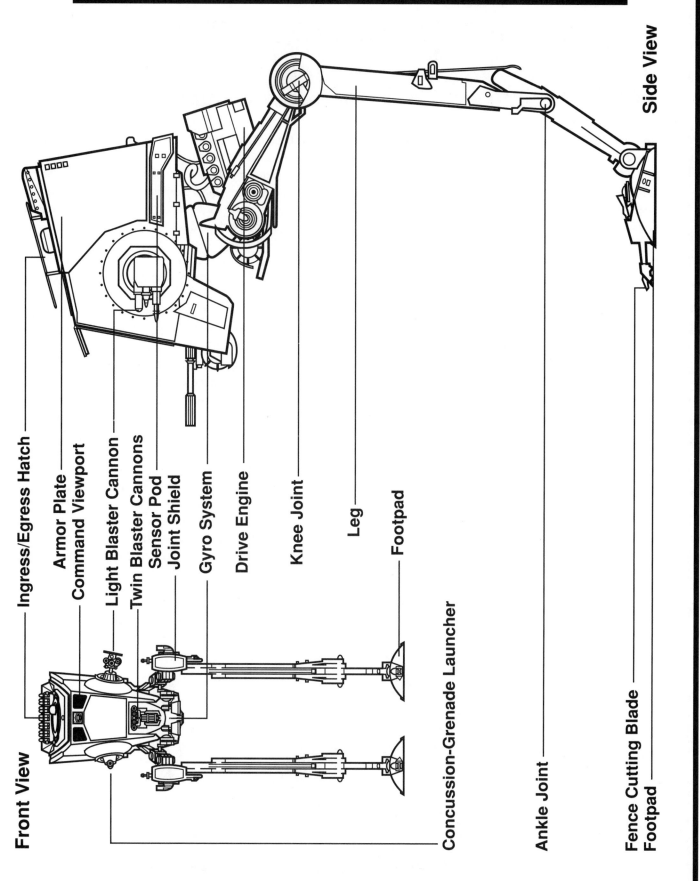

Side View

Front View

Ingress/Egress Hatch

Armor Plate
Command Viewport

Light Blaster Cannon
Twin Blaster Cannons
Sensor Pod
Joint Shield

Gyro System

Drive Engine

Knee Joint

Leg

Footpad

Concussion-Grenade Launcher

Ankle Joint

Fence Cutting Blade
Footpad

A-9 VIGILANCE

KUAT DRIVE YARDS A-9 VIGILANCE INTERCEPTOR

The A-9 Vigilance Interceptor is a short-range Imperial fighter that was introduced shortly after the defeat of Grand Admiral Thrawn, five years after the death of the Emperor at the Battle of Endor. Designed by Kuat Drive Yards, makers of the infamous Imperial Star Destroyer, the A-9 Vigilance represented an attempt by Kuat to steal some of the lucrative starfighter contracts Sienar Fleet Systems had received for its TIE fighter series.

While some Imperial factions purchased A-9s, the ship also fell into New Republic hands. Oppressed workers on a Kuat factory world managed to depose their planetary governor and turn a few A-9 prototypes over to the New Republic forces just as the Empire's offensive against Mon Calamari was heating up (a year after Thrawn's death).

The A-9 is typical of many Imperial fighters—it has no shields and no hyperdrive. Instead, it is compact, light, and fast and therefore was perfect for shock attacks against reinforced New Republic bases or slower capital ships and fighters. It is faster than the TIE interceptor and on a par with the New Republic's A-wing fighter.

The hull is a simple affair, with a central control cockpit pod that contains the Carbanti sensor arrays, weapons, and all computer systems. Two wings connect to the powerful KuatDriveSystems A-9x thrust engines. The engines are as long as the starframe

and have self-contained power generators. The laser cannons also have their own power generator, and the computer control system can reroute power from any of these generators to any other portion of the ship, allowing the pilot to cut power to the weapons and limp home even if the engine power generators fail (provided that the engines are still functional).

The A-9's weapons consist of two forward-firing laser cannons which pack more punch than do an X-wing's laser cannons. While they are generally fire-linked for simultaneous fire, a modification kit allows the laser cannons to be independently targeted. This kit includes a servo driver system that can depress the guns up to ninety degrees, making the A-9 capable of performing strafing missions against ground targets.

While Kuat Drive Yards promised the Empire a superior fighter, combat results have been consistently disappointing. While the ship is indeed faster than the TIE interceptor, it has been shown to be no more maneuverable, and its hull is actually significantly weaker. The Empire purchased a fighter that is as limited in its utility as is the New Republic's A-wing fighter. It is believed that Kuat designers are developing an *improved* A-9, which should be far tougher. New Republic technicians have thoroughly examined the A-9, and while not amazed by what they see, they intend to use some of its design elements in future New Republic fighters.

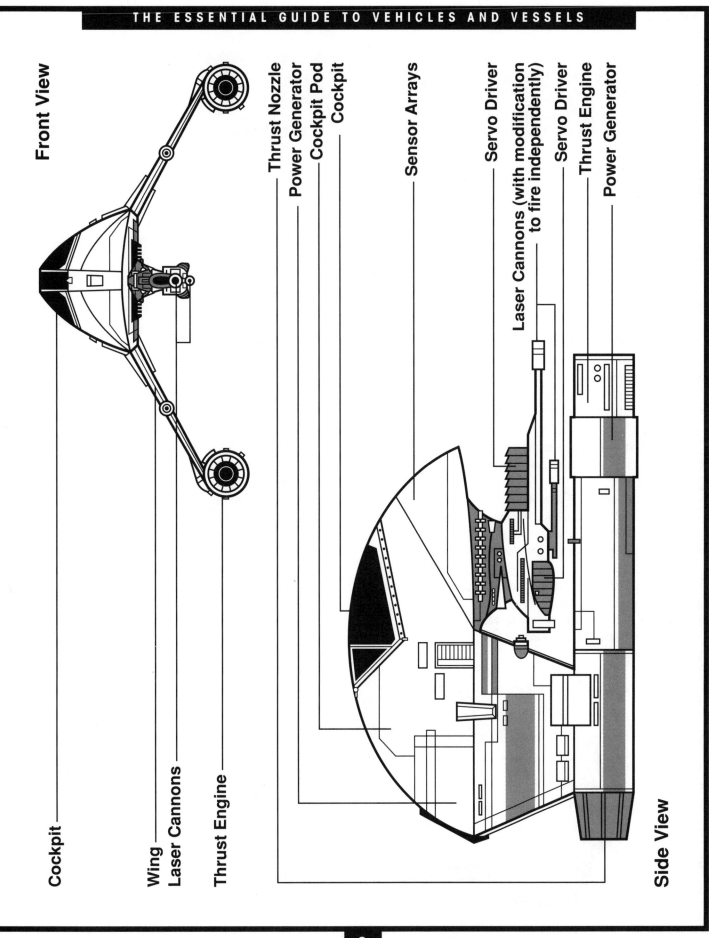

Front View

Cockpit

Wing
Laser Cannons

Thrust Engine

Thrust Nozzle
Power Generator
Cockpit Pod
Cockpit

Sensor Arrays

Servo Driver

Laser Cannons (with modification to fire independently)

Servo Driver
Thrust Engine
Power Generator

Side View

A-WING FIGHTER

ALLIANCE A-WING FIGHTER

The A-wing was the fastest starfighter in the galaxy at the time of the Battle of Endor. Designed by Alliance General Jan Dodonna and Rebel engineer Walex Blissex, the A-wing was intended to be a high-speed ship capable of outrunning anything in the Imperial Navy. At the battle, a single A-wing destroyed the Super Star Destroyer *Executor* when pilot Arvel Crynyd rammed the *Executor*'s bridge, causing the ship to crash into the Death Star.

The small, wedge-shaped ship continues to be the Alliance's main interceptor fighter. It is an exceptionally difficult ship to fly because it is constantly pushing the limits of performance. The A-wing is constantly subjected to incredible stresses, and its engines, hull, and weapons systems require constant maintenance. Since it is only 9.6 meters long, each ship component is wedged into the cramped hull, and even the lightest hit can cause critical system failures. The pilot is almost totally exposed to enemy fire.

While fast, the A-wing is fragile and is easily damaged by enemy fire. One hit is often enough to destroy the vessel. A-wing pilots must rely on the ship's blistering speed and their own willingness to take foolish chances to survive in combat.

The A-wing has two wing-mounted pivoting blaster cannons which can angle sixty degrees up or down. This gives the fighter a far wider field of fire than starfighters with fixed weapon emplace-

ments. A few A-wings have even been modified to fire straight back. Each laser cannon has its own power generator. A-wings sometimes are mounted with a pair of concussion-missile launchers; while these weapons are short-range, their destructive capability is superior to that of laser cannons.

The A-wing has an unusual sensor-jamming array which serves to disrupt enemy readings, although this unit is generally effective only against fighters. This array also jams communications, allowing A-wings to attack and get away before the enemy can summon help.

The A-wing gets its remarkable performance from two Novaldex J-77 "Event Horizon" engines, and relies on centered thruster-control jets for maneuverability, although the J-77 engines have adjustable thrust-vector controls for enhanced performance. Adjustable stabilizer wings assist in atmospheric flight. The wing-control units are tied into the engine's thrust-vector controls, so the wings visibly adjust even in space.

The A-wing was originally designed to defend Rebel bases and merchant ships from Imperial raids. However, Rebel tacticians eventually learned that it was far better for "hit-and-fade" assaults against Imperial vessels, where its superior speed allowed the A-wing to attack and flee before enemy fighters could be scrambled. The A-wing was also used in combination with other Rebel fighters: the "A-wing slash" was a devastating attack that used slower fighters to distract enemy TIEs while the A-wings closed in on the Imperial ships and cut them to ribbons.

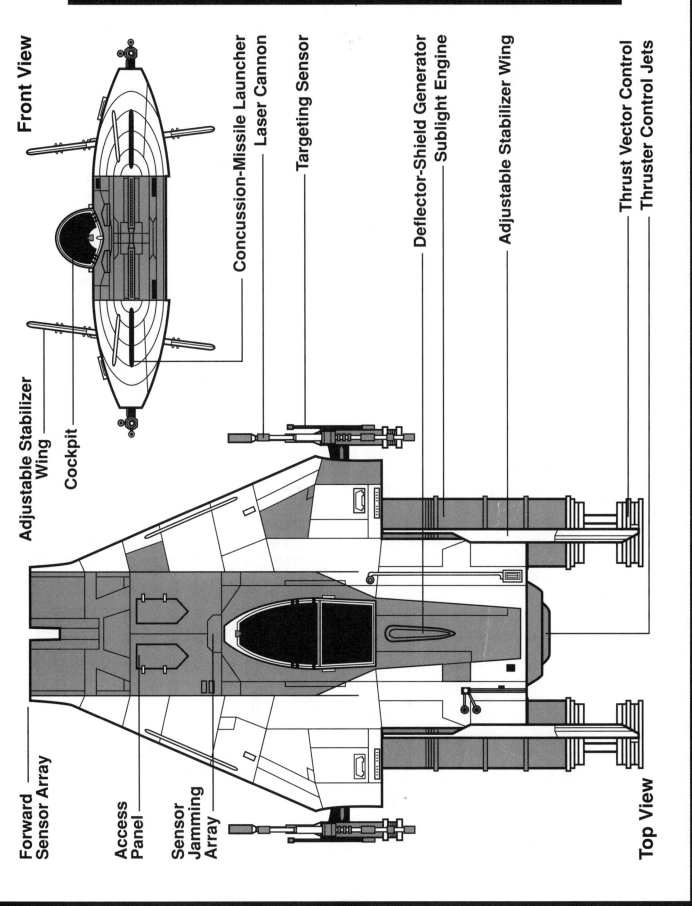

Front View

Adjustable Stabilizer Wing

Cockpit

Concussion-Missile Launcher

Laser Cannon

Targeting Sensor

Deflector-Shield Generator

Sublight Engine

Adjustable Stabilizer Wing

Thrust Vector Control

Thruster Control Jets

Forward Sensor Array

Access Panel

Sensor Jamming Array

Top View

AMPHIBION

SEDRIMOTORS LTD. AMPHIBION

Amphibions are water assault vehicles that played a prominent role in the Battle of Calamari, six years after the Battle of Endor. They are used by a number of aquatic and amphibious battle forces, including the Mon Calamari Defense Force and the New Republic Sea Commandos.

Amphibions were designed as troop carriers and normally work in teams of two to sixteen vehicles. They can quickly deliver troops over a large area, giving New Republic sea forces incredible flexibility.

They are surface hover vehicles; rather than using repulsorlift drives, they utilize a series of small, quiet hover engines to produce an air cushion that suspends the amphibion just a few centimeters above the surface level. The drive system can propel the amphibion up to one hundred kilometers per hour, and the hover unit allows the amphibion to work over both water and flat land.

The small hover engines are mounted between armor plates along the bottom and sides of the vehicle, while a triple bank of large hover drives are placed in the rear for propulsion. This system creates a dramatic saving in weight and cargo space, allowing the small vehicle to carry twenty troops and all their gear into combat. And thanks to the redundant hover-drive system, a number of the engines can fail and the amphibion will still be able to move, although at greatly reduced speed.

The hover system is far quieter than standard repulsorlift units, allowing troops to slip past enemy lines without alerting sentry posts. The hover engines have a reduced heat and energy profile, especially in aquatic operations, where water cools the engines. This means that scanners are also less likely to register the amphibions, making them the perfect vehicles for Sea Commandos on stealth assault missions.

Amphibions are lightly armored and not suited for heavy combat against heavy aquatic and repulsorlift craft. Only the command cabin and gunnery tower are adequately protected. The forward command cabin seats two and is fully sealed, while the gunner sits at the bottom of the rotating antipersonnel gun turret at the rear. The copilot can control the gun remotely, but at the cost of greatly reduced accuracy.

The amphibion's only other weaponry consists of whatever weapons the troops carry with them by hand. The amphibion has partial armor to give the troops some cover, but heavy laser blasts can easily penetrate the thin armor plates. The top of the vehicle is open for quick loading and unloading, although this makes the troops vulnerable to fire from above.

Amphibions are cheap, mass-produced vehicles. For heavy-combat missions they normally are supported by heavy repulsortanks, airspeeders, and heavy water-combat vehicles.

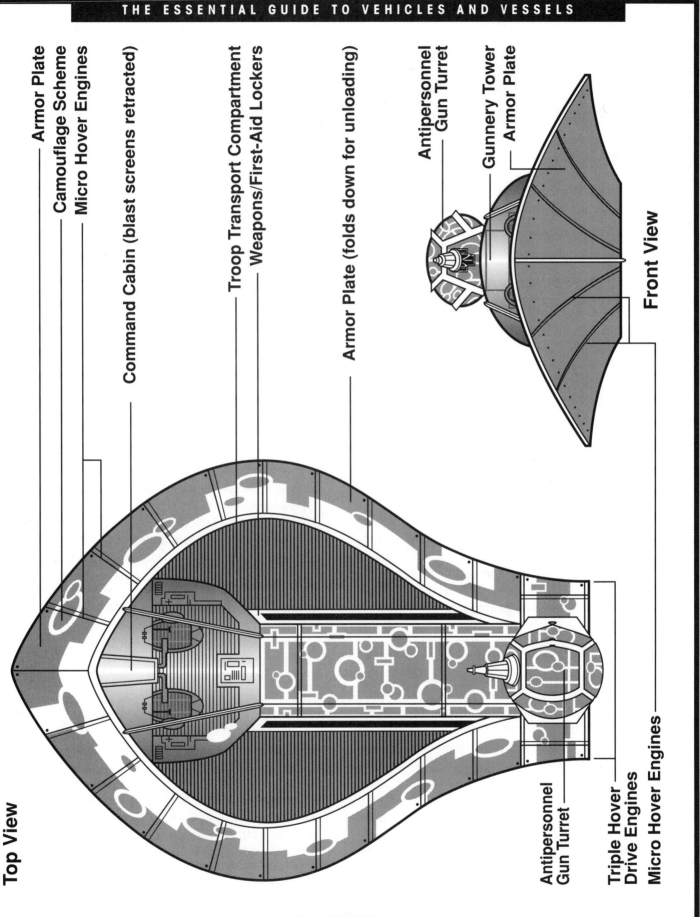

Top View

Armor Plate

Camouflage Scheme

Micro Hover Engines

Command Cabin (blast screens retracted)

Troop Transport Compartment

Weapons/First-Aid Lockers

Armor Plate (folds down for unloading)

Antipersonnel Gun Turret

Gunnery Tower

Armor Plate

Front View

Antipersonnel Gun Turret

Triple Hover Drive Engines

Micro Hover Engines

B-WING FIGHTER

SLAYN & KORPIL B-WING

The B-wing was the Rebel Alliance's most powerful heavy-assault starfighter. It was designed to take on much larger Imperial capital ships, thus providing the Alliance fighters with the punch of capital ships at a fraction of the cost. Although only about four meters longer than the famed X-wing, the B-wing had more firepower than many Imperial patrol ships.

The B-wing starfighter was designed by then-Commander Ackbar with the help of engineers from the Verpine Slayn and Korpil colonies. Later, the Verpine colonies and Ackbar worked to develop a two-man B-wing, adding a dedicated gunner. While the two-man B-wing, dubbed the B-wing/E (for B-wing/Expanded), was in many ways a superior ship, it was not widely accepted.

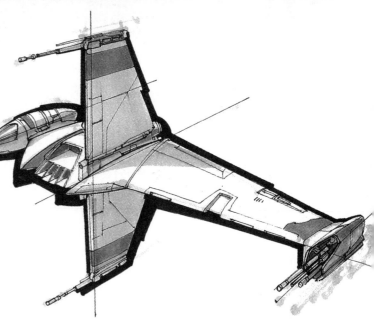

The original B-wing is essentially a long, flat wing with a cockpit on one end. Two folding airfoils near the midpoint of the primary wing extend out for combat. The fighter has an unusual cockpit gyro-stabilization system that allows the cockpit to remain stable while the rest of the ship rotates around it, significantly reducing stresses that result from sudden maneuvers. Unfortunately, this complex gyro-stabilizing system frequently breaks down. This locks the wing assembly in position, making it almost impossible to turn the ship without severely straining the spaceframe.

Because the B-wing is so difficult to handle, only a few of the Alliance's pilots were qualified to fly it. B-wing pilots tended to become very attached to their ships and liked to personally supervise every repair and modification.

The B-wing's advanced targeting computer links the performance of the ion cannons and proton-torpedo launchers, giving the ship maximum firepower against a single target, although the pilot also can split fire between different targets. The pilot can choose to fire a low-power targeting laser to "tag" enemy ships. While this gives the pilot nearly perfect range and vector information, it also gives away the B-wing's position.

In standard configuration, each secondary wing has one ion cannon, with a third ion cannon located at the base of the main wing. A laser cannon and an emission-type proton-torpedo launcher are also mounted on the end of the main wing. The engines sit just above the extending wings,

with another proton-torpedo launcher immediately above the engines. A pair of auto-blasters are in the nose of the cockpit module; technicians can opt to mount up to four auto-blasters in the nose section.

B-wing designers deliberately made the weapon-mounting points modular. Technicians can reconfigure auto-blaster, laser-cannon, and ion-cannon mounts within a few hours. A popular alternative B-wing weapon configuration is achieved by removing the auto-blasters and mounting the three ion cannons in the command pod, with a laser cannon placed on the end of the main wing and each airfoil.

Each fighter is powered by a single immense Quadex Kyromaster engine with four individually adjusted thrust nozzles. The engine is fed by a single Vinop 02 K ionization reactor and four Slayn & Korpil JZ-5g7 power convertors. The ship has four cooling plates to dissipate exhaust heat.

The B-wing has moderate sublight speed capability, and its hyperdrive, a Class Two unit, is only half as fast as comparable X-wing and A-wing hyperdrives. Unlike other Rebel starfighters, the B-wing does have a navigation computer, but it stores only two sets of jump coordinates.

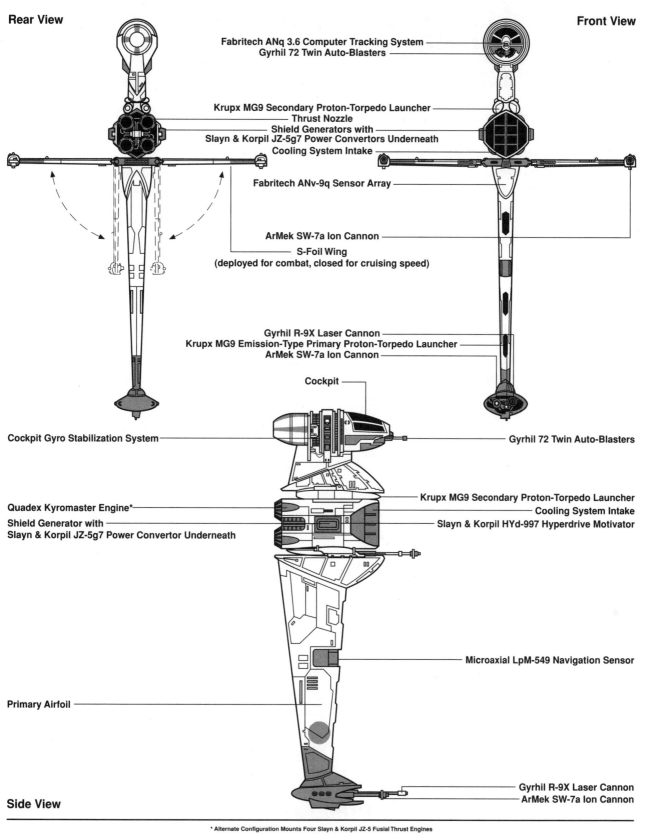

Rear View

Front View

Fabritech ANq 3.6 Computer Tracking System
Gyrhil 72 Twin Auto-Blasters

Krupx MG9 Secondary Proton-Torpedo Launcher
Thrust Nozzle
Shield Generators with
Slayn & Korpil JZ-5g7 Power Convertors Underneath
Cooling System Intake

Fabritech ANv-9q Sensor Array

ArMek SW-7a Ion Cannon
S-Foil Wing
(deployed for combat, closed for cruising speed)

Gyrhil R-9X Laser Cannon
Krupx MG9 Emission-Type Primary Proton-Torpedo Launcher
ArMek SW-7a Ion Cannon

Cockpit

Cockpit Gyro Stabilization System

Gyrhil 72 Twin Auto-Blasters

Quadex Kyromaster Engine*

Krupx MG9 Secondary Proton-Torpedo Launcher
Cooling System Intake

Shield Generator with
Slayn & Korpil JZ-5g7 Power Convertor Underneath

Slayn & Korpil HYd-997 Hyperdrive Motivator

Microaxial LpM-549 Navigation Sensor

Primary Airfoil

Gyrhil R-9X Laser Cannon
ArMek SW-7a Ion Cannon

Side View

* Alternate Configuration Mounts Four Slayn & Korpil JZ-5 Fusial Thrust Engines

Weapons Note: Alternate Weapon Configuration Mounts Three Gyrhil R-9X Laser Cannons, Three ArMek SW-7a Ion Cannons, and Two Krupx MG9 Proton-Torpedo Launchers.

CARRACK CRUISER

DAMORIAN MANUFACTURING *CARRACK*-CLASS LIGHT CRUISER

Carrack light cruisers are small combat cruisers that had been part of the Imperial Navy since the earliest days of the New Order. The Carrack's excellent design made it competitive even against newer ships, and the Imperial Navy was slow to retire these durable and capable craft.

At 350 meters long, Carracks are considered light cruisers, but they are quite heavily armed. The standard Imperial weapon configuration includes ten heavy turbolasers, twenty ion cannons, and five tractor-beam projectors. This weaponry gives the Carrack sufficient firepower to engage most Rebel capital starships. The Carrack can also be refitted with twenty laser cannons to replace the ion cannons, making the ship an excellent antistarfighter cruiser.

A major drawback of the Carrack is that it has no hangar bay. Instead, small external racks carry a mere five TIE fighters for courier or recon duty. The Carrack must rely on other ships or planetary bases for TIE fighter support. However, the ship has powerful sublight engines that give it the speed of an X-wing fighter, making it one of the fastest cruisers in the Imperial fleet.

Carrack cruisers feature an unusual compartmentalization system, giving the ship great resistance to hull damage. The system takes up a high percentage of the interior space but also increases crew survival rates; on many occasions, Imperial rescue crews found crewmen alive inside drifting wreckage. The Carrack's biggest weakness is insufficient armor plating around the power generators. A direct hit just aft of a Carrack's midline has a good chance of disabling the vessel.

Original Imperial protocols called for the Carrack to be a support cruiser, usually assigned to sector patrol in pacified Imperial sectors. Carracks were also assigned as rearguard vessels for fleet actions. Older Carracks were used as private transports for planetary governors, sector Moffs, and other dignitaries.

The decline of the Empire after the death of Emperor Palpatine forced Imperial commanders to place more and more of the vessels into frontline duty, where larger New Republic cruisers constantly bested them.

The Carrack cruiser *Dominant* was the main Imperial warship at Bakura. At the time of the encounter with the Ssi-ruuk, the ship was nearly a decade old and had served in a number of engagements against pirate and Rebel bases. It was reassigned to Bakura, under the command of Captain Pter Thanas, to assist Imperial Governor Nereus. The ship played a key role in the defense against the Ssi-ruuvi invasion force, but Thanas turned on his Rebel "allies" as soon as the Ssi-ruuk had retreated, and the *Dominant*'s guns destroyed the Alliance fighter cruiser-carrier *Flurry*. Thanas eventually surrendered the *Dominant* to the Alliance and defected. He was soon appointed commander of the *Dominant* in its new role as flagship of the newly created Bakuran Alliance system defense force.

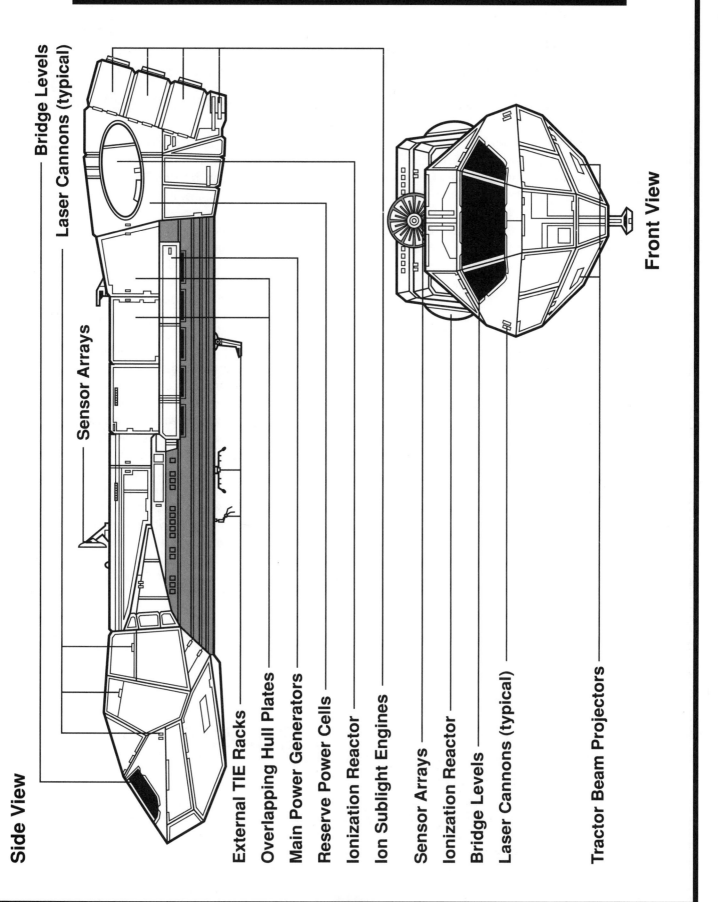

Side View

Bridge Levels

Laser Cannons (typical)

Sensor Arrays

Front View

External TIE Racks

Overlapping Hull Plates

Main Power Generators

Reserve Power Cells

Ionization Reactor

Ion Sublight Engines

Sensor Arrays

Ionization Reactor

Bridge Levels

Laser Cannons (typical)

Tractor Beam Projectors

CHARIOT LAV

UULSHOS LAVR QH-7 CHARIOT

The Uulshos QH-7 Chariot light assault vehicle (LAV) is a command speeder that was used extensively by Imperial Army command personnel. This modified military landspeeder is approximately twelve meters long and has a top speed of one hundred kilometers per hour. The Chariot flies at a maximum altitude of eight meters, allowing it to skim over most low-lying obstructions.

The Chariot was one of the more common command speeders in the Imperial Army; this was due more to its low per-unit cost than to exceptional performance. This vehicle seldom entered combat but instead acted as a rear-echelon command vehicle that could keep pace with advancing Imperial soldiers, repulsorcraft, and walkers. The Chariot command speeder was normally deployed with artillery or repulsorlift platoons, although it could also be assigned to scouting units for special missions.

Each Chariot has an armored canopy and layered armor plates to absorb low-power blasts. Electronic countermeasures fill the rear half of the craft, providing protection against electromagnetic bursts and other disruption tactics. The communications bay has a sophisticated signal scrambler for outgoing transmissions, making it virtually impossible for enemy units to intercept and decode enemy communiqués.

The assault vehicle has only a single short-range laser cannon for use in last-ditch defense, but accompanying escort vehicles normally are expected to handle any enemy troops foolish enough to attack. The onboard laser cannon drops out of a hatch beneath the main cabin and faces forward.

The vehicle normally only carries a crew of three: the driver, the commander, and the bodyguard/gunner. However, an entire command staff can be crammed aboard the vehicle if necessary. At least four communications droids are assigned to the communications array.

The Chariot's onboard computers are equipped with advanced battle-assistance programs, holographic tactical battlefield displays, and complete communications arrays, giving the commander access to the most detailed intelligence available. Imperial commanders could coordinate the actions of over a dozen combat units and were able to provide a continuous datafeed to central military command.

As Grand Admiral Thrawn prepared for his campaign against the New Republic, he conducted a systematic upgrade of the Chariot and other aging repulsorcraft. The Chariot's laser cannon was replaced with a more powerful swivel gun. Thrawn used a command speeder to coordinate his search for Luke Skywalker and Mara Jade in the dense forests of Myrkr, at least until that command speeder was crushed in the town square of Hyllyard City when Luke Skywalker toppled a ten-meter-tall stone arch on top of it.

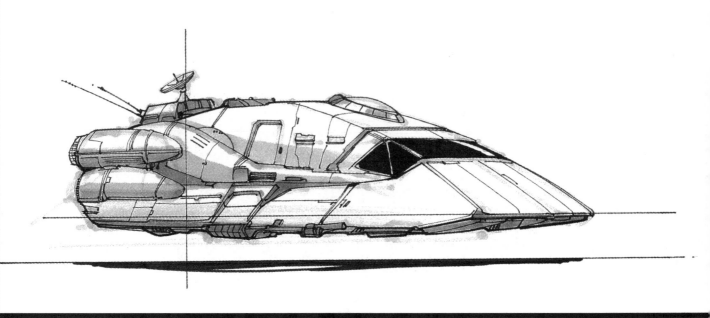

Front View

Side View

Long-Range Comm Transceiver

Blast Deflection Plate
Retractable Forward Armor Plate (shown retracted)
Air Intake/Filtration Unit
Intake Screen
Laser Cannon Mount (cannon retracted)
Repulsorlift Altitude/Angling Jet

Repulsorlift Engines (5)
Subspace Scrambler/Transceiver
Long-Range Comm Transceiver
Power Core Access
Maneuvering Flap
Comm Analysis Amplifier/Receptor
Armored Cooling Vanes
Low-Frequency Encryptor
Retractable Viewports
Armored Canopy
Layered Armor Plates

Main Access Hatch
Repulsorlift Altitude/Angling Jet

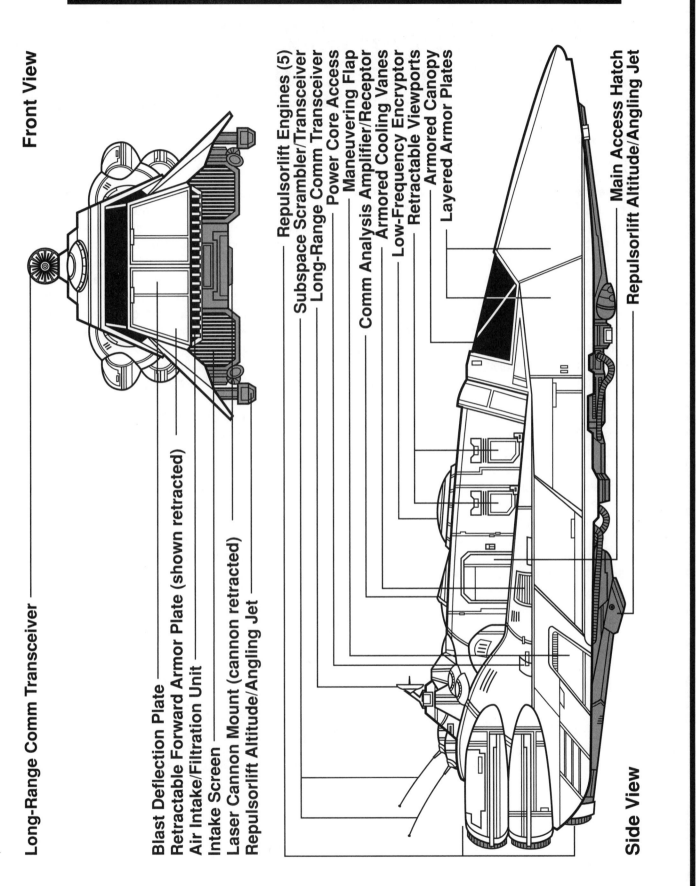

CHU'UNTHOR

REPUBLIC FLEET SYSTEMS *CHU'UNTHOR*

The *Chu'unthor* is a cruiser that dated back to the days of the Old Republic. Luke Skywalker discovered the ship's rusting wreckage on Dathomir and later learned that under the command of Yoda and a number of other Jedi Masters, it had served as a mobile training academy for groups of Jedi apprentices.

The ship was immense. At two kilometers long, a kilometer wide, and at least forty meters tall, the *Chu'unthor* had room for nearly 10,000 Jedi students, with hundreds of exercise and lightsaber sparring rooms used to hone every student's body to physical perfection. Workshops gave Jedi places to build lightsabers, while hundreds of meditation rooms offered students places to develop mental discipline. Dozens of healing and hospital rooms were used to teach young Jedi healing arts with which they could help the physically or mentally impaired. The ship also had several library rooms with texts covering Jedi teachings, advanced and theoretical sciences, history, literature, languages, the arts, and alien civilizations.

One severe problem for many species when traveling in space is the sense of confinement experienced in a starship. To alleviate this problem, the *Chu'unthor* had wide corridors with high ceilings, while dozens of rooms had domes or large viewports. By holding classes open to the stars, the Jedi effectively received a double boon. Not only did this help alleviate the sense of claustrophobia, but these rooms constantly reminded the Jedi in training that a

Jedi's gifts were not to be used for selfish ends—in time, every Jedi would be called on to go out and serve among the stars.

After defeating the evil Nightsisters of Dathomir, Luke Skywalker came to learn about the history of the *Chu'unthor*. The ship had been built just four centuries earlier to gather and train Jedi students from many parts of the galaxy. The *Chu'unthor*'s noble mission had been cut tragically short when it had crashed on the exile world of Dathomir, home to "witches," descendants of a fallen Jedi named Allya. These witches had mastered Dathomir's unique attunement to the Force, greatly expanding their inherited powers.

The damaged *Chu'unthor* had been surrounded and attacked by the witches and the rancors that were under their control. Master Yoda had saved the life of a young witch named Rell, and the two had negotiated a truce. The *Chu'unthor* and its reader tapes were to be left behind, but the Jedi were free to leave. Yoda asked Rell to keep the disks hidden until a young Jedi came to free her world from the Nightsisters, a group of witches who had turned to evil.

Nearly three centuries later Skywalker fulfilled Yoda's ancient prophecy by defeating the Nightsisters and the Imperial occupation forces. Rell, now old and feeble, gave Luke the tapes from the *Chu'unthor*, thus providing a solid foundation for the formation of his Jedi *praxeum*, or academy, on Yavin Four.

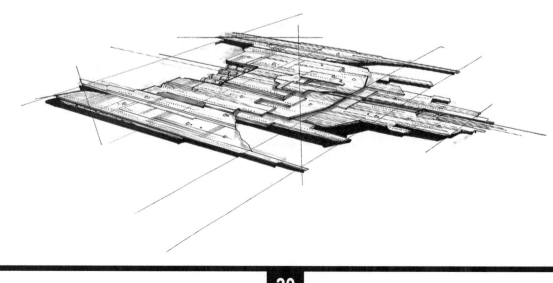

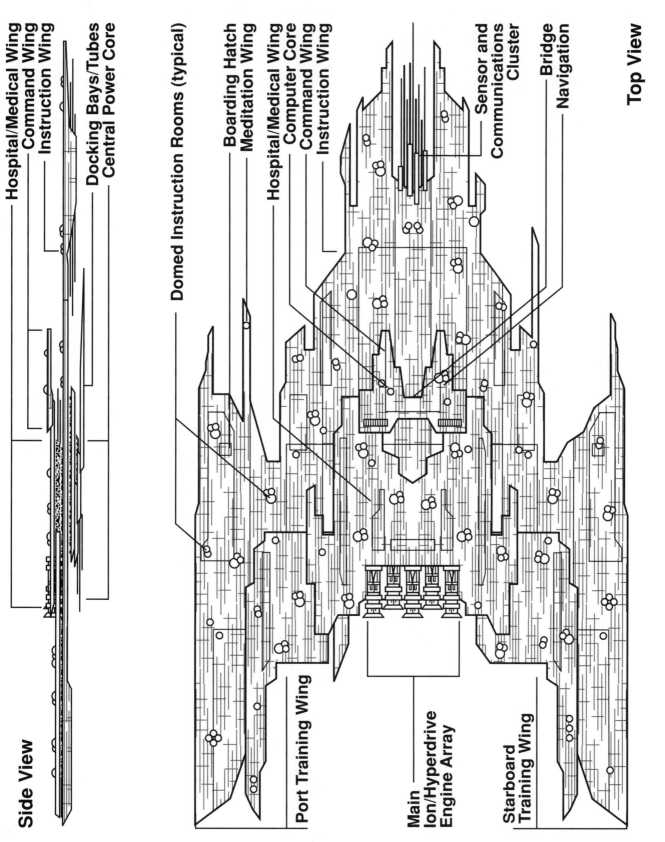

Side View

Hospital/Medical Wing
Command Wing
Instruction Wing

Docking Bays/Tubes
Central Power Core

Domed Instruction Rooms (typical)

Boarding Hatch
Meditation Wing

Hospital/Medical Wing
Computer Core
Command Wing
Instruction Wing

Sensor and
Communications
Cluster

Bridge
Navigation

Top View

Port Training Wing

Main
Ion/Hyperdrive
Engine Array

Starboard
Training Wing

CLOAKSHAPE FIGHTER

KUAT SYSTEMS ENGINEERING CLOAKSHAPE FIGHTER

The Kuat Systems Engineering CloakShape fighter is one of countless older starfighters. A CloakShape fighter pursued the *Millennium Falcon* on the smugglers' moon of Nar Shaddaa. The ship, owned by bounty hunters out to claim the Hutt bounty on Han Solo's head, was destroyed by the automated laser cannons in Shug Ninx's access tunnel.

Like the aging Z-95 Headhunter, the CloakShape isn't good enough for frontline combat missions, but many of these ships find a home in planetary defense forces or in the fleets of private companies and wealthy individuals. CloakShape fighters are used by bounty hunters, pirates, and other groups or individuals with a need for assault starships.

CloakShape fighters are designed for atmospheric and short-range space combat; their power plants aren't strong enough for prolonged missions in space. In stock form, they lack a hyperdrive and are often paired with carrier ships.

Like many older fighters, the CloakShape trades speed for durability: in an era when starfighter designers are favoring firepower over a sturdy hull, the CloakShape promises to take a beating and bring the pilot home.

CloakShapes have been around so long that few of these vessels still meet the manufacturer's stock specifications. The

designers built the ship to be easily modified, and it's not uncommon to find that only the original hull remains in a given ship. The hull has enough room for heavier thrusters, added weapons, or a larger fuel supply; with some work, a mechanic can even add shield generators.

There are also several after-market modification kits designed specifically for the CloakShape. One kit has a strap-on hyperdrive sled with a self-contained power generator, while another has a rear-mounted maneuvering fin that dramatically improves the CloakShape's handling. The maneuvering fin add-on is so common that most people think it is part of the ship's original design. Anyone with the time for hands-on work could probably produce a modified CloakShape that could compete with an Alliance Y-wing fighter, and have enough money left over to buy a used freighter.

The CloakShape destroyed on Nar Shaddaa included mounted fire-linked double laser cannons and a pair of concussion-missile launchers. Adding the launchers' large ammo bays meant stripping out the shield generators in order to make room. The bounty hunter thought his reinforced hull would be enough to get him through a battle; Shug Ninx's automated laser cannons proved him wrong.

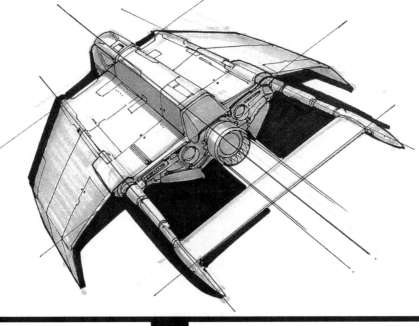

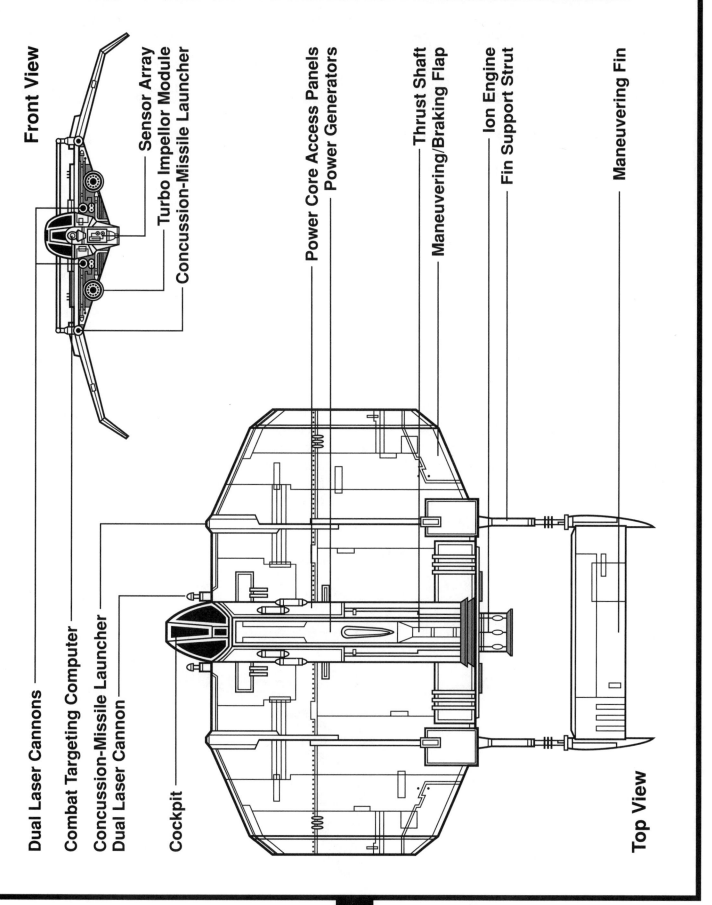

Front View

Dual Laser Cannons

Sensor Array

Turbo Impellor Module

Concussion-Missile Launcher

Power Core Access Panels

Power Generators

Thrust Shaft

Maneuvering/Braking Flap

Ion Engine

Fin Support Strut

Maneuvering Fin

Dual Laser Cannons

Combat Targeting Computer

Concussion-Missile Launcher

Dual Laser Cannon

Cockpit

Top View

CLOUD CITY

CUSTOM INCOM CORPORATION REPULSORLIFT CITY

Cloud City is a titanic floating metropolis suspended nearly 60,000 kilometers above the core of the gas giant of Bespin. Its main industry is Tibanna gas mining, but it is also a popular resort community and a center of trade. Cloud City features luxury hotels, casinos, and shopping plazas—all of them free of the Empire. This is because it is a remote colony with a population of only six million and represents a negligible percentage of the galactic Tibanna gas market.

Cloud City is sixteen kilometers in diameter and seventeen kilometers tall (including the immense unipod that hangs below the city proper). Its architecture gives the illusion of open space in what is essentially a closed environment. Cloud City's many plazas allow breathtaking views of the brilliantly colored clouds surrounding the city.

There are 392 levels and a surface plaza concourse. The upper levels contain resorts and casinos, while the middle levels are for heavy industry and for housing the working classes. The lower levels have Tibanna gas processing facilities and the 3,600 repulsorlift engines which keep the city anchored in place. A central wind tunnel nearly a kilometer in diameter allows Cloud City some "give" against Bespin's incredible storm winds.

The unipod hanging below the city has thirty-two tractor-beam projectors that reach down into the planet's atmosphere and draw spin-sealed Tibanna

gas up into the city's gas refineries. Tibanna gas is used as a hyperdrive coolant, and when spin-sealed by extremes in pressure and temperature, it serves as a fantastic energy source for blasters. Since Bespin's atmosphere naturally spin-seals Tibanna gas, the gas is relatively inexpensive to harvest.

Lando Calrissian "won" the position of Baron Administrator of Cloud City and worked for several years to earn an image of respectability both for himself and for the city. However, his shady past brought about the downfall of his beloved city. Former smuggling partner Han Solo, fleeing the forces of the Empire, sought refuge on Bespin. Lando was forced to turn Solo and his companions over to Darth Vader and Boba Fett, and Cloud City's independence was gone. Vader left a full Imperial garrison to maintain order, and Lando decided to join the Rebellion to save Solo.

The Imperial garrison commander, Captain Treece, turned Cloud City's Tibanna gas mining operations into Ugnaught slave camps, although Lando Calrissian ultimately helped free the Ugnaughts and repel the Imperial forces. The Empire retook Cloud City and used it as a supply base during Grand Admiral Thrawn's campaign against the New Republic. After the defeat of Thrawn, Cloud City was again freed, but its glamour and wealth were gone. The few remaining citizens have since decided to stay neutral, and Cloud City is now a sleepy mining colony that has seen better days.

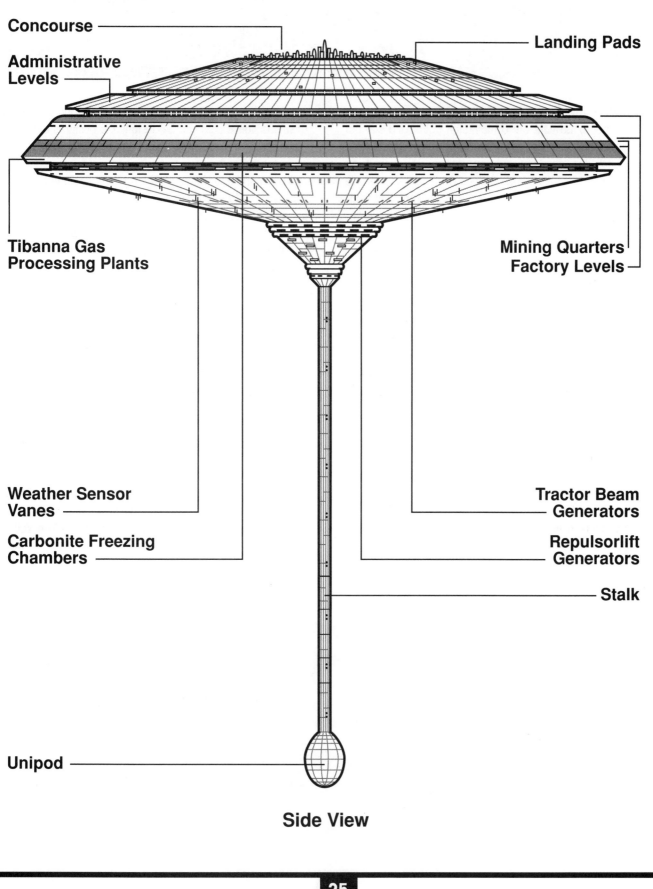

Concourse

Administrative Levels

Landing Pads

Tibanna Gas Processing Plants

Mining Quarters Factory Levels

Weather Sensor Vanes

Carbonite Freezing Chambers

Tractor Beam Generators

Repulsorlift Generators

Stalk

Unipod

Side View

COMBAT CLOUD CAR

UBRIKKIAN TALON I COMBAT CLOUD CAR

Combat cloud cars are combination patrol and combat vehicles that are used throughout the galaxy. These vehicles follow the standard cloud car design, with linked ion and repulsorlift engines and a sealed cabin for high-altitude flight. Many different models are offered by prominent vehicle manufacturers, including Bespin Motors, Ubrikkian, Aratech, Merkuun, and SoroSuub.

Combat cloud cars are popular because they fill a gap between airspeeders and starfighters. They have enough weaponry to stand up to fighters and freighters but are much cheaper than space-capable fighters. They are excellent for both lower- and upper-atmosphere duty, with a maximum altitude of around one hundred kilometers on most human-standard worlds. They have superior maneuverability and excellent speed: some combat cloud cars can reach up to 1,500 kilometers per hour, making them capable of outrunning most starships in an atmosphere setting.

They are significantly more reliable than heavily modified airspeeders, requiring far less maintenance and downtime. Replacement parts are standardized for several models, allowing technicians to perform improvised emergency repairs. Combat cloud cars can be deployed almost anywhere, and their ion engines allow them to be assigned to bases where repulsorlift-only vehicles can't work, such as planets with unusual gravitational fields.

Most combat cloud cars have extra hull plating and enhanced weapons systems. Aside from patrol and combat missions, these cars can be assigned to customs duty, forward scouting, and even traffic control over busy starports and speederways.

The Noghri use Ubrikkian Talon I combat cloud cars that were supplied by the Empire. The Talon I cars are used to patrol their homeworld of Honoghr, with support provided by small patrol ships orbiting the planet. When dispatching patrol craft, the Noghri follow typical Imperial protocols and send out the vehicles in pairs. This may be an exceptionally light defense web for most worlds, but Grand Admiral Thrawn considered the Noghri to be immensely loyal to the Empire—and Honoghr has few resources worth fighting for.

The Talon I cloud car has a single pod with two outstretched airfoils and a main fin for maneuverability. A double blaster cannon is mounted in the nose of the pod, and a single Ubrikkian Servant ion/repulsorlift engine is mounted in the rear of the vessel. The engine is low and exposed to the air for exceptional cooling. Each wing has a trio of maneuvering jets and emergency braking thrusters. Noghri technicians at the main starport in Nystao are responsible for the maintenance and repair of these vessels.

Honoghr's minimal defenses allowed Luke Skywalker to seek refuge among the Noghri. When he was escorted in for landing, two combat cloud cars guided him to a valley where the Noghri were modeling the reconstruction of their planet's ecosystem.

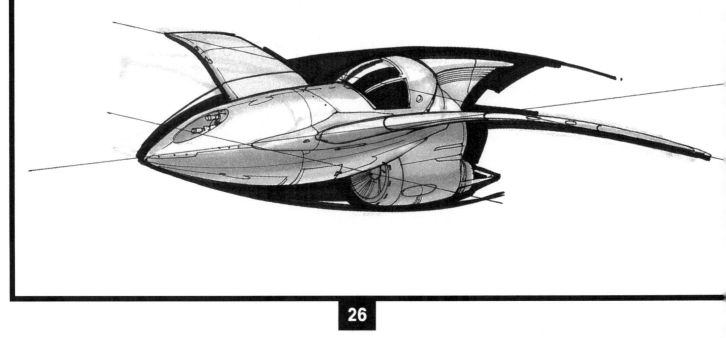

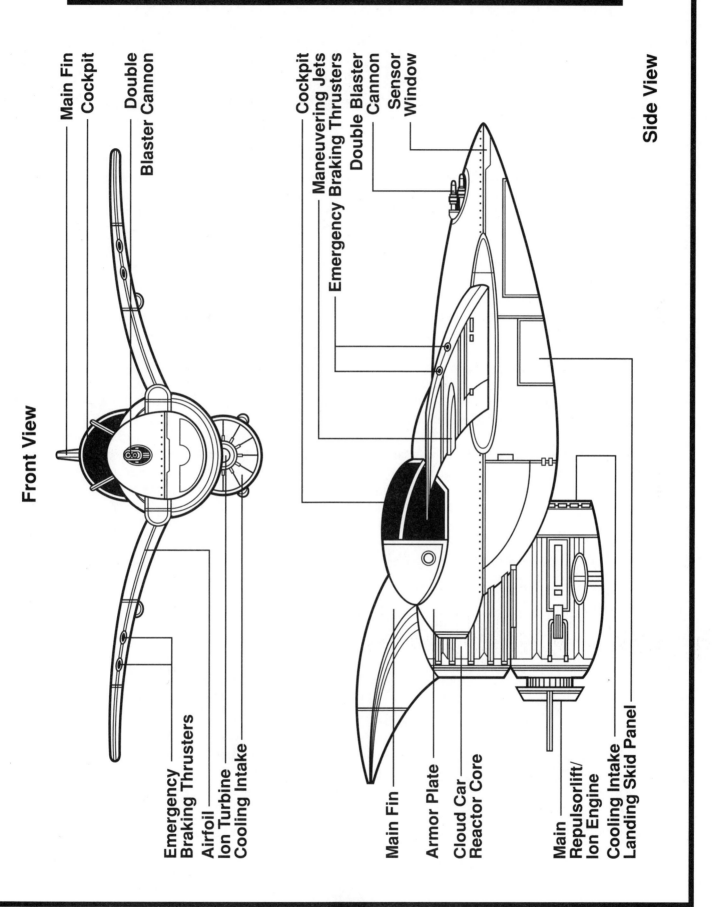

Front View

Main Fin
Cockpit
Double Blaster Cannon

Emergency Braking Thrusters
Airfoil
Ion Turbine
Cooling Intake

Side View

Cockpit
Maneuvering Jets
Emergency Braking Thrusters
Double Blaster Cannon
Sensor Window

Main Fin
Armor Plate
Cloud Car Reactor Core

Main Repulsorlift/Ion Engine
Cooling Intake
Landing Skid Panel

CORAL VANDA

PANTOLOMIN SHIPWRIGHTS CRUISER

The subocean liner *Coral Vanda* is a famous vacation cruiser that plies the oceans of the planet Pantolomin. The luxurious vessel offers three- and seven-day excursions through the exquisite coral reefs just off the continent of Tralla.

However, the *Coral Vanda* is famous for more than sight-seeing. Those who book a trip on the ship come to gamble. The ship's eight incredible casino rooms are among the most luxurious in the galaxy: scarlet *greel* wood paneling with inset Rodian sanriv gemstones lines every table. Each casino has multiple levels, a bar offering virtually any concoction, and even a serving window so gamblers need not leave the casinos to eat. Each casino contains transparisteel viewports that run the length and height of the room, allowing sight-seeing tourists to view Pantolomin's oceans as the ship slides through the coral reefs and colorful fish schools.

Virtually any game of chance can be found in the casino rooms, including tregald, lugjack, crinbid, and any of the hundreds of recognized sabacc variations. A local favorite is "halfback's bluff." The *Vanda* releases a colorful trinket into the middle of a school of Pantolomin halfbacks, local oceangoing creatures known for their playfulness and rippling, color-changing hides. Bets are placed on which halfback will carry off the trinket to its lair.

The *Coral Vanda* has sixteen luxury suites on the main concourse, and also offers four "adventure rooms" which re-create exotic galactic locations and are among the most sophisticated amusement facilities to be found anywhere. Each adventure room uses a combination of holographic generators, tactile arrays, and olfactory emitters to create a stunningly realistic simulation. Current offerings include Coruscant's Imperial Plaza, the sky cities of Tranthellix, an Ithorian herd ship bazaar, and the crystal caverns of Berchest.

The *Coral Vanda*'s central level has cabins for a contingent of up to six hundred passengers, with casinos immediately above and below. The cruise ship is unarmed, although it has a small security team to maintain order; in an emergency, they can be drafted for combat duty. The vessel has dozens of escape pods in the event of a collision or another accident.

The cruiser became a pawn in Grand Admiral Thrawn's bid to defeat the New Republic when Han Solo and Lando Calrissian came to the famous cruise liner while searching for the *Katana* fleet. Starship thief Niles Ferrier led Thrawn right to the *Coral Vanda*, but Solo and Calrissian managed to avoid capture. This incident allowed Thrawn the extra time he needed to find and secure most of the *Katana* fleet Dreadnaughts.

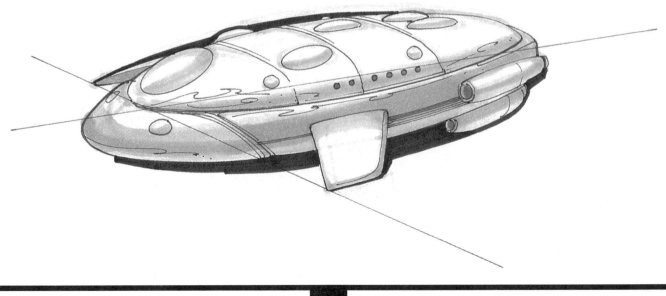

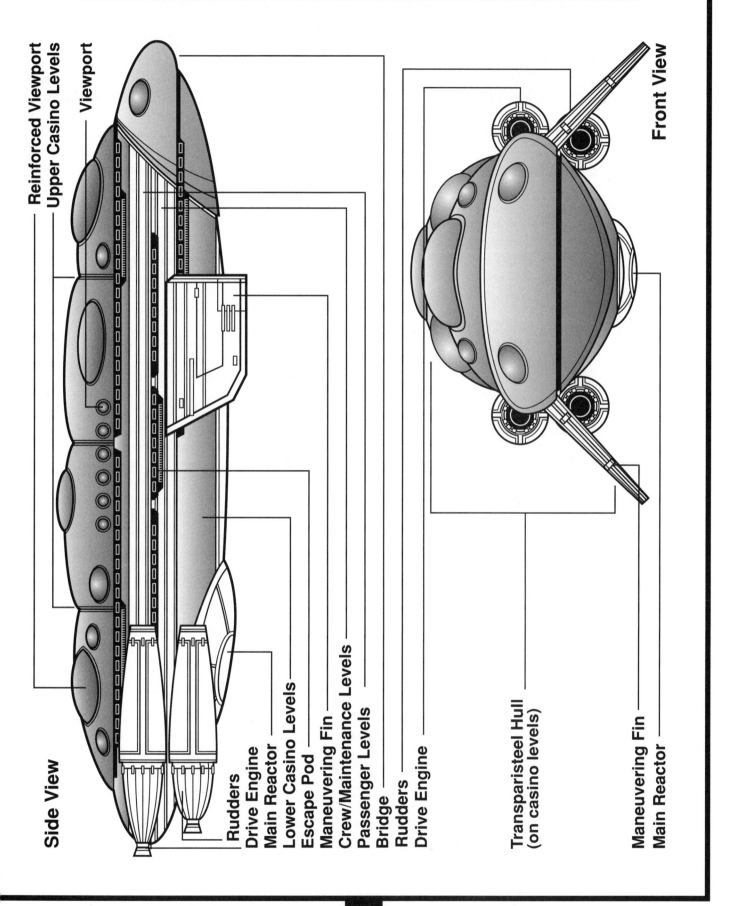

Side View

Reinforced Viewport
Upper Casino Levels
Viewport

Rudders
Drive Engine
Main Reactor
Lower Casino Levels
Escape Pod
Maneuvering Fin
Crew/Maintenance Levels
Passenger Levels
Bridge
Rudders
Drive Engine

Front View

Transparisteel Hull
(on casino levels)

Maneuvering Fin
Main Reactor

DARTH VADER'S TIE FIGHTER

SIENAR FLEET SYSTEMS TIE ADVANCED X1 PROTOTYPE

The TIE Advanced x1 Prototype was the fighter used by Lord Darth Vader at the Battle of Yavin. This particular vessel was one of several TIE prototypes fielded by the Sienar Fleet Systems design team during the critical years between the Battle of Yavin and the death of the Emperor at Endor. The TIE Advanced x1 was perhaps the most successful of these prototypes, and many of the refinements in that vessel were later incorporated into the TIE interceptor and the TIE Advanced (TIE/Ad) ship dubbed the "TIE Avenger."

The TIE Advanced x1 featured a custom-designed spaceframe and a reinforced durasteel-alloy hull, with an elongated rear deck and matching bent wings covered with solar panels. The vessel mounted a Sienar Fleet Systems (SFS) I-S3a solar ionization reactor and paired SFS P-s5.6 twin ion engines for a far more powerful drive system than that of the standard TIE/ln. Speed was only slightly improved over earlier models, due to the added mass and to the fact that a good deal of the extra power was bled off to the shield generators. The TIE Advanced x1 was less maneuverable than standard TIE fighters, but it could take far more punishment than could the fragile TIE/ln ships.

The TIE Advanced x1 sported twin heavy blaster cannons in a fixed, front-mounted position. In a major exception to standard Imperial military policy, the TIE Advanced x1 featured shield generators and a modest hyperdrive

(although the navigation computer could store only ten sets of jump coordinates).

The TIE Advanced x1 lacked a life-support system, and the pilot had to wear a fully contained flight suit with an internal oxygen supply. Pilots were strapped into an adjustable shock couch with foot yokes and a hand control panel.

The TIE Advanced x1 was initially produced in only very modest numbers. Lord Darth Vader received one of the vessels for his personal missions; most of the other ships were deployed to elite Imperial squadrons for field testing. By the time of the Battle of Hoth, TIE Advanced x1 fighters had been deployed to a number of Navy fleets, including Lord Vader's Star Destroyer squadron.

The Empire decided not to order the TIE Advanced x1 in large quantities, citing the excessive cost. Privately, some Imperial Navy strategists admitted that the Navy was afraid to purchase a fighter with a hyperdrive, fearing that it would provide an excuse to slash orders for new capital starships.

The Empire instead opted for the TIE interceptor, which featured the TIE Advanced x1's drive system, but in a more compact ship. While the TIE interceptor lacked hyperdrives and shields, it was blindingly fast, incredibly maneuverable, and significantly cheaper than the TIE Advanced x1. By the Battle of Endor, the large increase in TIE interceptor production meant the end of production for the TIE Advanced x1.

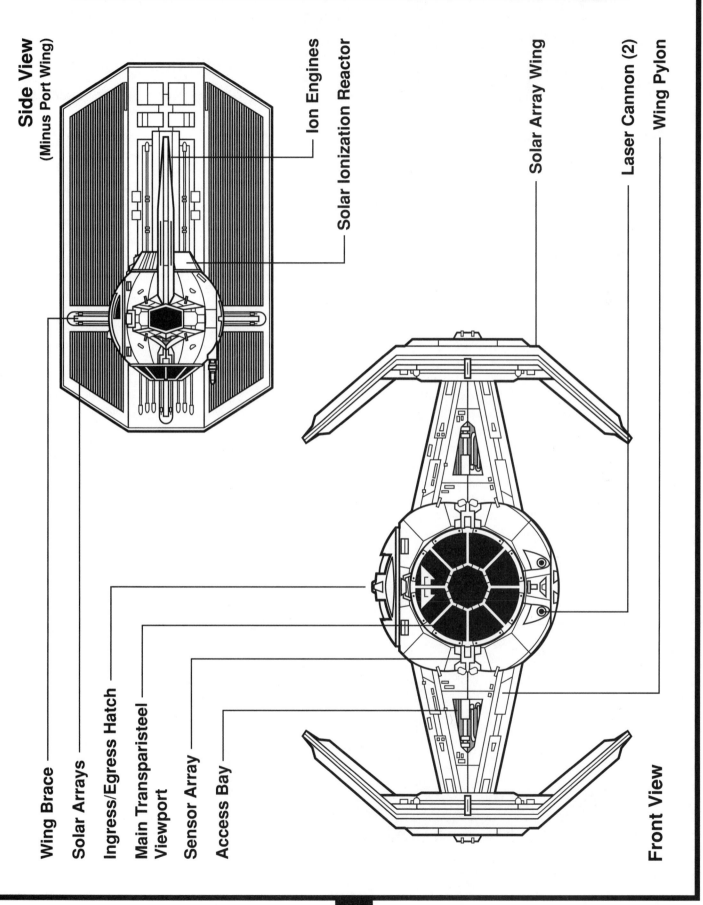

Side View
(Minus Port Wing)

Ion Engines

Solar Ionization Reactor

Solar Array Wing

Laser Cannon (2)

Wing Pylon

Wing Brace

Solar Arrays

Ingress/Egress Hatch

Main Transparisteel Viewport

Sensor Array

Access Bay

Front View

DASH RENDAR'S *OUTRIDER*

CORELLIAN ENGINEERING CORPORATION YT-2400 FREIGHTER

Dash Rendar is a cocky smuggler who, despite his abrasive and mercenary personality, aids the Rebel Alliance in the fight to overthrow the Empire. Dash flew with the Rebels at the Battle of Hoth and uses his ship, the *Outrider*, as a smuggling and courier vessel for Rebel missions.

The *Outrider* is an ebony Corellian YT-2400 freighter converted for smuggling duty. The ship features the trademark saucer-shaped hull of the YT series, but it is a more modern YT-2400 (as opposed to the older YT-1300s, such as the *Millennium Falcon*). This newer ship is like most Corellian designs: fast, tough, and endlessly modifiable.

With thick armor plating and bulky engines, the YT-2400 can easily handle the strain of deep-space combat. The vessel has power to spare and an oversize hull begging for hot-rodded engines and powerful weapons; it's obvious that when the Corellian Engineering Corporation sold this ship as a "stock cargo hauler," it was with a wink and a grin.

Rendar's YT-2400 features a rounded hull with a pair of starboard bracing arms that connect to the cockpit compartment, which is essentially a long tube. The aft section of the cockpit tube contains the primary escape pod, which seats six. The bracing arm's interior space generally is used for crew quarters and living space.

The rounded hull area is devoted to cargo holds and ship's systems. In practice, much of the interior hull space is taken up by modified engines, power generators, weapons systems, and all the other illegal "goodies" any self-respecting smuggling ship needs. A second escape pod, as well as the air lock, is located on the far side of the cargo compartment, directly opposite the bracing arms.

Dash, being a typical smuggler, decided to take advantage of the YT-2400's adaptability. His first step was to replace the engines with three stolen KonGar KGDefender military-grade ion engines. A modified SoroSuub Griffyn/Y2TG hyperdrive gives the *Outrider* a Class 0.75 hyperspace speed rating—slower than the *Millennium Falcon*'s Class 0.50 hyperdrive but far faster than most military vessels, which are either Class One or Class Two. Powerful shield generators and a *highly* illegal sensor stealth system make the *Outrider* a perfect smuggling ship.

A pair of heavy Dymek double laser cannons, personally modified by Dash for greater range, are dorsal- and ventral-mounted on standard Corellian 1D servo turrets. They normally are manned but can be controlled via the targeting computer in the cockpit, although accuracy is then significantly reduced. Two forward-firing concussion-missile launchers are mounted on the cockpit tube and have a magazine of three missiles each.

Dash has relied on this ship to save his life countless times. It's not uncommon for smugglers and other spacers to get emotionally attached to their vessels, and Dash is no exception. He has been heard saying, "I owe the *Outrider* the best . . . she's brought me home when any other ship would have scattered me across space."

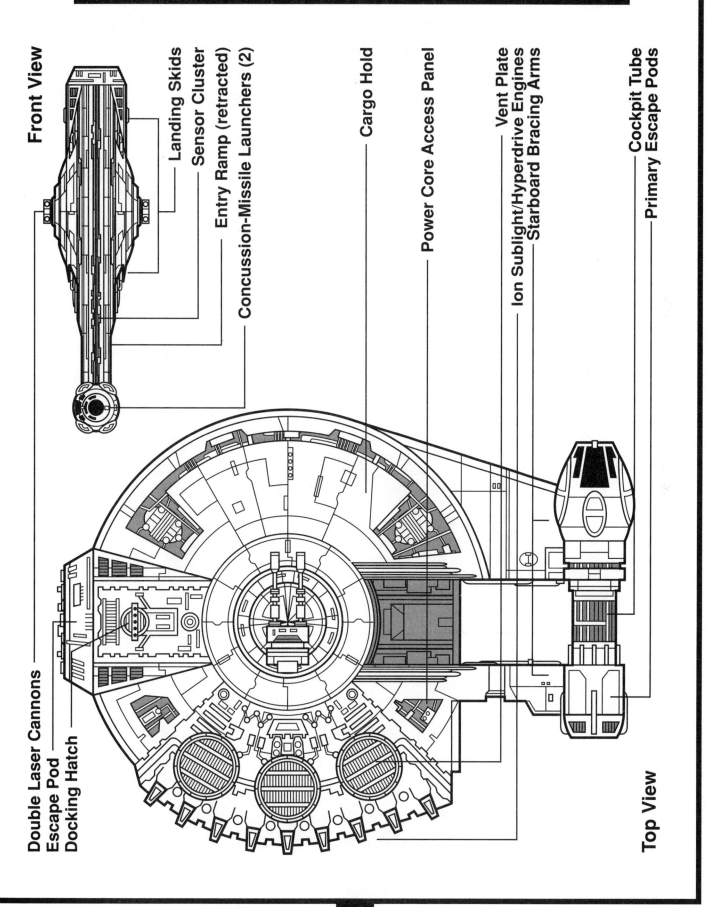

Front View

Landing Skids
Sensor Cluster
Entry Ramp (retracted)
Concussion-Missile Launchers (2)

Cargo Hold

Power Core Access Panel

Vent Plate
Ion Sublight/Hyperdrive Engines
Starboard Bracing Arms

Cockpit Tube
Primary Escape Pods

Double Laser Cannons
Escape Pod
Docking Hatch

Top View

DEATH STAR

CUSTOM DEEP-SPACE BATTLE STATION

In an Empire ruled through fear, nothing symbolized Emperor Palpatine's oppression better than the infamous Death Star battle station. However, the Death Star also represented the Empire's greatest weakness: the tendency to consider technology supreme, and to underestimate its foes. This weakness resulted in the first Death Star's destruction over Yavin, although not before it had destroyed the peaceful world of Alderaan, killing billions of innocent people.

The Death Star was conceived by Grand Moff Tarkin and approved by the Emperor. Drawing on concepts pioneered at many secret military installations, Chief Engineer Bevel Lemelisk designed the massive space station. The Death Star was commanded by Tarkin, but Lord Darth Vader served as the Emperor's emissary and wielded the widest possible authority to enforce the Emperor's will.

The Death Star's centerpiece was an awesome, planet-destroying superlaser. The weapon was used only twice: first to destroy the penal world of Despayre (where the Death Star was built) and second to obliterate Alderaan.

Everything about the Death Star boggles the imagination. At 120 kilometers in diameter, it was the size of a Class IV moon and was the largest starship ever built (at least until the construction of the larger *second* Death Star). Fully half of the battle station's interior was filled by the reactor core, the sublight and hyperdrive systems, and the superlaser housing.

The station had a crew of over 265,000 soldiers. Gunners, ground troops, starship support crew, and pilots brought the total onboard personnel to nearly 1 million beings. Even more amazing, these figures indicated *minimum* crew standards.

For weaponry, in addition to the superlaser, the Death Star had 15,000 capital ship turbolasers and over 700 tractor-beam projectors. These projectors could capture virtually any ship and, when working in conjunction with one another, could reel in even an Imperial Star Destroyer. The Death Star also maintained an awesome array of support ships and vehicles, with 7,000 TIE fighters, four strike cruisers, over 20,000 military and transport vessels, and over 11,000 combat vehicles.

Despite all these awesome advantages, simple errors doomed the station. First, the Death Star's defenses were built around the idea of repelling a capital ship attack; starfighters were considered "insignificant" by Imperial military strategists. And when the Alliance mounted its assault over Yavin, the Rebels could send only a small force of X-wing and Y-wing fighters. Grand Moff Tarkin considered the attack inconsequential. He refused to launch TIE fighters in defense of the station, and only the TIE fighters under Lord Vader's direct command were deployed against the Alliance's fighters.

As a result of those errors of arrogance, the mightiest weapon in the history of the galaxy was destroyed by a simple proton torpedo fired down an unshielded exhaust vent. This Achilles' heel allowed the Empire's enemies to detonate the Death Star's power core and win the day.

Front View

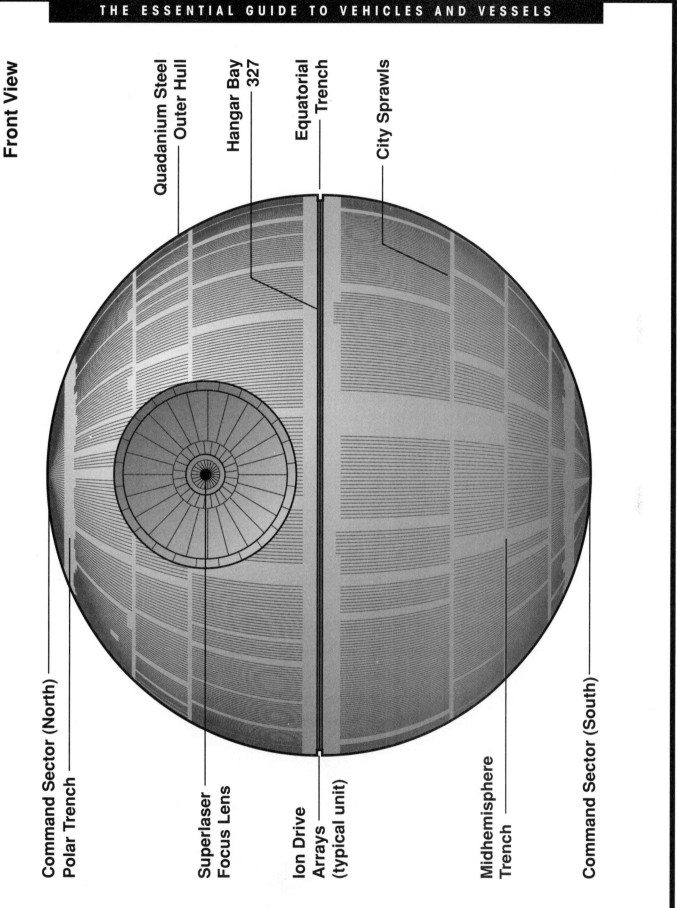

Command Sector (North)

Polar Trench

Quadanium Steel
Outer Hull

Hangar Bay
327

Equatorial
Trench

City Sprawls

Superlaser
Focus Lens

Ion Drive
Arrays
(typical unit)

Midhemisphere
Trench

Command Sector (South)

DEATH STAR II

CUSTOM DEEP-SPACE BATTLE STATION

The destruction of the first Death Star over the fourth moon of Yavin represented a devastating defeat for the Empire. In typical fashion, Emperor Palpatine decided that the best revenge would be to again confront the Rebellion with its greatest fear—a resurrected Death Star.

Palpatine summoned the original Death Star's lead designer, Bevel Lemelisk, ordering him to produce an even more advanced battle station. After finishing work on the *Tarkin* battle station, Lemelisk's design team soon completed the second Death Star's design.

Not only was the second Death Star larger and more deadly, but several flaws in the original design were corrected. The vulnerable thermal exhaust ports were replaced with millimeter-wide heat dispersion ducts, leaving no weak spots in this battle station's armor. The finished design increased the overall size of the new Death Star to 160 kilometers in diameter. The north pole of the station featured a one-hundred-story tower topped by the Emperor's private observation chamber—perhaps the most heavily armored and shielded portion of the station.

This new Death Star's central weapon, the terrifying superlaser, featured substantially increased power, allowing it to be recharged in a matter of minutes rather than hours. The superlaser's targeting and power-control systems were refined so the weapon could be turned on capital starships.

Lemelisk added 20,000 turbolasers

to repel attacks from starfighters and capital ships. Once completed, this station would have carried thousands of TIE fighters, troops, and ground combat vehicles. This new Death Star would have been invincible; the only way to stop it would have been to destroy it while it was still under construction.

Of course, the Death Star was also part of an elaborate trap set by Emperor Palpatine to lure the Rebels out of hiding. For nearly four years the Rebels had managed to avoid Imperial war fleets. The Emperor provided a target so dangerous that the Rebels could not afford to pass it up.

Palpatine allowed the Alliance's Bothan spies to learn the location of the Death Star; he did *not* disclose the fact that the superlaser would be fully operational by the time the Rebel fleet arrived. The Rebels fell for his simple trap.

Imperial engineers built an immense shield generator on the forest moon of Endor to protect the partially completed Death Star. However, the Empire underestimated the "primitive" Ewoks indigenous to Endor's moon. A small team of Rebel commandos was able to enlist the Ewoks' aid and destroy the shield generator, thus allowing the *Millennium Falcon*, commanded by General Lando Calrissian, to fly inside the partially completed battle station and destroy its power core.

As the second Death Star exploded over the forest moon, the Emperor was killed and his war fleet was flung into disarray. A month later Rebel leader Mon Mothma declared the end of the Rebellion and announced the formation of the New Republic.

Front View

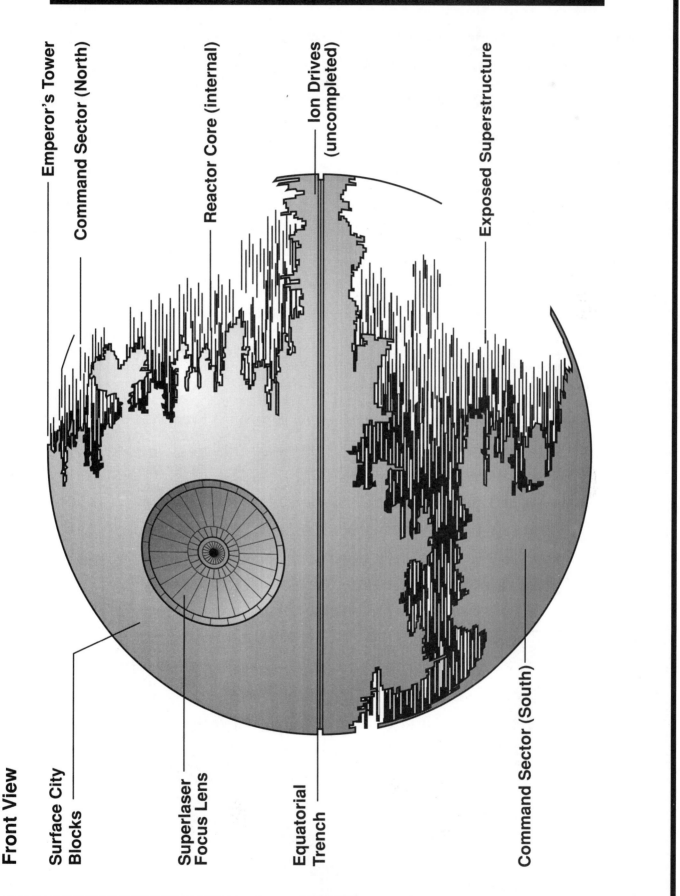

Emperor's Tower

Command Sector (North)

Reactor Core (internal)

Ion Drives (uncompleted)

Exposed Superstructure

Surface City Blocks

Superlaser Focus Lens

Equatorial Trench

Command Sector (South)

DEATH STAR PROTOTYPE

PROTOTYPE CUSTOM DEEP-SPACE BATTLE STATION

The prototype Death Star was built at the Maw Installation before the construction of the first Death Star battle station at Despayre, a planet in the Horuz system. Many of the original Death Star's systems were conceived and designed by famed starship engineer Bevel Lemelisk and others who worked at the Maw Installation. Under the direction of Tol Sivron, the Twi'lek chief scientist, the installation's specialists built a limited prototype specifically to see if an operational planet-destroying superlaser could be created.

Initial construction efforts were a success, and soon Lemelisk and Tarkin were headed to Despayre for the construction of a full Death Star. The Maw Installation . . . and the prototype Death Star . . . were left behind and forgotten.

The prototype was never fully completed; its mission had been fulfilled, and it was simply anchored above the Maw Installation planetoids. The construct had an open frame with support beams forming a giant globe 120 kilometers in diameter. The only visible components inside the frame were the giant reactor core, a few engines for sublight movement, and the prototype superlaser itself.

The prototype superlaser had several disadvantages compared with the working model of the first Death Star. For example, the firepower was "only" sufficient to destroy the core of a planet: while the planet would inevitably be rendered uninhabitable, the weapon did not completely vaporize the victim world. The targeting system was never perfected, plus the superlaser was also incredibly wasteful of power and the weapon's storage batteries took several hours to recharge fully. While the weapon could be fired at reduced power, the superlaser's destructive ability was reduced significantly.

The prototype Death Star was never intended to be a practical weapon of war, so there was no need to install the maintenance and repair machinery, the immense computer core, or the hyperdrive engines that took up a huge amount of space in the actual Death Star space station. Instead, the prototype had only a small command cabin with slave-rigged computer systems to control the superlaser and drive units. This computer system minimized personnel requirements, but such linked computer systems are prone to failure without constant maintenance and are not practical for military starships.

The prototype was activated by Tol Sivron after the Maw Installation was attacked by a New Republic task force. The space station was finally destroyed when Kyp Durron, piloting the Sun Crusher, lured the prototype Death Star into one of the Maw's black holes, where it was crushed by incredible gravitational forces.

Front View

Superlaser Power
Distribution Shaft

Power Cell
Coupling

Ion Engines
(for sublight
movement)

Main Reactor

Frame

Power Distribution Shaft

Power Amplification
System

Focus Lens Frame

Superlaser
Focus Lens

Amplification
Crystal Prototype

Laser Crystal

Command
Cabin

Reactor
Core

Frame

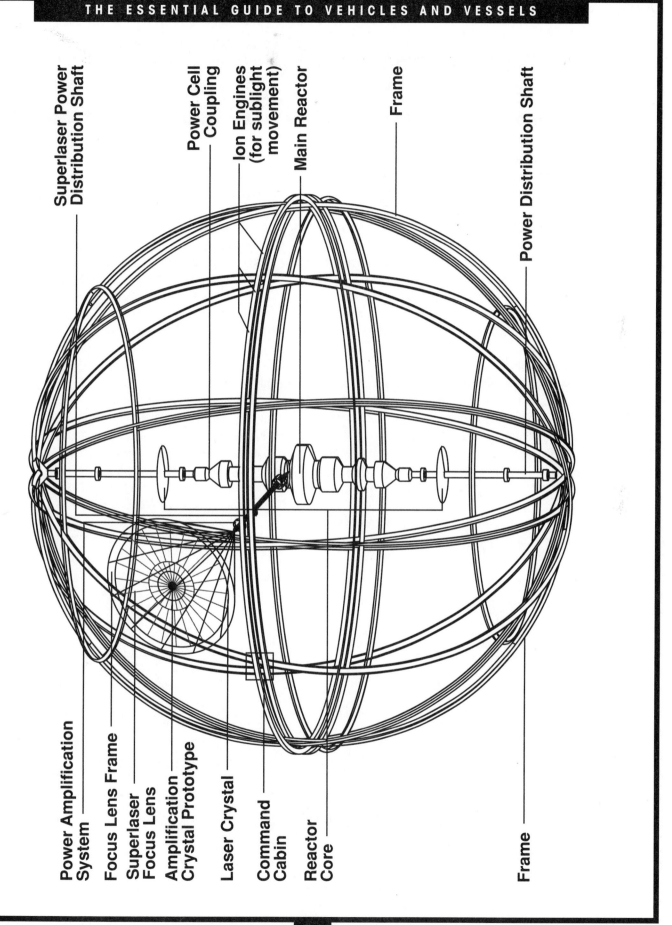

DESERT SKIFF

Ubrikkian Bantha II Cargo Skiff

Skiffs are utility repulsorlift vehicles that often are used to move cargo or passengers. Jabba the Hutt used a number of skiffs as escorts for his sail barge. His henchmen used them to rush to a raiding site, allowing the passengers on the sail barge to enjoy the battle from a safe distance.

Skiffs are common in ports and warehouse districts across the galaxy. Depending on their work detail, they can be open or enclosed, and can handle over one hundred tons of cargo—often volume, rather than mass, provides the limiting factor in cargo transportation. Skiffs can reach speeds of 250 kilometers per hour and can fly as high as 50 meters above a planet's surface.

These are very basic vehicles. The whole deck is open and the driver control station is normally located at the rear of the vehicle. Skiffs are so simple that even labor droids can control them. Since they are intended to move at slow speeds, often the driver must stand while driving. A single repulsorlift engine provides forward thrust, while steering is handled by angling two steering vanes that hang off the back of the hull.

Cargo can be loaded by hand, or the driver can extend magnetic lifters to pull cargo modules up onto the deck.

These modules are locked in place with magnetic fasteners and reinforced with standard cargo straps.

Skiffs are sometimes used as mass-transit vehicles, especially on poor worlds that can't afford anything better. They can be fitted with up to sixteen seats and are often supplied with rain screens to keep passengers dry.

Skiffs do not make good combat vehicles. They are neither maneuverable nor sturdy enough to stand up in battle. A single blast from a hand blaster can disable the repulsorlift unit or smash a steering vane. If the repulsorlift unit is damaged, the skiff can topple if weight shifts too quickly—something that a number of Jabba's henchmen learned the hard way when they tumbled down into the Sarlacc's mouth.

Jabba the Hutt used a number of Ubrikkian Bantha II cargo skiffs as patrol and escort vehicles for his sail barge. While they were armor-plated, they were still unsuited to combat, as Luke Skywalker quickly proved. Jabba had had extendable gangplanks affixed to the skiffs to increase the entertainment value of his Sarlacc feedings. After the rescue of Han Solo, Luke Skywalker and other Rebel heroes used one of Jabba's skiffs to escape from the Great Pit of Carkoon even as Jabba's sail barge exploded spectacularly.

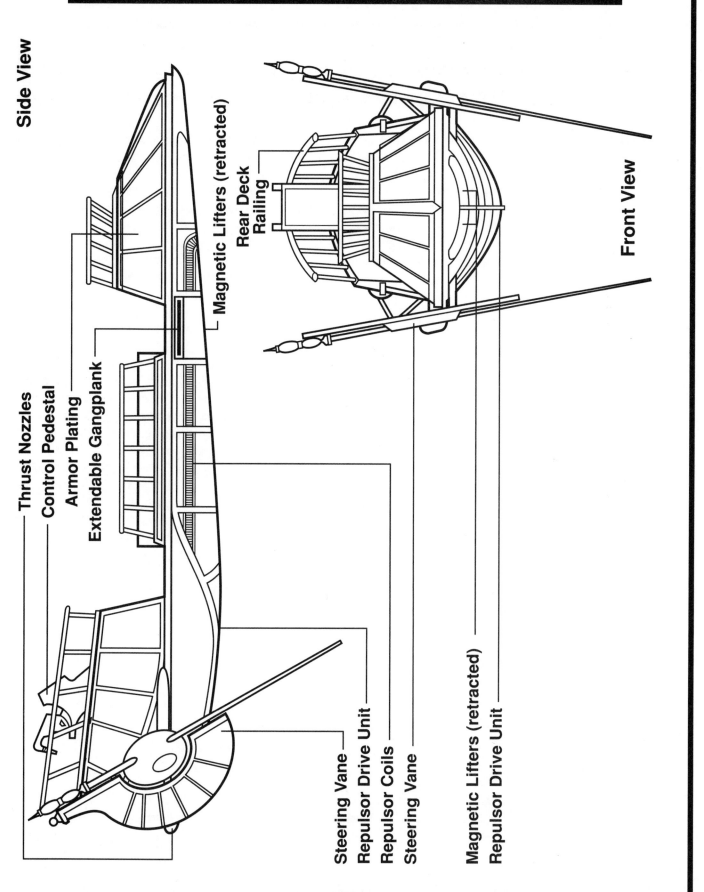

Side View

Thrust Nozzles

Control Pedestal

Armor Plating

Extendable Gangplank

Magnetic Lifters (retracted)

Rear Deck Railing

Front View

Steering Vane

Repulsor Drive Unit

Repulsor Coils

Steering Vane

Magnetic Lifters (retracted)

Repulsor Drive Unit

DREADNAUGHT

RENDILI STARDRIVE DREADNAUGHT HEAVY CRUISER

Dreadnaughts are large, ancient heavy cruisers that originally were commissioned by the Old Republic. These six-hundred-meter-long ships were among the largest ships in the Old Republic Navy before the introduction of the Victory Star Destroyer. While the cruisers are slow and poorly armed by modern starship standards, a number of Dreadnaughts had been refitted over the years for service in both the Empire and the Rebel Alliance.

The standard Dreadnaught in the Imperial Navy was not significantly different from the original ship the Old Republic had used. The ship maintained ten turbolaser cannons, twenty quad turbolaser cannons, and ten turbolaser batteries. Even after refitting, a Dreadnaught's sublight speed barely matched that of the Victory Star Destroyer. The hyperdrive had a slow Class Two rating, and the hull and shields were weak for a ship of its size. Refitted Dreadnaughts still required a crew of 16,000 soldiers. The Empire was able to construct flight decks in most of its Dreadnaughts, allowing them to carry a squadron of twelve TIE fighters. Imperial Dreadnaughts were normally assigned to patrol duties in outlying portions of the Empire or sent to protect supply convoys.

The Rebel Alliance took a fundamentally different approach when refitting its Dreadnaughts for duty. The resulting ships were known as Rebel assault frigates. Alliance technicians removed most of the superstructure to increase fuel efficiency and sublight speed. Dorsal fins with banks of maneuvering jets increased maneuverability, and by using large-scale automation, Alliance technicians were able to reduce the crew requirement to just under 5,000. Rebel assault frigates carried no fighters, but their weaponry included fifteen laser cannons, twenty quad laser cannons, and fifteen turbolaser batteries. Unfortunately, these modifications required time and money, and so the Alliance had very few assault frigates.

With the advent of Grand Admiral Thrawn's quest to capture the *Katana* fleet of Rendili StarDrive Dreadnaughts, historians around the galaxy showed renewed interest in this "cursed" battle fleet, known as "the Dark Force" because of its dark gray hull surfacing. Each *Katana* Dreadnaught was completely refitted with slave-rigging units. This reduced each ship's crew to about 2,000 soldiers, but it also tied each ship's vital systems into a central computer. One Dreadnaught could seize control of the entire fleet . . . and that is exactly what happened.

A hive virus quickly spread through the fleet, driving its victims insane; the *Katana* fleet crew members slaved their ships together and jumped into hyperspace, disappearing for nearly half a century. Only after the New Republic contacted Talon Karrde was the Dark Force rediscovered, but Grand Admiral Thrawn had already learned the location of the *Katana* fleet. The Empire captured most of the two hundred ships, and Thrawn filled the Dreadnaughts with his clone stormtroopers, giving the Imperial Grand Admiral a decisive advantage in his own campaign against the New Republic.

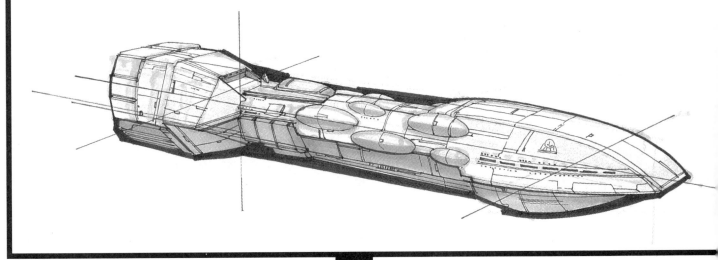

Front View

Side View

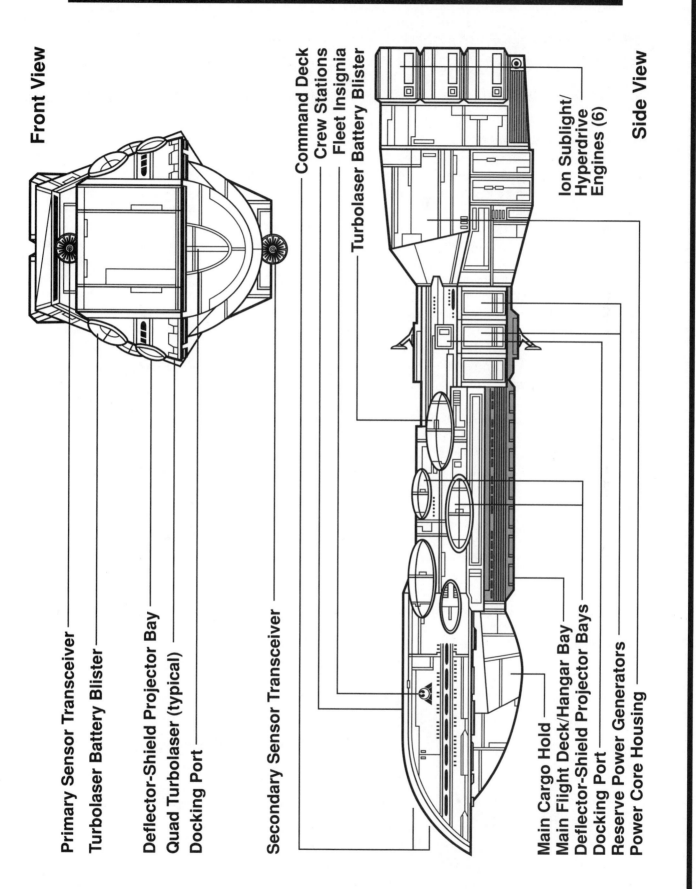

Primary Sensor Transceiver

Turbolaser Battery Blister

Deflector-Shield Projector Bay

Quad Turbolaser (typical)

Docking Port

Secondary Sensor Transceiver

Command Deck

Crew Stations

Fleet Insignia

Turbolaser Battery Blister

Ion Sublight/
Hyperdrive
Engines (6)

Main Cargo Hold

Main Flight Deck/Hangar Bay

Deflector-Shield Projector Bays

Docking Port

Reserve Power Generators

Power Core Housing

E-WING FIGHTER

FreiTek, Inc. E-wing Starfighter

The FreiTek E-wing starfighter was introduced during Grand Admiral Thrawn's campaign against the New Republic. A year later, when the revived Emperor made his bid for power, the ship had become a key element of the New Republic's starfighter forces.

The E-wing was designed by the former Incom Corporation designers who created the fabulously successful X-wing starfighter. The E-wing gave their new company, FreiTek, a design that ranked with the best fighters any company was producing. Initial engagements with Imperial fighters convinced the New Republic's pilots that they had an incredible ship at their disposal. The E-wing was initially designed with the same mission profile as the older A-wing: to protect New Republic convoys from Imperial raiding missions.

The ship provides respectable speed, but its greatest asset is firepower. The primary weapons are fire-linked triple laser cannons: one cannon on the end of each wing, with the third cannon directly above the cockpit.

The E-wing also serves as an excellent medium assault and close-support fighter because of its sixteen proton torpedoes. These heavy weapons can severely damage capital ships and reinforced military bases, giving New Republic strategists another option when B-wings are too slow for a mission.

The E-wing offers performance that until recently was thought to be impossible. FreiTek's engineers incorporated several remarkable advances in flight control and power regulation. The resulting ship is as fast and maneuverable as the TIE interceptor, and its heavily reinforced hull allows the E-wing to absorb more damage than the New Republic's famed X-wings can.

Unfortunately, those advancements have come at a price. The E-wing's advanced computer systems have proved overwhelming for R2 astromech droids. The New Republic has had to switch over to the new Industrial Automaton R7 astromechs, which were designed specifically to handle the more advanced systems and hyperdrive interfaces aboard the E-wing.

The E-wing has a reliable fixed-wing design. While some designers consider movable wings essential to top combat performance, FreiTek's designers produced a ship that is superior to any movable-wing design. The E-wing is easy to repair between missions; modular parts, from laser cannon actuators to power couplings, enable New Republic technicians to strip and rebuild an E-wing in almost half the time it would take to perform a similar operation on an X-wing.

Initial battles showed that the laser cannons were underpowered because they used synthetically spin-coiled Tibanna gas, which broke down quickly, greatly reducing the fire range. Because of the Battle of Calamari, New Republic technicians lacked the time to design a permanent solution, such as refitting the weapons for a more suitable blaster gas. Instead, they rigged the laser cannons to accept three times the standard power feed, increasing the weapon range to acceptable levels but also risking a terminal power overload. These modified ships have been dubbed E-wing: Type B.

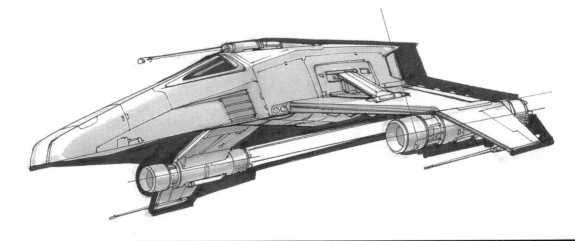

Front View

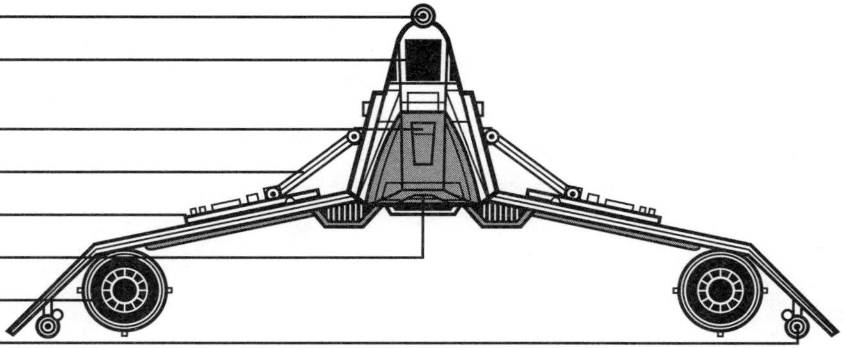

Laser Cannon
Cockpit
Sensor Window
Support Strut
Wing
Proton-Torpedo Launcher
Drive Engine
Laser Cannon

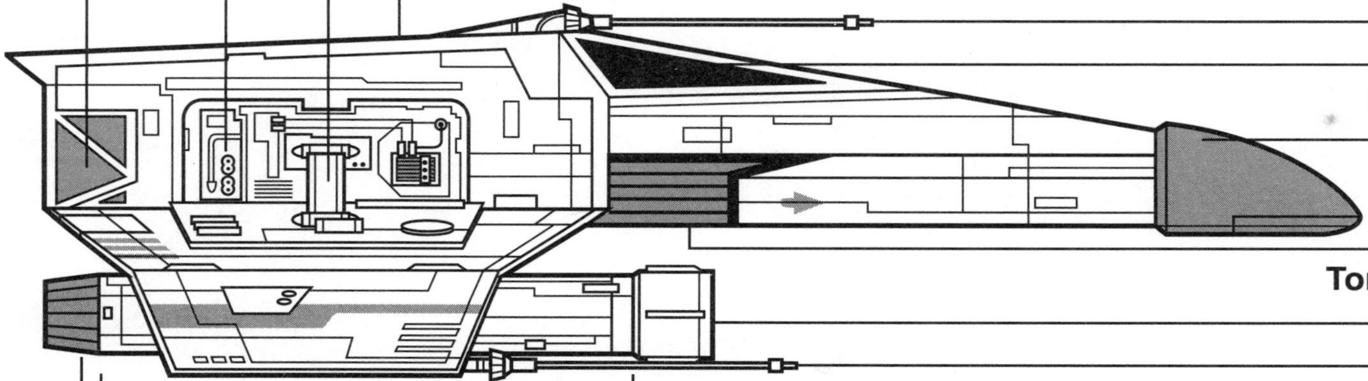

Power Generator
Deflector-Shield Generator
Support Strut
R7 Astromech Droid (in sealed compartment)
Laser Cannon
Cockpit
Nose Cone with Sensor Array
Proton-Torpedo Launcher
Cooling Intake
Laser Cannon
Drive Engine
Exhaust Nacelle

Side View

ECLIPSE STAR DESTROYER

KUAT DRIVE YARDS *ECLIPSE*-CLASS SUPER STAR DESTROYER

Emperor Palpatine was never one for subtlety. His Empire had been built on a foundation of rule through terror. When he reappeared on the galactic stage six years after his apparent "death" at the Battle of Endor, he returned to his old ways of grandiose weapons and attacks of stunning brutality. Renewed in a fresh clone body, Palpatine gathered his allies from the remaining Imperial factions and directed his forces from a new command vessel, the *Eclipse*.

The *Eclipse* was a new Super Star Destroyer that was a stunning 17.5 kilometers long: it was twice the size of the original Super Star Destroyer and over ten times the size of Imperial Star Destroyers. The Emperor's new flagship was as much a symbol of Palpatine's thirst for power as it was military matériel.

The incredible ship was deliberately designed to frighten enemy forces, for a frightened enemy is a defeated enemy. The ship was solid black, and its hull resembled that of naval warships of eras long past. The *Eclipse* easily achieved its objective of demoralizing enemy troops.

In combat, the *Eclipse*'s hull and shields were so strong that it could ram enemy vessels without hesitation. The ship was equipped with ten gravity-well projectors to prevent enemy vessels from escaping to hyperspace. Five hundred heavy laser cannons and 550 turbolasers made the ship capable of engaging entire New Republic fleets. The *Eclipse* carried fifty squadrons of TIE interceptors (six hundred ships) and eight squadrons of TIE bombers.

The *Eclipse* was also intended to devastate entire worlds. Its main weapon was a superlaser weapon, although its power was only two-thirds that of the main weapon aboard the first Death Star—it was "merely" powerful enough to crack the crust of a planet rather than destroy it outright.

For ground assaults, the *Eclipse* carried five prefabricated garrison bases and one hundred AT-AT walkers. With a crew of over 700,000 beings and 150,000 troops, the destroyer rivaled the Death Star in sheer manpower.

The *Eclipse* was stopped over the Pinnacle Moon when Luke Skywalker and Leia Organa Solo joined Force energies to engulf Emperor Palpatine in a wave of life energy. This action stunned Palpatine, forcing him to lose control over the Force storms he had summoned. As Luke and Leia escaped from the *Eclipse*, the storms consumed and destroyed the vessel.

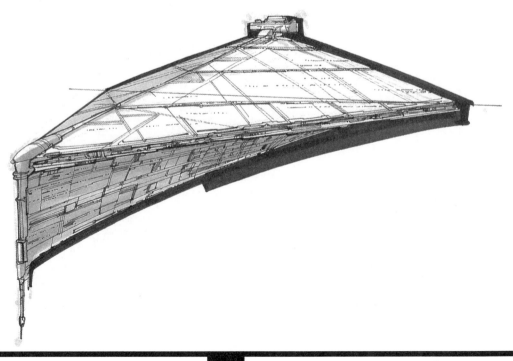

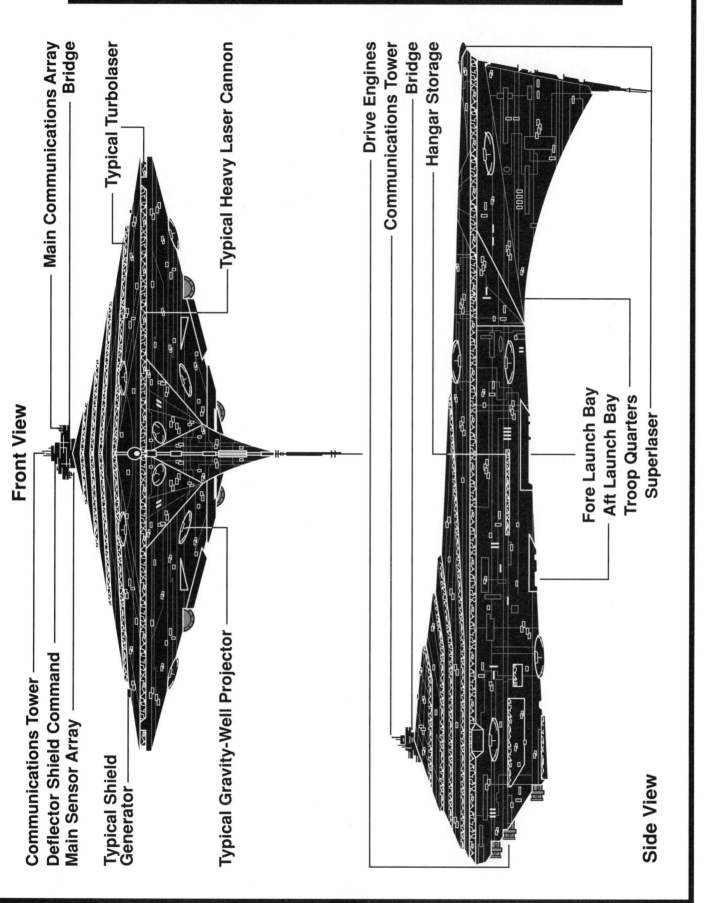

Front View

Main Communications Array
Bridge
Typical Turbolaser
Typical Heavy Laser Cannon

Communications Tower
Deflector Shield Command
Main Sensor Array

Typical Shield Generator

Typical Gravity-Well Projector

Drive Engines
Communications Tower
Bridge
Hangar Storage

Fore Launch Bay
Aft Launch Bay
Troop Quarters
Superlaser

Side View

ENFORCER ONE

CORE GALAXY SYSTEMS DREADNAUGHT

Enforcer One was Bogga the Hutt's military dreadnaught and the flagship of his space fleet, a vessel that repeatedly demonstrated the Hutt's power and was responsible for many of Bogga's great victories, including the raid on the Nematiec Gang asteroid base and the capture of Finhead Stonebone's pirate ships. Commanded by Captain Norufu, an enslaved near-human, the ship's home port was Bogga's palace on Taboon's moon.

The *Enforcer One* was a heavily modified Core Galaxy Systems dreadnaught originally designed for planetary occupations. This type of ship normally used its turbolasers to blast through planetary defense armadas, then entered a planet's upper atmosphere to allow its drop ships to deliver a planetary invasion force.

Bogga acquired this ship after it had been decommissioned by the Republic and shipped to the salvage yards on Ord Trasi. Even in its stripped-down state, *Enforcer One*'s weapons and shields were still powerful. Captain Norufu had been known to allow attackers the luxury of a few opening shots, believing that having enemies watch their blasts dissipate harmlessly would inspire terror.

The *Enforcer One*'s main offensive weapon was a fixed heavy turbolaser. The power core and laser actuator had an advanced cooling system to allow the weapon extended usage, while the long laser barrel was modified with experimental galven circuitry to more tightly focus the beam and increase the range.

Additional weapons included sixteen laser cannons mounted on turrets, fast enough to accurately target small fighters, although they lacked the punch to damage large capital ships. *Enforcer One* also had four tractor-beam projectors; one of Norufu's favorite tactics was to use the tractor beams to capture a ship and then haul it around to point-blank range for the heavy turbolaser. Bogga's dreadnaught had an interior landing bay nearly three hundred meters long and a pair of immense ship loading arms that could be used to pull captured ships into the bay.

The ship carried six light tactical fighters, which Bogga ended up replacing with alarming frequency. The Hutt's pilots seldom received much training in fighter combat, and the Hutt considered the ships expendable, too. Stonebone's gunners destroyed one of these ships in an incident that killed the pilot, Dreebo. Demonstrating why he had earned the title "the Merciful One," Bogga decided to withhold Dreebo's service bonus and *not* charge Dreebo's home clan for the fighter's replacement.

Enforcer One was crewed by the usual assortment of multispecies Hutt underlings. Captain Norufu was responsible for the down-and-out spacers who handled the control, navigation, and weapons systems. Bogga's chief enforcer, the Weequay known as Grimorg, had the unenviable job of keeping control of the many Weequays, Nikto, Klatooinans, and Vodrans who served as crew hands and boarding troops.

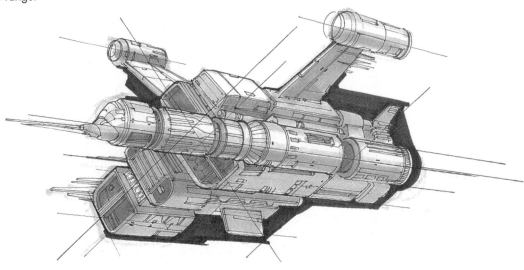

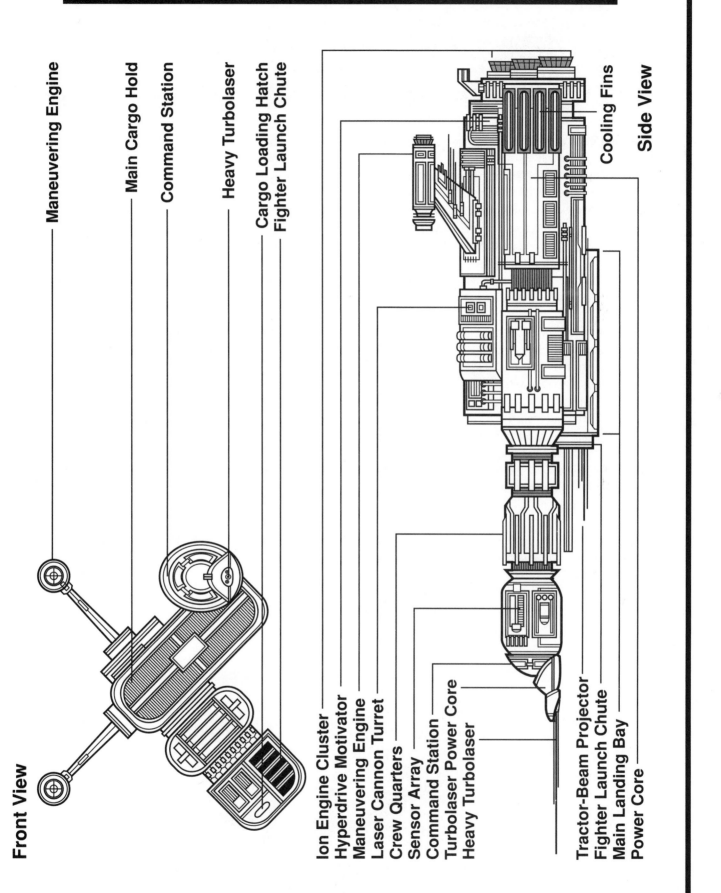

Front View

Maneuvering Engine

Main Cargo Hold

Command Station

Heavy Turbolaser

Cargo Loading Hatch

Fighter Launch Chute

Side View

Cooling Fins

Ion Engine Cluster

Hyperdrive Motivator

Maneuvering Engine

Laser Cannon Turret

Crew Quarters

Sensor Array

Command Station

Turbolaser Power Core

Heavy Turbolaser

Tractor-Beam Projector

Fighter Launch Chute

Main Landing Bay

Power Core

ESCAPE POD

CORELLIAN ENGINEERING CORPORATION CLASS-6 ESCAPE POD

Without the efforts of the astromech droid known as R2-D2, Princess Leia's efforts to stop the Empire would have ended in failure over the desert world of Tatooine. However, Artoo, following direct orders from the Princess, commandeered an escape pod and blasted away from the captured *Tantive IV*, taking with him C-3PO and the plans to the Death Star. Imperial gunners assumed that the launch was due to a system malfunction and decided not to destroy the pod.

Only Leia's orders allowed Artoo access to the pod, since Imperial law requires giving organics first priority access to escape equipment in the event of a deep-space disaster, while droids are often left aboard ship.

Escape pods are standard aboard all deep-space starships. The *Tantive IV* carried eight six-being escape pods, all very simple in construction. Explosive separator charges eject such pods away from the ship, and the escape pod's distress beacon is automatically activated upon launch, although R2-D2 deactivated the distress beacon just before touchdown on Tatooine in order to throw off Imperial pursuit.

While there are probably as many different types of escape pods as there are starships, they all share a few characteristics. The interior of an escape pod is spartan: passengers are expected to use the pod only for a few hours. Some pods seat as few as two people, while larger pods carry over a dozen beings. Padded gee-couches protect occupants from injury. A simple piloting station provides access to the sensor, communication, and flight control systems, although the shipboard systems are heavily automated so the escape pod can land without a pilot at the controls. Sensors provide atmosphere as well as radiation and gravitational information about nearby planets, and a limited comm transceiver scans for activity on standard communication frequencies.

The interior compartments carry up to two weeks' worth of rations, including food, water, survival shelters, medpacs, breath masks, glow rods, and comlinks. Sometimes an escape pod's emergency supplies include a civilian hunting blaster. In emergencies, survivors can use the escape pod as a shelter while seeking more adequate protection.

Escape pods have simple drive systems with just enough fuel to orient the pod toward the nearest habitable planet and assist in emergency braking during landing. In some pods, parachutes, maneuvering jets, flotation devices, or repulsorlift drive units slow planetary descent and cushion landing.

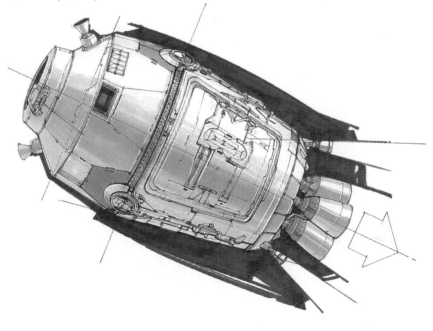

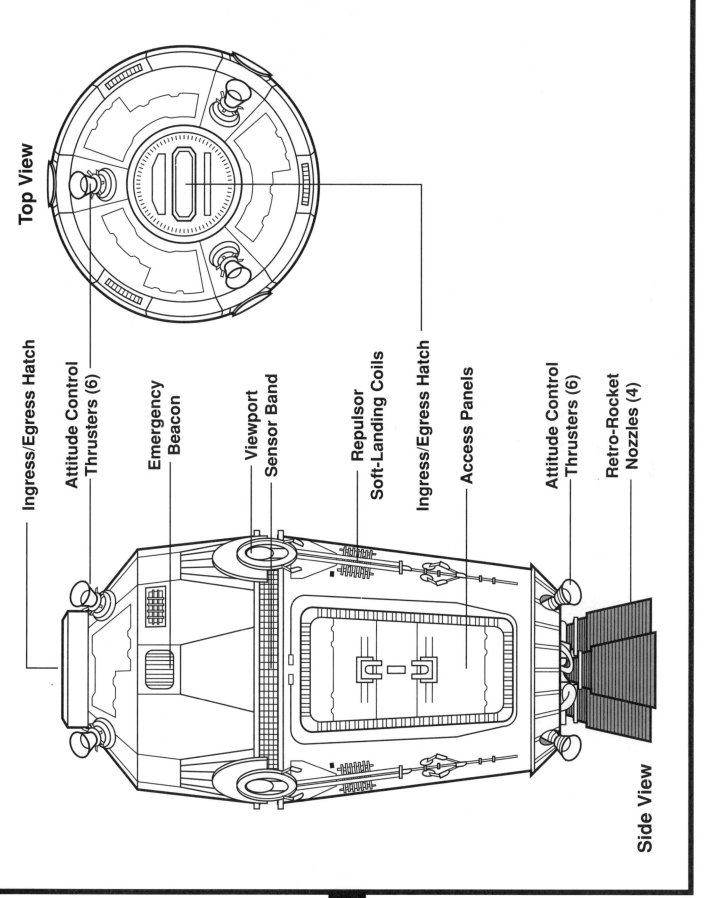

Top View

Ingress/Egress Hatch

Attitude Control Thrusters (6)

Emergency Beacon

Viewport Sensor Band

Repulsor Soft-Landing Coils

Ingress/Egress Hatch

Access Panels

Attitude Control Thrusters (6)

Retro-Rocket Nozzles (4)

Side View

EXPANDED B-WING FIGHTER

SLAYN & KORPIL B-WING/E2 ASSAULT FIGHTER

Admiral Ackbar used an expanded B-wing fighter dubbed the B-wing/E2 (for "enhanced model two") as his personal diplomatic shuttle. The B-wing/E2 is the second version of the *two-man* B-wing starfighter, the first of which was originally designed by Ackbar and the engineers of the Verpine Hive colonies Slayn and Korpil shortly after the Battle of Yavin.

The original two-man ship, later dubbed the B-wing/E, was designed at Research Station Shantipole, an asteroid design facility deep within the Roche Asteroid Field. Imperial spies nearly captured the design specs, but a group of Rebel operatives foiled the Imperial espionage operation. One year later Slayn & Korpil produced the premier B-wing/E2.

Physically, the B-wing E-models look very similar to the original Alliance B-wing fighter. The only major difference is that the command cabin has been stretched out another three meters to accommodate a gunner, who sits directly behind the pilot. Adding the gunner has resulted in a dramatic increase in enemy kills, because previously the lone pilot had to handle flying and gunnery simultaneously. The new gunner's compartment is mounted on an independent gyro-stabilizer to ensure a stable field of fire regardless of any evasive maneuvers the B-wing may be making.

The B-wing/E is faster and tougher but less maneuverable than the standard B-wing. The modified ship is as fast as the Y-wing fighter. Increased shield generators have added to the ship's ability to withstand damage, making the vessel a true threat to Imperial ships. The standard weapon configuration for the B-wing/E consists of two fire-linked laser cannons, three ion cannons, and a proton-torpedo launcher with eight torpedoes. The B-wing/E2 added an extra proton-torpedo launcher for a faster rate of fire but kept the same standard load of eight torpedoes. Recently, New Republic technicians designed a removable ammo magazine that can be mounted on the "neck" of the fighter. This attachment carries an additional twelve proton torpedoes and feeds directly into the launchers, although it disrupts the fighter's mass balance enough to reduce maneuverability.

Ackbar's personal B-wing/E2 was modified from the standard design, with the second seat placed beside the pilot. The additional space behind the pilot's station was converted into a cargo compartment.

It was Ackbar's B-wing that crashed while on final approach to the planet Vortex and smashed through the Vors' Cathedral of Winds, killing thousands of the avian aliens. New Republic intelligence later learned that the ship had been sabotaged by Terpfen, Ackbar's chief starship mechanic and an unwilling Imperial spy serving Ambassador Furgan of Carida.

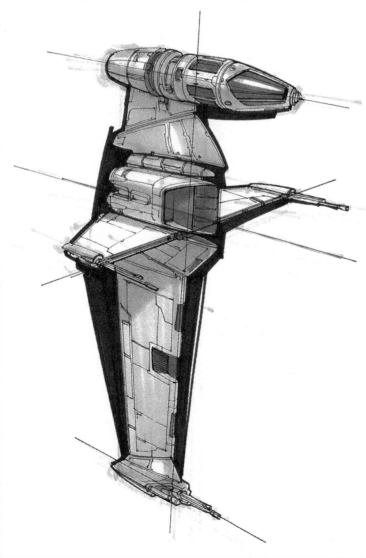

Front View

Side View (wings closed)

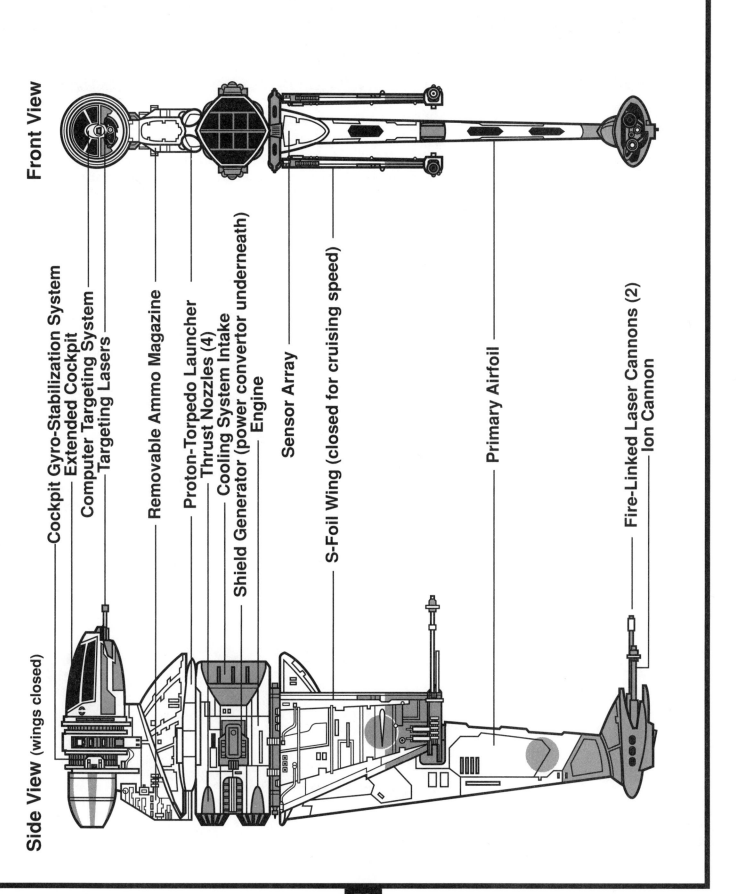

Cockpit Gyro-Stabilization System
Extended Cockpit
Computer Targeting System
Targeting Lasers

Removable Ammo Magazine

Proton-Torpedo Launcher
Thrust Nozzles (4)
Cooling System Intake
Shield Generator (power convertor underneath)
Engine

Sensor Array

S-Foil Wing (closed for cruising speed)

Primary Airfoil

Fire-Linked Laser Cannons (2)
Ion Cannon

EXECUTOR

KUAT DRIVE YARDS SUPER STAR DESTROYER

The first of four *Super*-class Star Destroyers in service before the Battle of Hoth, the *Executor* was Darth Vader's command ship while he hunted down the main Rebel Alliance base. At 8,000 meters long, it was the largest traditional starship constructed by the Imperial Navy—only the Death Stars and torpedo spheres were larger. Super Star Destroyers were Imperial Navy command ships and were assigned only to the most important and prestigious missions. Being assigned to the *Executor* was regarded by Navy officers as the fast track to promotion.

In a military sense, the Super Star Destroyer was somewhat impractical, since a smaller ship could fulfill its mission duties. Rather, the Super Star Destroyers represented the Emperor's unlimited power and resources. The Imperial Star Destroyer frightened worlds into submission; the Super Star Destroyer terrorized them beyond the capability for resistance. At over five times the length of a standard Star Destroyer, it could conquer without firing a shot, and so win the battle before engaging the enemy.

Bristling with over a thousand weapons, including turbolasers, concussion-missile tubes, tractor-beam projectors, and ion cannons, Super Star Destroyers wielded awesome firepower. They held two full wings of TIE fighters, for 144 ships, as well as 200 other combat and support ships. For ground assaults, Super Star Destroyers maintained a full corps of stormtroopers, 38,000 ground troopers, three prefabricated Imperial garrison bases, and enough walkers to decimate any Rebel base.

The *Executor* was built at the starship yards of Fondor after being designed by Lira Wessex, designer of the Imperial Star Destroyer. Upon its completion, the ship was presented to Lord Vader as a headquarters ship for his quest to find the Rebel Alliance's command base. It was originally commanded by Admiral Ozzel, but after his unfortunate death, Admiral Piett was given command of the vessel by Lord Vader.

The *Executor* was destroyed at the Battle of Endor. After its shield generators were destroyed, Rebel fighter pilot Arvel Crynyd smashed his A-wing fighter into the *Executor*'s bridge. With the ship crippled and damage-control crews unable to seize command using the auxiliary control centers, the Death Star's gravity pulled the *Executor* into the immense battle station. The *Executor* exploded on impact with the Death Star, also causing significant damage to the incomplete battle station. Many of the Empire's best young officers were killed in that incident, making the New Republic's eventual victory over the Empire far easier.

While only four Super Star Destroyers were in service by the Battle of Hoth, it is known that several more were under construction. It is unknown how many of these ships were completed before the Battle of Endor, but several are thought to be in the hands of rogue Imperial warlords.

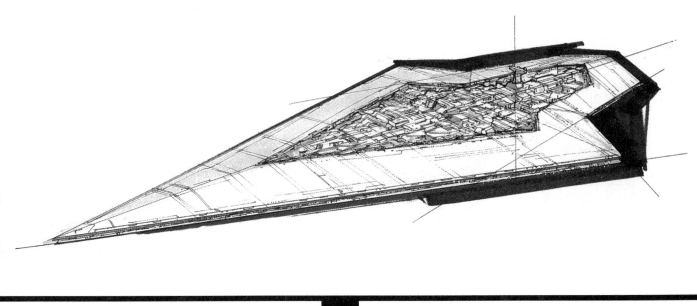

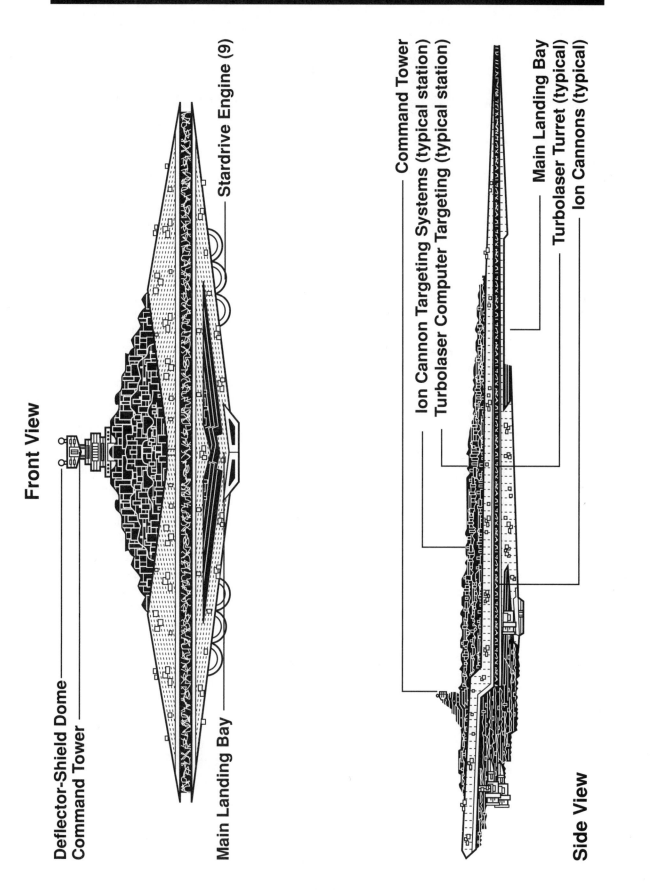

Front View

Deflector-Shield Dome
Command Tower

Stardrive Engine (9)

Main Landing Bay

Command Tower

Ion Cannon Targeting Systems (typical station)
Turbolaser Computer Targeting (typical station)

Main Landing Bay
Turbolaser Turret (typical)
Ion Cannons (typical)

Side View

FLURRY

MODIFIED SOROSUUB *QUASAR FIRE*–CLASS BULK CRUISER

The *Flurry* was a cruiser-carrier, commanded by Captain Tessa Manchisco, used by the Rebel Alliance in the battle against the Ssi-ruuk. The ship was a modified SoroSuub *Quasar Fire*–class bulk cruiser that had served with distinction in the Virgillian Civil War.

The Sullustans donated several of the stripped-down bulk freighters to the Virgillian Alignment forces, having first modified the ships by removing the main cargo brackets, leaving only the main hull brace, the drives, and the command pod. Then the ships were fitted with hangar bays for fighters. Upon receiving the fleet of carriers, the Virgillians promptly installed stolen Imperial military-grade weapons and shield generators.

The *Flurry* was eventually commissioned in the Rebel Alliance fleet after being donated by the Rebel-sympathetic Virgillian Alignment, which had ousted Imperial occupation forces from its system shortly before the Battle of Endor.

The *Flurry* was 340 meters long, with almost all the interior space taken up by its single starfighter hangar bay. It could carry nearly fifty fighters, a significant improvement over the three dozen ships a standard Mon Calamari Star Cruiser could carry. Complete repair and maintenance facilities were stationed behind the main flight deck. The *Flurry* had only a pair of heavy turbolasers for defense, while a pair of tractor-beam projectors guided fighters in for safe docking.

The cruiser's mission profile was to deliver fighters into combat and then retreat to a safe distance. If attacked by larger ships, the *Flurry* was to call back its fighters for defense or flee until the fighters could regroup.

The *Flurry* carried a crew of 250, although over half those crewers were devoted to starfighter maintenance and repair. The Quasar Fire carrier-cruisers are lean combat vehicles with a small bridge and support crew. A single astromech droid on the bridge helps with navigation and control, while each gunnery station has an additional astromech droid to provide targeting telemetry.

For the Bakura mission against the Ssi-ruuk incursion, the *Flurry* was equipped with a prototype battle analysis computer (BAC). The creation of famed Alliance strategist General Jan Dodonna, the BAC was linked to every navigation and combat computer in the Alliance task force to provide detailed composite images of the battle.

As a result of the emergency nature of the Bakura relief effort, the *Flurry* was assigned whatever Alliance starfighters were still operational: Captain Manchisco got twenty X-wings, three A-wings, and four B-wings. Fortunately, the X-wings included Rogue Squadron, under the command of Wedge Antilles. While Alliance command knew that the B-wings were quite likely to break down (because there hadn't been time for a thorough maintenance overhaul following the Battle of Endor), it was thought that their firepower would give the task force some much-needed punch, even if that help would be only temporary.

The *Flurry* was destroyed over Bakura when the Imperial Carrack cruiser *Dominant* suddenly opened fire on her. All hands were lost and were posthumously decorated for their heroic sacrifice.

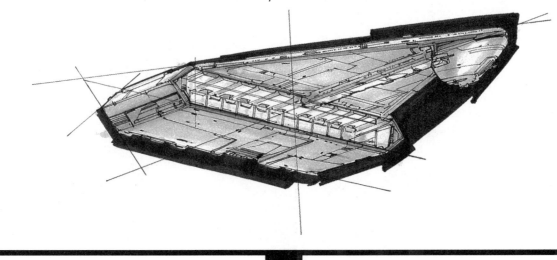

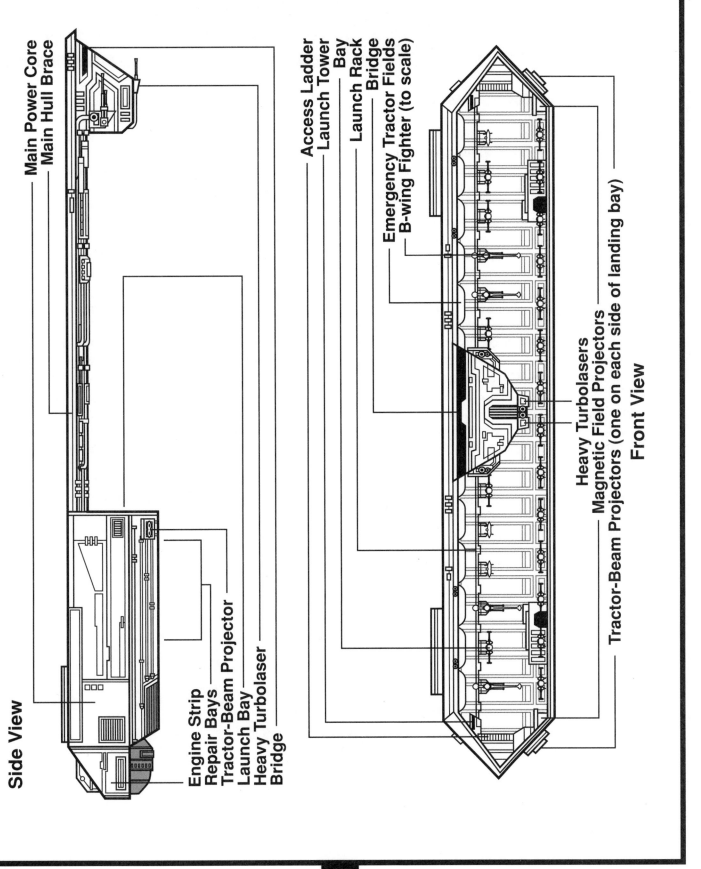

Side View

Main Power Core
Main Hull Brace

Engine Strip
Repair Bays
Tractor-Beam Projector
Launch Bay
Heavy Turbolaser
Bridge

Access Ladder
Launch Tower
Bay
Launch Rack
Bridge
Emergency Tractor Fields
B-wing Fighter (to scale)

Heavy Turbolasers
Magnetic Field Projectors
Tractor-Beam Projectors (one on each side of landing bay)
Front View

GURI'S STINGER

MODIFIED SURRONIAN CONQUEROR ASSAULT SHIP

The enigmatic woman known only as Guri is a bodyguard and operative for the powerful criminal overlord Prince Xizor. Little is known of Guri's history before she began working for Xizor, and despite her prominent status within Xizor's organization, she remains a being of mystery.

Guri pilots the modified assault ship *Stinger*. The distinctive profile of the *Stinger* is known and feared by criminals throughout the Empire, from the capital of Coruscant to distant trading worlds like Nar Shaddaa, Celanon, and Ord Mantell.

The *Stinger* is a modified Surronian assault ship that Xizor owned long before he entrusted it to Guri. Guri uses the ship as a mobile base of operations when she is commanding Xizor's various paramilitary groups, but she has also been known to use it to smuggle precious cargoes for Xizor.

The *Stinger* is roughly twenty-eight meters long, with a hull that is curved and appears to be somehow *sculpted*. The ship is powered by a cluster of four Surronian A2-grade and four A2.50-grade ion engines, with a sublight speed faster than that of an X-wing and only slightly slower than that of a TIE fighter. In an atmosphere, the *Stinger* can achieve a top speed of 1,150 kilometers per hour. Its maneuverability is enhanced by having the pilot individual-

ly adjust each engine's exhaust nozzles through the onboard computer system; this eliminates the need for maneuvering jets. Guri has installed a set of four emergency braking jets in the forward wings and on more than one occasion has used them to slow the *Stinger* so rapidly that pursuing ships overtook it, thus providing an easy target for her weapons. The modified Corellian Engineering Corporation H2-1 hyperdrive gives the ship a Class One hyperdrive rating.

The weaponry consists of a pair of fire-linked ion cannons facing forward as well as a turret-mounted double laser cannon. The laser cannons can be handled from the turret's gunnery position or controlled from the cockpit, although at significantly reduced accuracy.

The forward compartment has the cockpit, with seating for the pilot and two passengers. The small emergency escape pod is set immediately behind the cockpit. Behind the ship's "neck" is the main cargo hold, although cargo space aboard the *Stinger* is at a premium. Most of the rear compartment has been filled by the *Stinger*'s large power core, reserve engine components, and modified shield generators. The *Stinger*'s internal systems are monitored by an advanced MicroThrust computer system that automatically reroutes power and activates reserve systems if there is a major system overload, leaving Guri free to concentrate on piloting and combat duties.

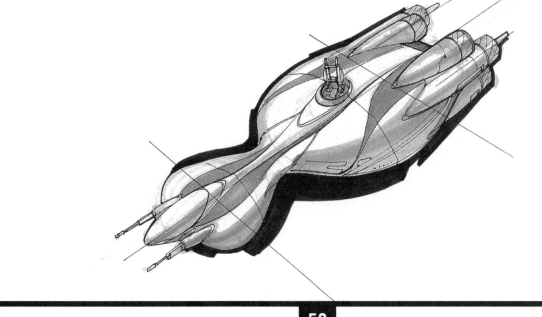

Side View

Landing Skid (retracted)

Entry Ramp (retracted)

Landing Skid (retracted)

Sensor Cluster

Emergency Escape Pod

Main Cargo Hold

Laser Cannon Turret

Access to Main Power Core

A2.50-Grade Ion Engine (4)

A2-Grade Ion Engine (4)

Reactor Core Exhaust Valves

Emergency Braking Jets

Cockpit

Fire-Linked Ion Cannon

Top View

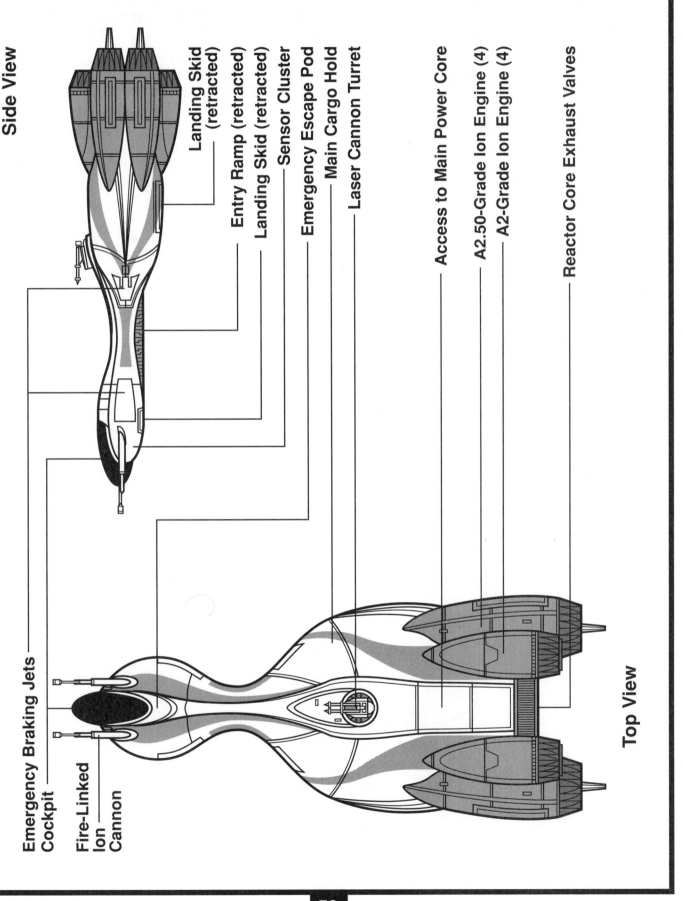

HAPAN BATTLE DRAGON

OLANJII/CHARUBAH BATTLE DRAGON

The Hapans are a rich and powerful people who have maintained extreme militancy in defending their borders. They have designed many combat starships, including the famed Hapan Battle Dragons.

Battle Dragons are roughly five hundred meters in diameter and are instantly recognizable with their prominent double saucers. Each Battle Dragon has forty turbolasers, forty ion cannons, dorsal and ventral triple ion cannons, ten proton-torpedo launchers, a single tractor-beam projector, and four pulse mass generator tubes.

Hapes lags significantly behind in turbolaser technology, with a weapon-recharge rate only one-third that of comparable Imperial weapons. While the actual blasts are as damaging, the slow recharge rate is a significant liability.

The Hapans compensated for this by developing a superior "weapon rotation" system. All the weapons are mounted on a drive system that rotates around the saucer: weapons are moved to the optimal target point, fired, and immediately moved away for recharging, while new weapons are instantly moved into place.

The Hapans also link weapons banks to a single targeting computer; each Battle Dragon has only four targeting computers. These linked weapons offer pinpoint targeting against a single target but cannot accurately target multiple ships. Against enemy groups, Battle Dragons must throw up a "wall of energy," firing all their weapons into a single vector with the hope of scoring significant hits. Thus, Hapans normally deploy Battle Dragons in groups to give them the ability to attack more than one target.

They have adopted the gravity well–projector technology that was developed by the Empire for Imperial Interdictor heavy cruisers. Hapan scientists have also developed "pulse mass mines" which produce "mass shadows," simulating the effects of planetary bodies and deterring ships from jumping into hyperspace. Each Battle Dragon carries sixteen pulse mass mines.

The Battle Dragon's hangar bays can carry three squadrons of fighters (thirty-six fighters) and an enhanced fighter for the wing commander. The Hapans have their own Miy'til fighters but also use X-wings and other designs. Support ships generally include four Hapan gunboats, six drop ships, and four personnel shuttles. Hapan Battle Dragons carry five hundred troops for ground assault.

In Prince Isolder's bid for the hand of Leia Organa, the Hapans brought sixty-three Battle Dragons to Coruscant: one to represent each inhabited world in their home star cluster. Each Battle Dragon is painted to honor the world it is pledged to. Prince Isolder's personal Battle Dragon, the *Song of War*, is painted a deep battle red to represent his courage and bravery. The Battle Dragons also came to the assistance of the New Republic in the Battle of Dathomir, where the combined forces routed the Warlord Zsinj's fleet.

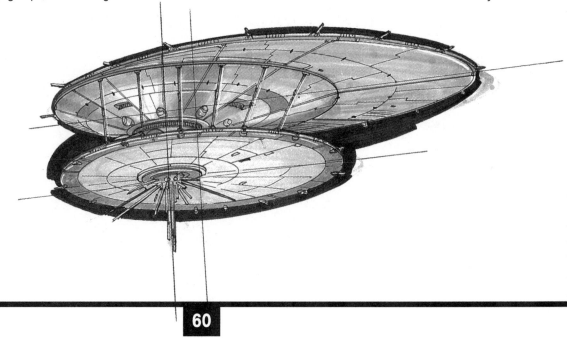

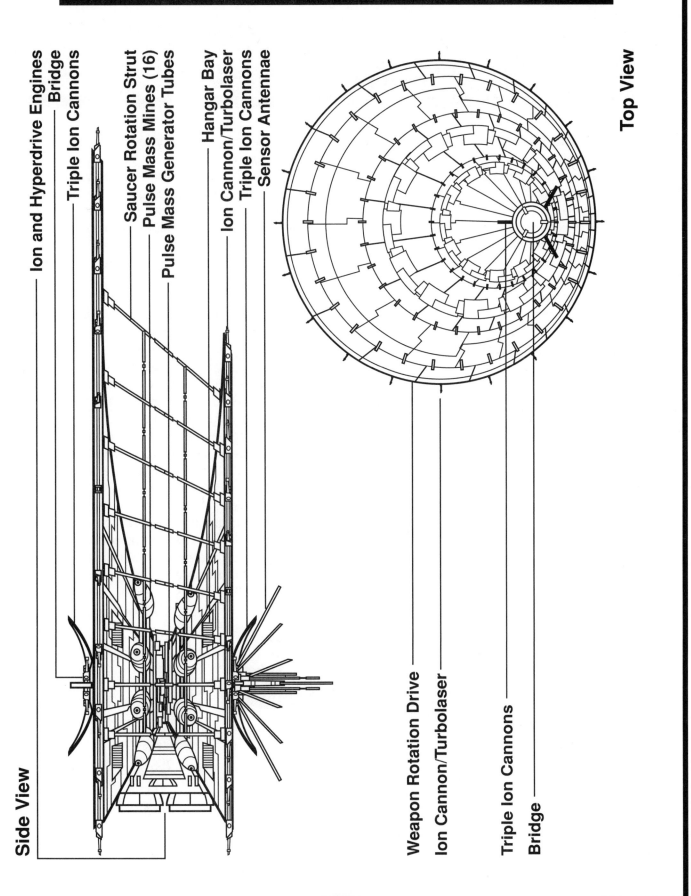

Top View

Side View

Ion and Hyperdrive Engines
Bridge
Triple Ion Cannons

Saucer Rotation Strut
Pulse Mass Mines (16)
Pulse Mass Generator Tubes

Hangar Bay
Ion Cannon/Turbolaser
Triple Ion Cannons
Sensor Antennae

Weapon Rotation Drive
Ion Cannon/Turbolaser

Triple Ion Cannons

Bridge

HAPES NOVA BATTLE CRUISER

HAPAN CONSORTIUM *HAPES NOVA*–CLASS BATTLE CRUISER

Hapes Nova–class battle cruisers are fast combat cruisers designed to supplement Hapan Battle Dragons. These battle cruisers are four hundred meters long and bristle with weaponry; they often command task forces charged with guarding the borders of the Hapan Cluster. Hapes Nova cruisers maintain sufficient supplies for a year of continuous operation. These fearsome ships have proved powerful enough to discourage many pirates and smugglers from trying to enter the Hapan Cluster.

The Hapes Nova battle cruiser is less than a decade old and incorporates the latest Hapan breakthroughs in technology—not to mention a number of advances that were stolen from Imperial corporations such as Kuat Drive Yards and SoroSuub. The result is a cruiser that is exceptionally swift at sublight *and* light speeds.

The Hapes Nova battle cruiser's main weapons are twenty-five turbolasers utilized for engaging capital ships. Ten laser cannons are mounted to handle fighters and small freighters, and another ten ion cannons are added to enable the ships to disable and capture enemy vessels. The Hapes Nova battle cruisers carry two squadrons of Hapan Miy'til fighters and six Hetrinar assault bombers. They can carry drop ships or landing barges as well as ground troops and combat vehicles, but normally Hapes Nova

cruisers are assigned to escort large troop ships for planetary invasions.

Because of the Hapans' limited turbolaser technology, Hapes Nova cruisers must choose their battles carefully. Since the Hapan turbolasers take nearly three times as long as Imperial turbolasers to recycle, a Hapes Nova cruiser can find itself incapable of returning fire at the most inopportune time. To counteract this weakness, the Hapans often assign Hapes Nova cruisers in groups of three or more ships. Hapan captains tend to favor swift, brutal assaults, intending to destroy all enemy ships with the first attack. This approach has added to the Hapans' reputation for vigorously defending their borders.

Taking a cue from Mon Calamari designs, Hapes Nova battle cruisers built in recent years have added backup shield generators. These newer ships also have been refitted with larger power generators so that they do not suffer from the power shortages that tend to plague Hapan Battle Dragons. However, these additions take up a great deal of the ship's interior space, eliminating the second squadron of fighters.

Prince Isolder, in his quest to earn Leia's hand in marriage, offered to give a Hapes Nova battle cruiser to Han Solo if he would cease his efforts to win Leia's heart. Solo refused, instead kidnapping Leia and spiriting her away to the distant world of Dathomir.

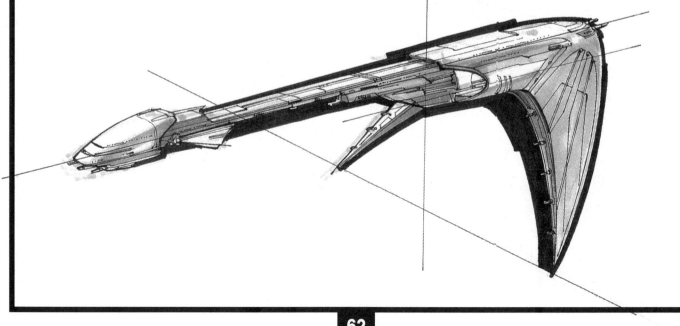

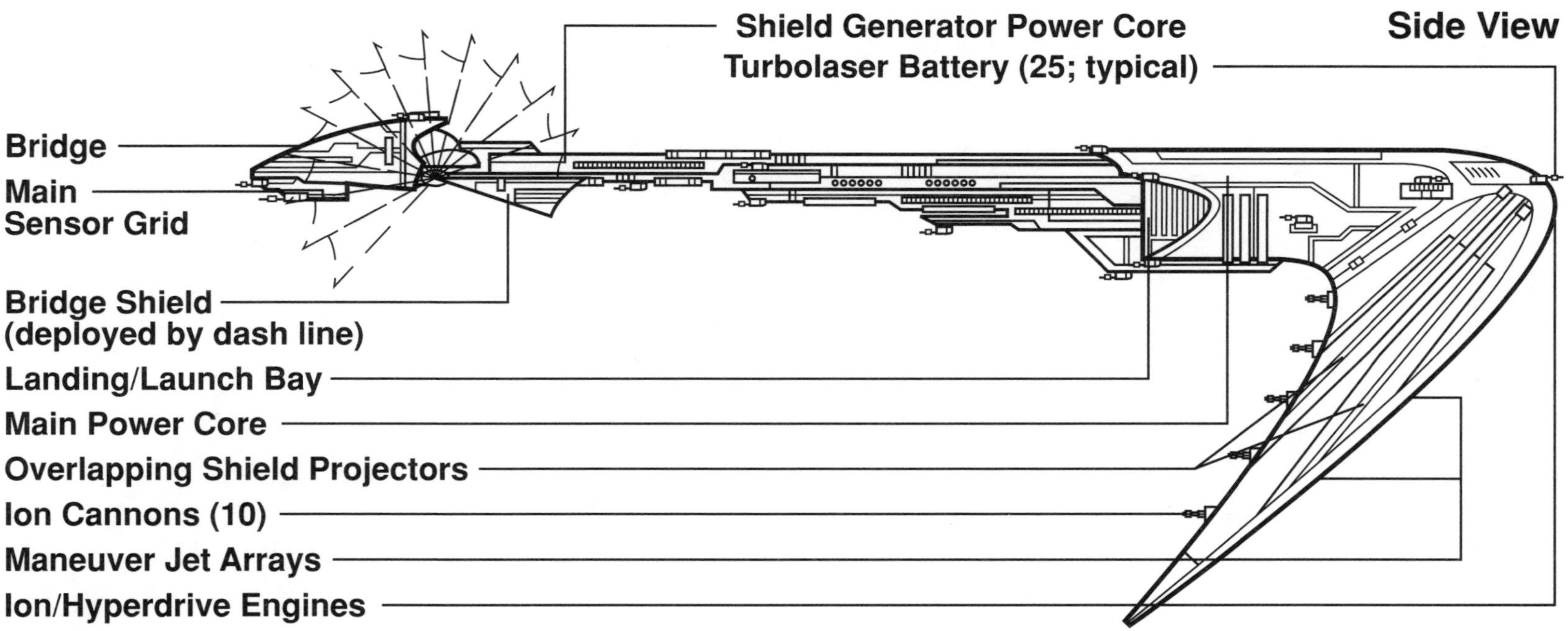

Side View

Shield Generator Power Core

Turbolaser Battery (25; typical)

Bridge

Main
Sensor Grid

Bridge Shield
(deployed by dash line)

Landing/Launch Bay

Main Power Core

Overlapping Shield Projectors

Ion Cannons (10)

Maneuver Jet Arrays

Ion/Hyperdrive Engines

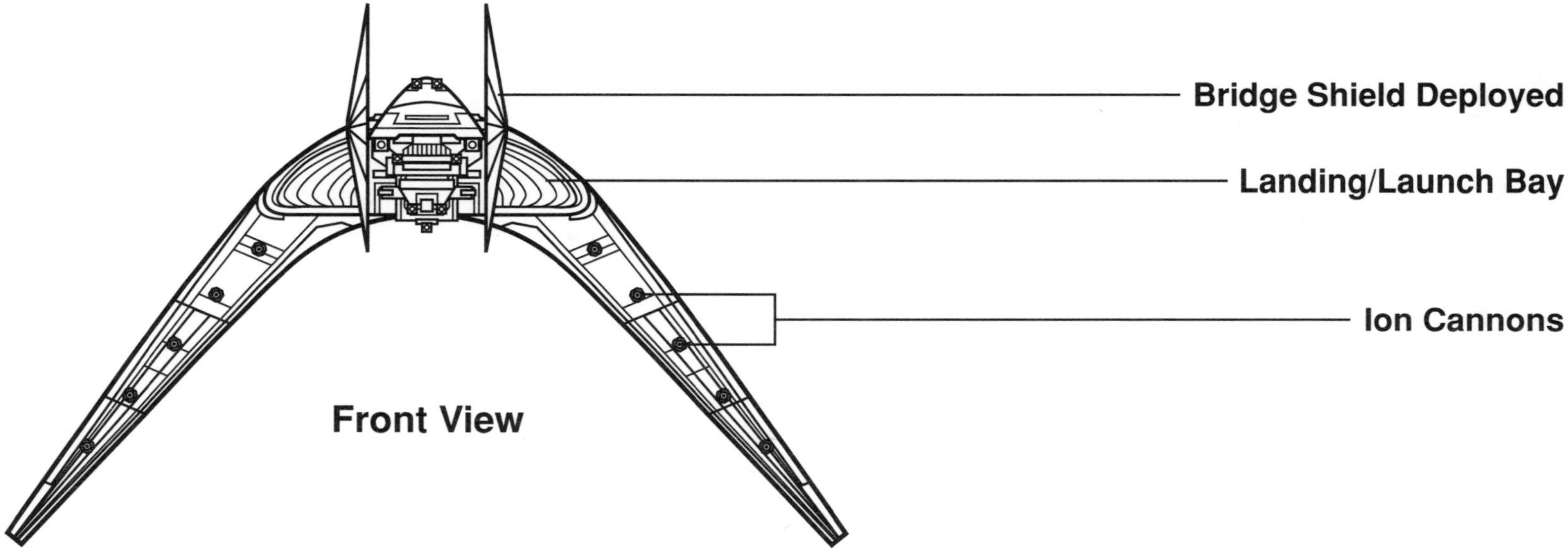

Bridge Shield Deployed

Landing/Launch Bay

Ion Cannons

Front View

HORNET INTERCEPTOR

MODIFIED TENLOSS HORNET INTERCEPTOR

The Hornet Interceptor is a sleek air and space fighter built by groups in the galactic black market and commonly found in the hands of pirates, smugglers, and other criminals.

The ship was originally designed by a consortium of freelance starship engineers who were hired by the mysterious Tenloss Syndicate, a shadowy criminal organization specializing in gunrunning, extortion, and smuggling. The Tenloss *Leukish* (governing council) desired a short-range fighter for combating mercenary and pirate forces . . . and the occasional TIE fighter patrol that got too nosy. Amid the upheaval that followed the death of Emperor Palpatine, these engineers were forced to hire their services out indiscriminately just to earn a living. Fortunately for the Tenloss Syndicate, the engineers more than earned their money.

The Tenloss Syndicate required a ship that was similar to the TIE fighter in mission profile: fast, lightweight, and easily mass-produced. The Hornet has a thin, rounded fuselage with insectile wings for atmospheric flight. The cockpit is placed in a self-contained command pod which can be ejected in an emergency. To save on mass, hull armor plating has been kept to a minimum except on the rear fuselage, where enemy strikes are most likely. The lack of armor is made up for by two small shield generators which provide a modest degree of protection.

The Hornet's greatest asset is its maneuverability. While only marginally faster at sublight than the X-wing, the

Hornet has engines and maneuvering jets that are placed amidships and triangulated at equidistant points around the hull. This gives pilots a decided edge in dogfights, where maneuverability is often the key to survival. Since the ship is designed only for short-range duty, the Hornet has no hyperdrives.

The Hornet's weaponry is an unusual hybrid of turbocharged laser cannons. While not full turbolasers, these weapons have more punch than do standard laser cannons, although they also become dangerously unstable after only a few uses.

The Hornet Interceptor has been made available only to groups affiliated with the Tenloss Syndicate. Because of the excellent performance of the ship, there is a high demand for these vessels. In the year after the death of the *renewed* Emperor, a great many of these ships were stolen from the Syndicate and sold to other criminal groups. Naturally, many of these deals were put together under questionable circumstances, and more often than not the buyers found that their illicit credits had paid for Hornets that had been stripped down and rebuilt with second-rate, cast-off parts from old Z-95 Headhunters and Y-wings.

Han Solo battled a Hornet Interceptor while on a diplomatic mission to Kessel. The administrator at that time, Moruth Doole, longed to exact revenge on Solo for past transgressions and ordered his fleet of fighters to shoot down the *Millennium Falcon*. One of those ships included a Hornet.

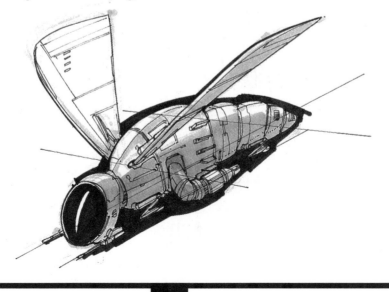

Front View

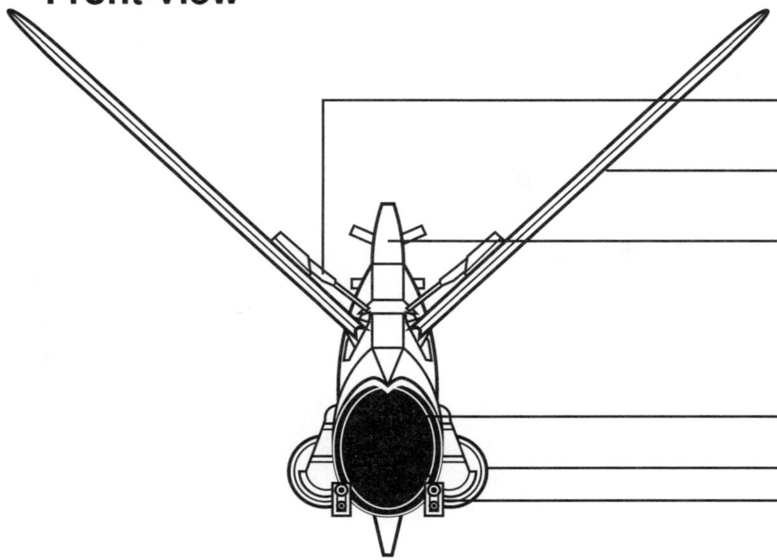

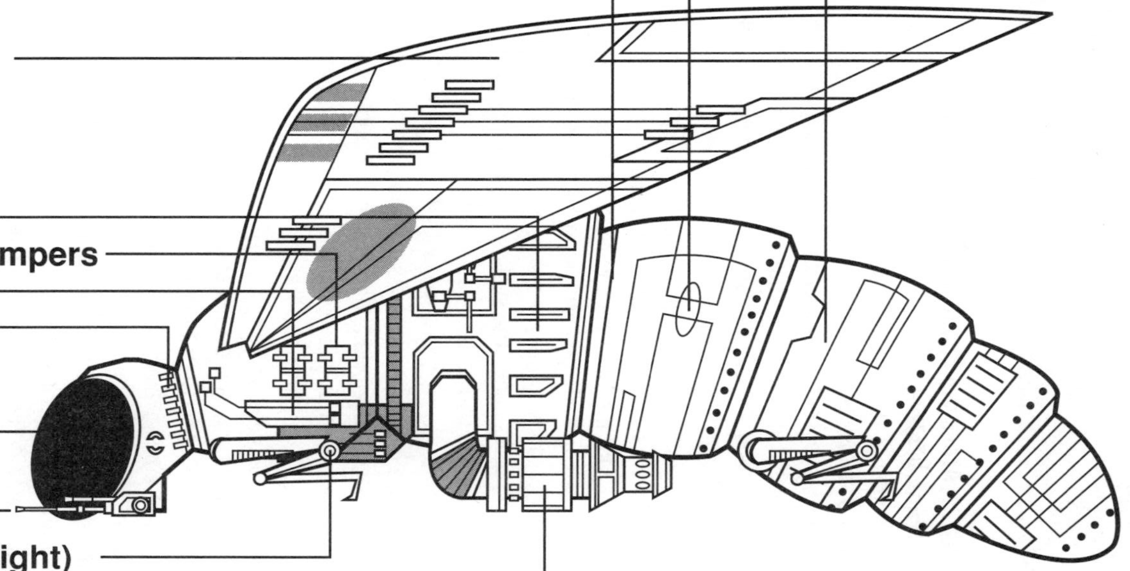

Wing Support Strut

Wing (for atmospheric flight)

Main Drive Engines

Cockpit

Maneuvering Jet

Turbocharged Laser Cannons

Central Fuel Bays

Fueling Port

Main Fuselage

Side View

Wing (for atmospheric flight)

Power Generator

Deflector-Shield Overload Dampers

Deflector-Shield Projector

Ejection Jets

Cockpit

Turbocharged Laser Cannons

Landing Strut (retracted for flight)

Maneuvering Jet

HOSK STATION

CUSTOMIZED ALDERAAN ROYAL ENGINEERS *ESSELES*-CLASS SPACE STATION

Hosk Station is a major trading port and space station that sprawls across Kalarba's largest moon. The station's close proximity to several influential systems allowed it to become a center of commerce and political influence. The droids C-3PO and R2-D2 had several adventures in and around Hosk Station while in the company of Nak Pitareeze, the grandson of a skilled starship designer.

The station was originally built to be a supply and maintenance facility for the Old Republic Navy. It was an excellent choice because of its proximity to then-new colonies, while the moon's low gravity proved convenient for capital ships coming in to dock. The system's asteroid belts provided a convenient source of metals and ores.

After thousands of years of activity, Hosk Station became a base in search of a mission. The former colonies had become stable worlds, and galactic trouble spots increasingly cropped up in areas close to *other* supply stations. So the Republic sold the station to civilian interests.

Transports, liners, and courier ships have come to use Hosk Station as a docking and transfer point. It is typical of many major space stations and is so large that it is a full community unto itself, with 5 million permanent residents. Artificial gravity and atmosphere generators provide a comfortable climate for humans, while different sectors of the station have different gravities and atmospheres to accommodate exotic life-forms. A fully computerized map of the station can be accessed from any public data terminal.

Hosk Station maintains virtually any business one could want, from small shops and droid dealerships to opulent restaurants and luxurious hotels. The station's interior is filled with starship repair and construction bays.

For defense, the station has ten turbolasers and a contingent of eight Hyrotii Zebra short-range fighters. A dozen tractor-beam projectors are mounted near the main docking bay clusters. Incoming ships are required to slave their computers to the starport controllers and allow the tractor beams to handle docking procedures.

Any facility that sprawls across a moon is going to have its share of wild stories, and Hosk Station is no exception. It has long been rumored that predatory animals nearly forty meters long live in the long-abandoned lowest sections of the station. R2-D2 and C-3PO learned that these rumors were true when they ventured down to Hosk's lowest levels and confronted a voracious creature called a hulgren.

Hosk Station was nearly destroyed by businessman Olag Greck when, during an attempt to steal a cargo shipment of ash ore, he sabotaged the station's power core, forcing the evacuation of the entire station. Fortunately, R2-D2 and C-3PO, working with the Hosk security droid Zed, saved the facility by channeling the explosion through the upper purge vents and into open space. Shortly thereafter a new power core was installed, and life on Hosk Station returned to normal.

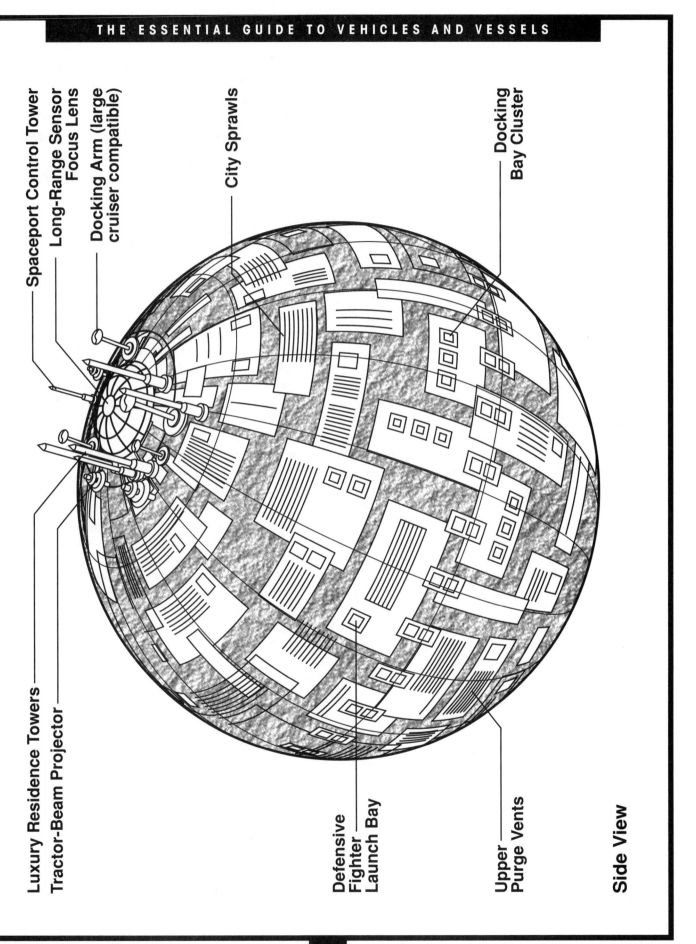

Spaceport Control Tower

Long-Range Sensor Focus Lens

Docking Arm (large cruiser compatible)

City Sprawls

Docking Bay Cluster

Luxury Residence Towers

Tractor-Beam Projector

Defensive Fighter Launch Bay

Upper Purge Vents

Side View

HOUND'S TOOTH

MODIFIED CORELLIAN YV-666 LIGHT FREIGHTER

The modified light freighter *Hound's Tooth* was purchased by the enigmatic Trandoshan bounty hunter known only as Bossk shortly after his previous ship was destroyed on Gandolo IV by the infamous Wookiee named Chewbacca and his human sidekick, Han Solo.

The aggressive Trandoshan (and famed Wookiee hunter) chose a modern Corellian design, the YV-666 freighter, and had the ship modified to suit his needs. The main hull is long, tall, and narrow with large maneuvering fins attached to the rear engine compartment. The bridge sits atop the ship and is connected to the main deck, which contains Bossk's quarters, the ship's computers and controls, and Bossk's training room. The engines, power core, and weapons systems take up the entire bottom half of the ship. The engines' two main drive nozzles are located between the maneuvering fins and can be individually attuned for thrust angles. The fins themselves contain miniature arrays of maneuvering thrusters. The *Hound's Tooth* is fast for a light freighter and has several banks of shield generators to enhance the already reinforced hull.

The *Hound's Tooth* has a retractable lower quad laser turret which can be handled by a gunner or controlled from the bridge. There is also a concussion-missile launcher with a magazine of six missiles.

The ship's controls have been modified for Trandoshans. Bossk rests his arms in a pair of troughs on the control grid. Microsensors along each trough respond to Bossk's every move, allowing the bounty hunter to control any system with minimal effort.

Bossk is a bounty hunter who likes to work alone, so he has installed an X10-D droid brain to control shipboard systems. The unit will respond to Bossk's verbal commands and can regulate weapons, thrusters, interior atmosphere, and security systems. The droid brain allows Bossk to control *Hound's Tooth* either from the bridge or from his personal cabin.

Bossk has also equipped the ship with redundant sensor and security systems in order to detect prisoner breakouts. An interior scanning system analyzes all cargo brought aboard the ship, and the holds are sensor-screened. The prisoner-holding cages in the aft cargo section are magnetically reinforced for added strength and are activated by motion sensors linked to a force-field generator. Bossk also keeps an automated skinning table (for Wookiees and other, similar prey) and his complete stock of hunting weapons in this hold. Unauthorized entry into any of several compartments triggers neural stunners, sub-q injectors, shock panels, or other security systems. Bossk has a voice-recognition system that enables him to secure the vessel from the outside.

Bossk also has an interior scout ship, the *Nashtah Pup*, for emergency operations. A large dorsal hatch on *Hound's Tooth* opens to release the short-range ship. The *Nashtah Pup* has room for only two and has almost no cargo space.

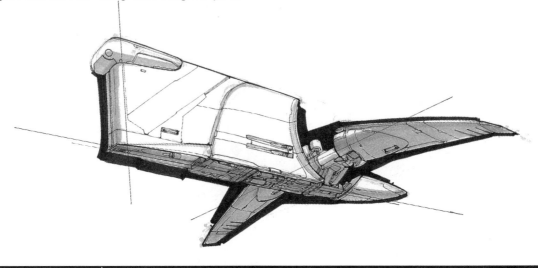

Front View

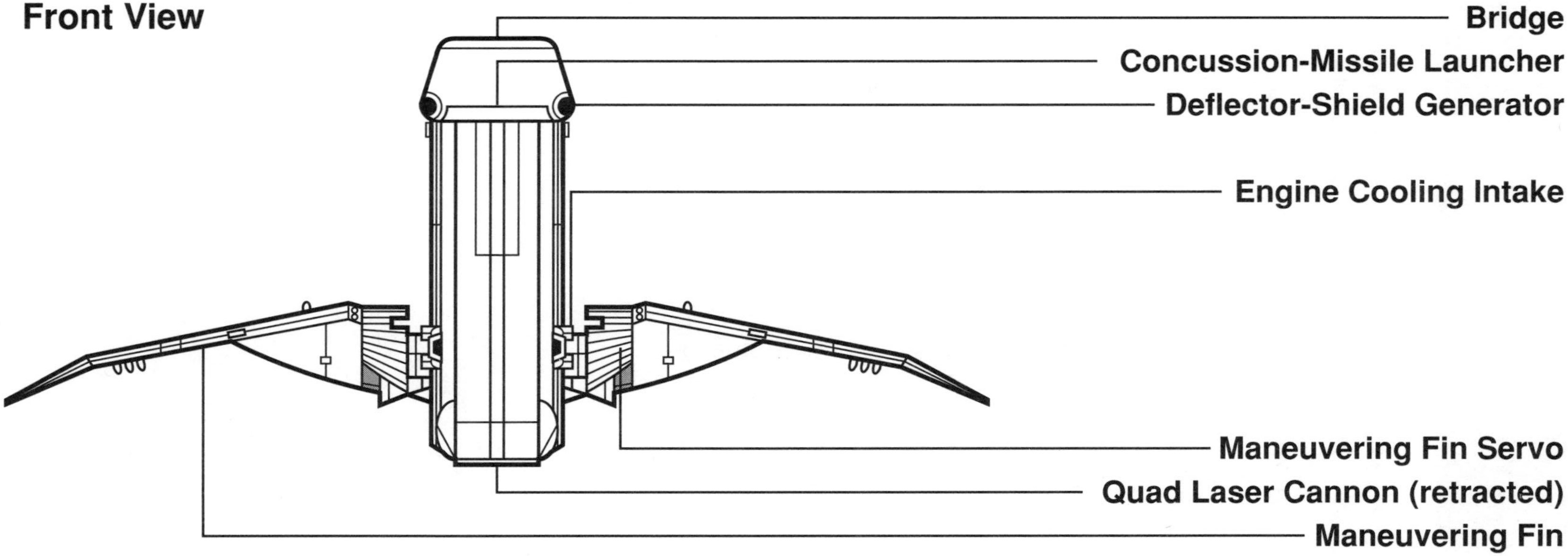

Bridge
Concussion-Missile Launcher
Deflector-Shield Generator

Engine Cooling Intake

Maneuvering Fin Servo
Quad Laser Cannon (retracted)
Maneuvering Fin

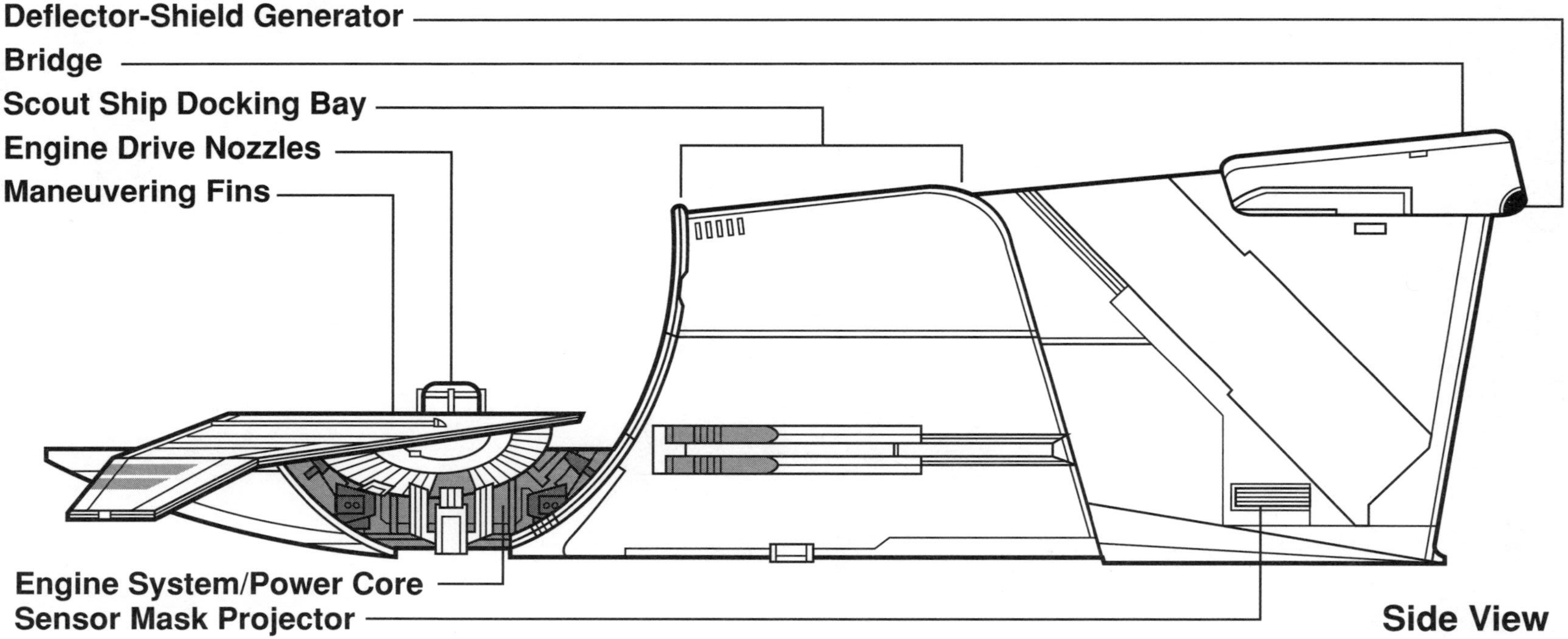

Deflector-Shield Generator
Bridge
Scout Ship Docking Bay
Engine Drive Nozzles
Maneuvering Fins

Side View

Engine System/Power Core
Sensor Mask Projector

HUTT CARAVEL

UBRIKKIAN SELTISS-2 CARAVEL

Hutts are beings that demand their own version of "style" in everything. Hutt caravels are a mark of that culture; to the outsider, these opulent vessels are decadence incarnate. To a Hutt, such a vessel is considered a just reward for displaying the keen ability to survive. These ships are commonly seen traveling between the adopted Hutt homeworld of Nal Hutta and the nearby smugglers' moon of Nar Shaddaa. No two Hutt caravels are identical; trying to purchase the most distinctive caravel is the basis of a long-standing competition among rival Hutt traders and crime bosses.

The Ubrikkian Seltiss-2 (pictured) is considered a "modest" vehicle that is typical of the caravels owned by Hutts who may be only a couple of centuries old. The Seltiss-2 appears to be a large, spacegoing sail barge, and the main sail, steering vanes, and repulsorlift drives propel the ship on leisurely voyages through Nal Hutta's upper atmosphere. The ion engines are small, compact, and wedged into the back of the hull. Since the caravel is used only for trips between Nal Hutta and Nar Shaddaa, it has no hyperdrive.

Caravels may be outfitted for combat, although the Hutts prefer to hide their weapons in order to lull attackers into a false sense of confidence. This particular ship has two hidden laser cannons which can be controlled from the bridge or the main cabin; when not being used, the cannons are retracted behind armor panels. This caravel has hull plating and shield generators on the main deck.

The main cabin is situated in the forward section of the hull, where armor plating panels can be retracted to give passengers a spectacular view of space. The main cabin is designed so that the Hutt is strategically positioned on a dais, looming over all guests—as is only fitting. Finished in *greel* wood and chrall-crystal, the cabin alone cost nearly 400,000 credits and can act as a self-contained transport vehicle, with independent repulsorlift and ion drives. When the caravel docks on a planet, the cabin detaches from the main hull and shuttles down to the surface. If there is a space emergency, the cabin can be ejected like an escape pod.

Interior corridors wind back to the engineering section and allow access to the rear outdoor deck. The level above the cabin has the bridge, a kitchen, and four small servant cabins. Sadly, there are no escape pods for the pilots or chefs, but the Hutts seem to have no problem finding new servants.

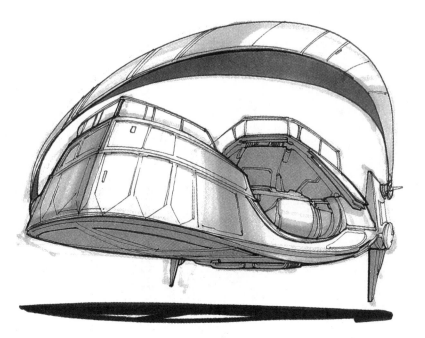

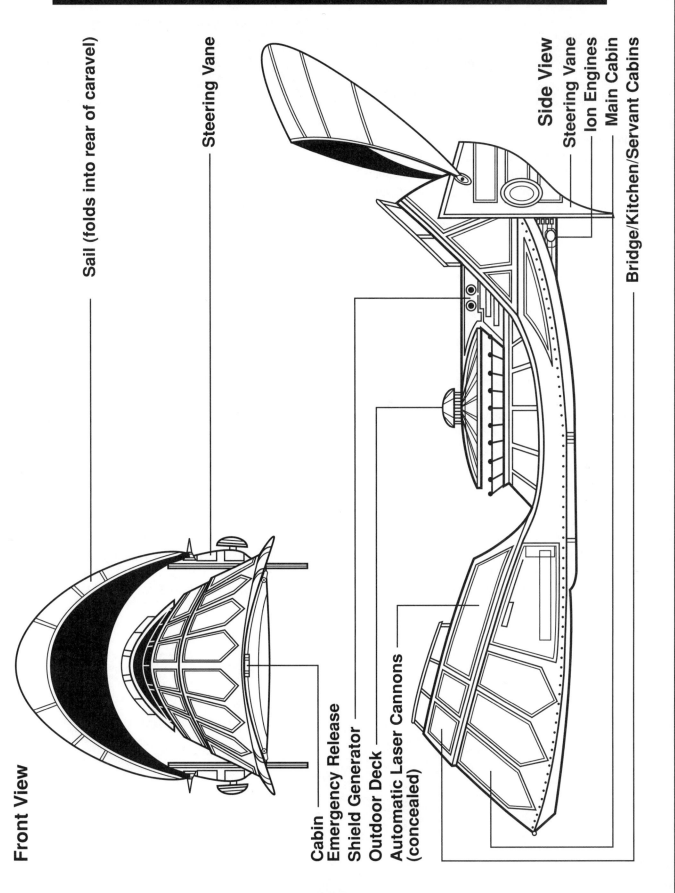

Front View

Sail (folds into rear of caravel)

Steering Vane

Cabin
Emergency Release
Shield Generator
Outdoor Deck
Automatic Laser Cannons
(concealed)

Side View

Steering Vane
Ion Engines
Main Cabin
Bridge/Kitchen/Servant Cabins

HYPERSPACE MARAUDER

TransGalMeg *Xiytiar*-Class Transport

The *Hyperspace Marauder* is a large freighter converted to smuggling duty. Owned and operated by Lo Khan and his Yaka cyborg partner, Luwingo, the *Hyperspace Marauder* is one of many ships licensed to haul military goods to the Deep Galactic Core, the area of space that the reincarnated Emperor Palpatine used as his base of operations.

At 165 meters long, the *Hyperspace Marauder* is far larger than most smuggling vessels. Lo Khan insists that this just gives him more room to hide his contraband.

The freighter tends to stick to more civilized routes; Lo Khan is someone who has always tended to play it safe—he has worked both sides of the Civil War but keeps a low profile, taking great care to ensure that he makes few enemies.

The *Marauder* is an oddity among space smuggling ships because it is lightly armed. Lo Khan finally added a pair of 700-Penetrator laser cannons, but the ship had gone unarmed for many years. The vessel is slow and lumbering, with heavy-duty shields. Its apparent vulnerability is a key part of Lo Khan's game plan.

In the instance of a raid, when a boarding party is sent over, Lo Khan uses the *Marauder*'s unusual computer and communications system to take over the other ship's computer systems. Before the aggressors can cut through the *Marauder*'s hull plating, they find that their ship is no longer under their control. Lo Khan has placed himself in an excellent bargaining position, since he can choose to shut down weapons, drives, or even life-support systems.

Of course, Lo Khan is a charitable being. He'll normally strip the valuable gear from the other ship but leave life support and low-level ion thrusters operational. While he travels on to his destination with a few extra goodies to sell to his underworld "friends," those who sought to rob him have several weeks to reflect on their misdeeds.

Lo Khan and Luwingo ended up saving Han Solo and the Corellian's companions on Byss when he allowed Salla Zend to hide the *Millennium Falcon* inside the *Marauder*. Unfortunately for Lo Khan, the *Hyperspace Marauder* wasn't nearly as good a hiding spot as Salla hoped. Giant Imperial Hunter-Killer probots quickly spotted the *Falcon* by scanning the freighter's interior. The H-K probots opened fire, but Salla and Shug Ninx raced the *Falcon* away from the Imperial H-Ks.

The *Marauder* was impounded by the furious Imperials, stranding Lo Khan and Luwingo on Byss. However, a new assault by the New Republic just weeks later gave the two smugglers the chance to recapture their ship. During the confusion of the New Republic attack, Khan and Luwingo infiltrated Byss's Imperial impound yards. They later used the *Marauder* to rescue New Republic forces commanded by General Lando Calrissian, who had been pinned down during a secret assault on Byss.

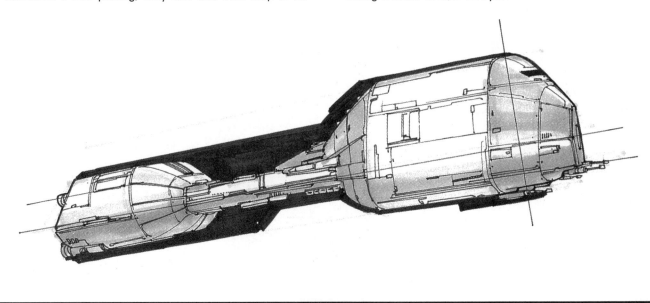

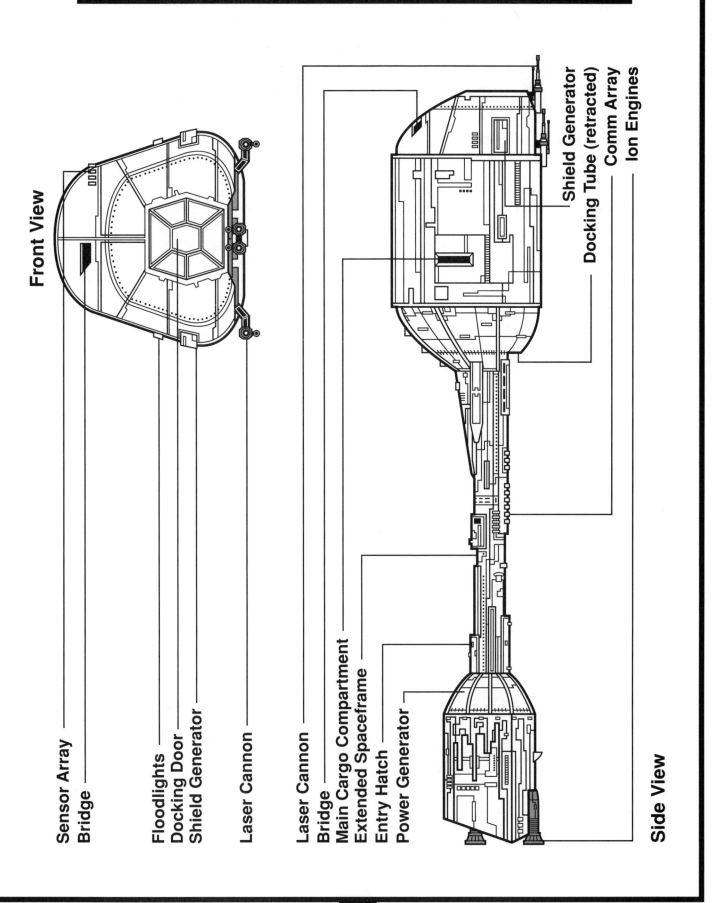

Front View

Sensor Array
Bridge

Floodlights
Docking Door
Shield Generator

Laser Cannon

Laser Cannon
Bridge
Main Cargo Compartment
Extended Spaceframe
Entry Hatch
Power Generator

Shield Generator
Docking Tube (retracted)
Comm Array
Ion Engines

Side View

I-7 HOWLRUNNER

INCOM CORPORATION I-7 "HOWLRUNNER"

The Incom Corporation I-7 "Howlrunner" is an Imperial fighter that was introduced during the chaotic days of the return of the Emperor. The short-range I-7 Howlrunners were first used by one of the major Imperial factions during the Imperial Civil War, and the *Millennium Falcon* had a brief run-in with a squadron of Howlrunners while on a mission to Coruscant to rescue Lando Calrissian and Luke Skywalker.

The short-range fighter has a streamlined, fixed-wing design and is at home in deep space and planetary atmospheres; it is fast compared with the older X-wings and Y-wings, but both the new E-wings and TIE interceptors can easily outrace this ship. Its weapons and targeting systems are nothing to brag about, either, with only a pair of foward-firing laser cannons that match the TIE interceptor for accuracy but aren't as powerful.

Unlike most Imperial fighters, the I-7 Howlrunner has dedicated shield generators, giving the ship the ability to take as much punishment as an X-wing can. The ship's low mass gives it excellent maneuverability, meaning that an I-7 could probably decimate a heavy assault ship such as a B-wing in a head-to-head battle. However, like TIE fighters, I-7s must rely on numerical superiority when going up against most New Republic fighters.

The I-7 was the first design from Incom Corporation since that company was nationalized by the Empire nearly a decade before the Civil War. Incom's proud legacy of ships like the Z-95 Headhunter had been overshadowed when their rogue design team delivered the T-65 X-wing to the Rebel Alliance, and the I-7 was an attempt to prove to the Empire's military procurers that Incom could still produce a fighter that could compete with both Sienar's TIE series and Kuat Drive Yards' new A-9 Vigilance Interceptor.

I-7 Howlrunners were welcome additions to many Imperial planetary bases, which tended to get last pick on new ships and equipment. While the I-7s aren't fantastic fighters, they represented a marked improvement over the aging TIE/ln fighters that these bases had been using for over a decade.

With the return of the Emperor and the reuniting of the Imperial factions, the I-7 Howlrunners were slowly deployed throughout the Imperial Navy, but no one showed great love for the new ships. I-7s have been routinely carried aboard smaller capital ships such as Dreadnaughts, Nebulon-B escort frigates, and old Victory Star Destroyers. Only a few have been stationed aboard Imperial Star Destroyers because of Naval Command's reluctance to shift away from the TIE series of fighters.

It is thought that some of those who acted as the Emperor's closest advisers have a particular liking for the ships and ordered several squadrons for "personal business."

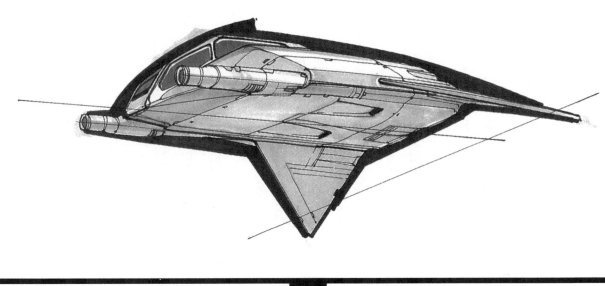

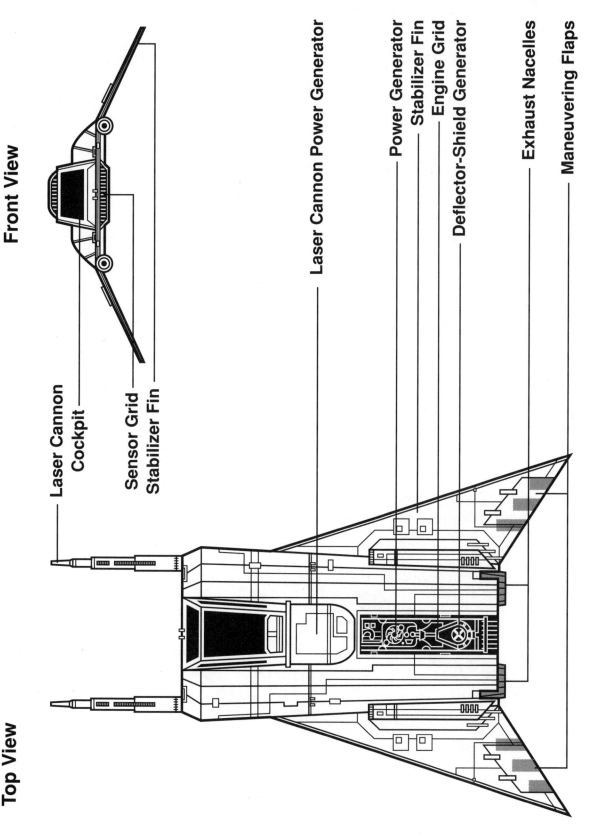

Front View

Top View

Laser Cannon
Cockpit

Sensor Grid
Stabilizer Fin

Laser Cannon Power Generator

Power Generator
Stabilizer Fin
Engine Grid
Deflector-Shield Generator

Exhaust Nacelles
Maneuvering Flaps

IG-2000

MODIFIED TRILON, INC. AGGRESSOR ASSAULT FIGHTER

IG-2000 was the assault starfighter utilized by the infamous assassin droid IG-88. Roughly twenty meters long, the ship was designed specifically for combat. While its mass was significantly higher than that of most starfighters, the majority of the interior space was devoted to engines and weapon systems.

This fighter's power came from a single Kuat Galaxy-15 ion engine stolen from a decommissioned Nebulon-B escort frigate. The engine was force-fed from three converted Quadex power cores, with a sublight speed that matched that of Boba Fett's *Slave I* and the Alliance's Y-wing fighter. To handle possible power overloads, the engine cowling had eight bleed-off vents that would direct discharges away from the power core.

Maneuverability was enhanced via a pair of extendable vanes. These were pulled flush with the hull for normal starflight, but for combat they were extended out. The vanes had several ailerons for atmospheric maneuvers and braking. The ship's inertial compensators were often disabled, since IG-88 had no reason to fear the gravitational effects of sudden maneuvers; the droid could perform maneuvers that would kill an organic pilot.

IG-2000's weaponry consisted of a pair of forward laser cannons, a single ion cannon mounted below the cockpit, and a pair of tractor-beam projectors mounted in the forward mandibles. Because bounties are often offered for *live* captures, the droid preferred to use the ion cannon to disable enemy ships, then use the tractor beams to maneuver ships to the air lock. IG-88 kept four assault drones in the air lock and used them as advance scouts for boarding actions in case his targets preferred to fight rather than surrender.

The forward cockpit section was IG-88's domain, with a weapons locker and a small maintenance area placed just behind the pilot station. The prisoner hold, the only area on the ship with a life support system, filled the middle deck of the ship. *IG-2000* had room for up to eight captives and featured a single stasis tube for keeping critically injured captives alive. The hold also had a small medbay (with an old FX-7 medical assistant droid) and an interrogation room.

The *IG-2000* was destroyed over Tatooine when IG-88 attempted to steal the carbonite-imprisoned Han Solo from Boba Fett. IG-88 used a decoy of the *IG-2000* to distract Fett in order to mount a sneak attack on *Slave I*. However, Fett outmaneuvered the assassin droid, capturing *IG-2000* with *Slave I*'s tractor beams and then destroying it with a volley of concussion missiles. Rumors abound that another assassin droid calling itself IG-88 has been spotted operating in bounty hunter circles, but those reports are unsubstantiated . . .

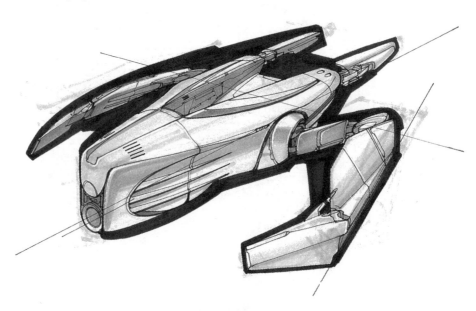

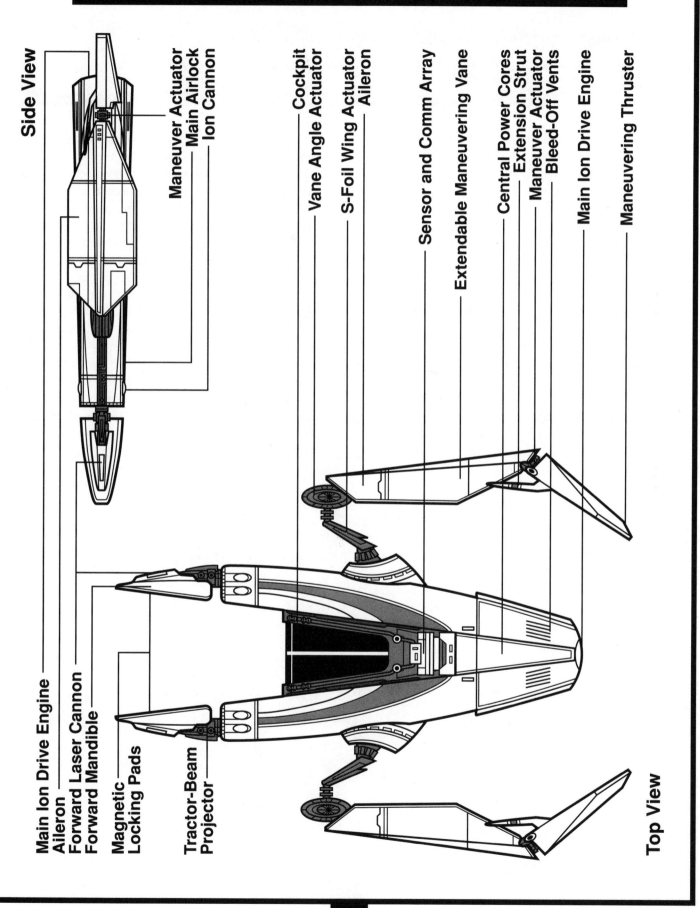

Side View

Maneuver Actuator
Main Airlock
Ion Cannon

Cockpit
Vane Angle Actuator
S-Foil Wing Actuator
Aileron

Sensor and Comm Array

Extendable Maneuvering Vane

Central Power Cores
Extension Strut
Maneuver Actuator
Bleed-Off Vents

Main Ion Drive Engine

Maneuvering Thruster

Main Ion Drive Engine
Aileron
Forward Laser Cannon
Forward Mandible

Magnetic
Locking Pads

Tractor-Beam
Projector

Top View

IMPERIAL LANDING CRAFT

SIENAR FLEET SYSTEMS/CYGNUS SPACEWORKS *SENTINEL*-CLASS LANDING CRAFT

The *Sentinel*-class landing shuttle is a primary Imperial landing craft that was derived from the Sienar Fleet Systems *Lambda*-class shuttle. As in the standard Lambda design, the ship features a stationary top wing with two folding lower wings. The Sentinel has a larger cargo area, and it is heavily armed and armored to enter combat.

The Sentinel shuttle has a command crew of five, including the pilot, the copilot/sensor officer, the head gunner, and two secondary gunners. The head gunner handles the four retractable laser cannons mounted in pairs on each side of the main troop compartment. One gunner handles the two concussion-missile launchers, which draw from individual magazines of eight missiles each. The final gunner handles the ion cannon and rotating repeating blasters. The ion cannon is mounted in a retractable turret in front of the stationary wing and is used to delay and disable enemy vessels. Rotating repeating blasters are deployed upon landing to provide covering fire.

The ship's combat modifications can include armor plating that is nearly 25 percent heavier than standard Lambda armor. Four deflector-shield generators, mounted fore and aft in pairs, supplement the hull's protection. Cygnus HD7 engines that match those found aboard Imperial XG-1 assault gunboats allow the ship to reach atmospheric speeds of 1,000 kilometers per hour, while sublight speed is roughly equivalent to that of the Alliance's Y-wing starfighter. The Cygnus HD7 hyperdrive unit gives the ship a Class One hyperdrive rating, matching the original Lambda's hyperdrive speed, despite the heavier armor.

The ship's troop compartment can carry six squads, for a total of fifty-four soldiers. The hold behind the troop compartment has room for a dozen repeating blasters as well as six speeder bikes. The Sentinel's removable seating units allow the ship to be converted quickly to a straight combat vehicle delivery vessel or to a combat-ready cargo ship. In this mode, the landing craft can carry three dozen speeder bikes or a dozen compact assault vehicles.

Each Sentinel landing craft is equipped with a reconnaissance speeder bike with a slaved communications terminal; the comm frequency is randomly determined before each mission to prevent opposing techs from intercepting transmissions. The shuttle also has a full comm array for standard fleet and ground-unit communications.

The craft was new at the time of the Battle of Yavin and was found aboard only a few Imperial vessels. Deployment was targeted to key forces, including Lord Vader's personal squadron, the fleet that maintained order in Virgillian space, and eventually the fleet that assembled in the distant Endor system.

After the death of Emperor Palpatine, Sienar and Cygnus continued production of the Sentinels, and both companies sold them to a number of private concerns, including front companies for the New Republic. The ships became quite common within two years after the defeat at Endor.

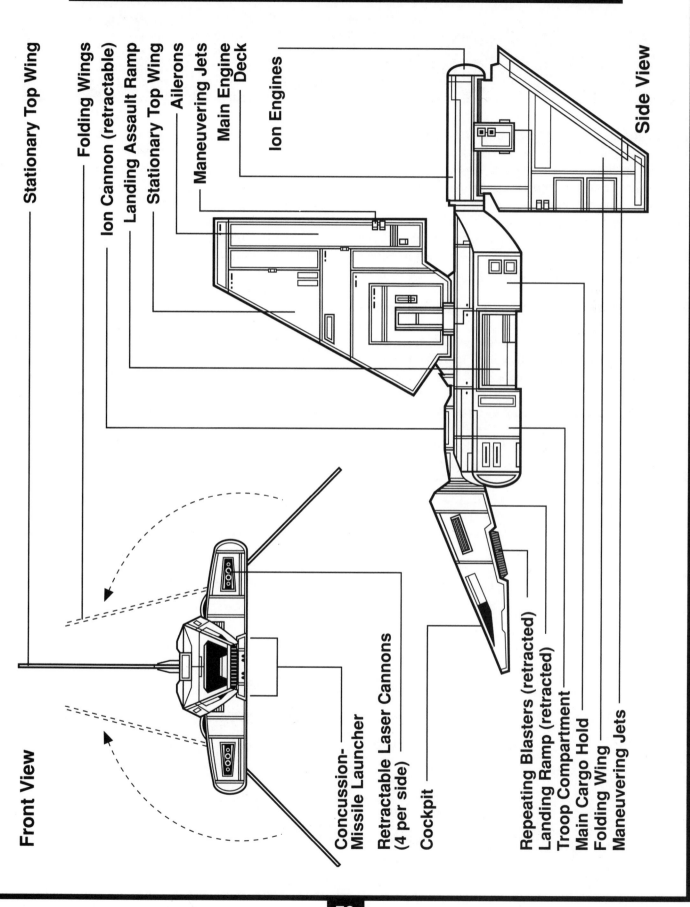

Stationary Top Wing

Folding Wings

Ion Cannon (retractable)

Landing Assault Ramp

Stationary Top Wing

Ailerons

Maneuvering Jets

Main Engine Deck

Ion Engines

Side View

Front View

Concussion-Missile Launcher

Retractable Laser Cannons (4 per side)

Cockpit

Repeating Blasters (retracted)

Landing Ramp (retracted)

Troop Compartment

Main Cargo Hold

Folding Wing

Maneuvering Jets

IMPERIAL STAR DESTROYER

KUAT DRIVE YARDS IMPERIAL STAR DESTROYER

The Empire's awesome wedge-shaped *Imperial*-class Star Destroyers form the core of the Imperial Navy. True marvels of starship engineering, Star Destroyers are 1,600 meters long and have over one hundred weapon emplacements for deep-space combat.

The mere presence of such a vessel in orbit is often enough to quell uprisings on Rebel-sympathetic worlds, and Star Destroyer commanders can engage whole Rebel fleets and still expect victory.

Standard Imperial Star Destroyers have sixty turbolasers for ship-to-ship combat and planetary assault. A Star Destroyer's sixty ion cannons are used to disable enemy ships in preparation for boarding. The Star Destroyer's superstructure features an immense command tower housing essential systems, computer controls, and the bridge. The command tower is topped by a pair of deflector-shield generator domes.

Star Destroyers have two ventral landing bays. The aft docking bay—the main launch and landing bay for shuttles, support and cargo ships, and TIE fighters—accommodates ships at least 150 meters long. It connects to forward interior bays and storage sections, all of which connect to immense lift shafts. Ahead of the storage sections is the forward launch bay.

The forward launch bay is used primarily to deploy assault shuttles, walker landing barges, and ground forces

vehicles; it also can serve as an auxiliary launch or landing bay for TIE fighters if the main docking bay is disabled.

A full wing of seventy-two TIE fighters (six squadrons of twelve ships each) is standard aboard each Destroyer. As of the Battle of Yavin, a standard Star Destroyer maintained four squadrons of standard TIE/Ins, one squadron of TIE interceptors, and one squadron of TIE bombers. (Lower-priority vessels have a squadron of TIE/gts.) By the time of the Battle of Endor, an additional TIE interceptor squadron had replaced one of the TIE/In squadrons.

Support ships, all maintained aboard the Destroyer, include eight *Lambda*-class shuttles, fifteen stormtrooper transports, five assault gunboats, and a variable number of Skipray blastboats and *Gamma*-class assault shuttles.

Star Destroyers carry planetary assault teams, with landing barges, drop ships, 20 AT-AT walkers, 30 AT-ST scout walkers, and 9,700 ground troops. For a long-term planetary occupation, the Destroyer can deploy a prefabricated garrison base with eight hundred troops, ten AT-ATs, ten AT-STs, and forty TIE fighters. Full planetary invasions often require a full fleet, normally six Destroyers, heavy and light cruisers, and carrier ships.

An upgraded version called the Imperial II began appearing shortly after the Battle of Yavin, boasting a heavily reinforced hull and more powerful heavy turbolaser batteries and cannons. In addition, there are several Star Destroyer variants for specialty missions.

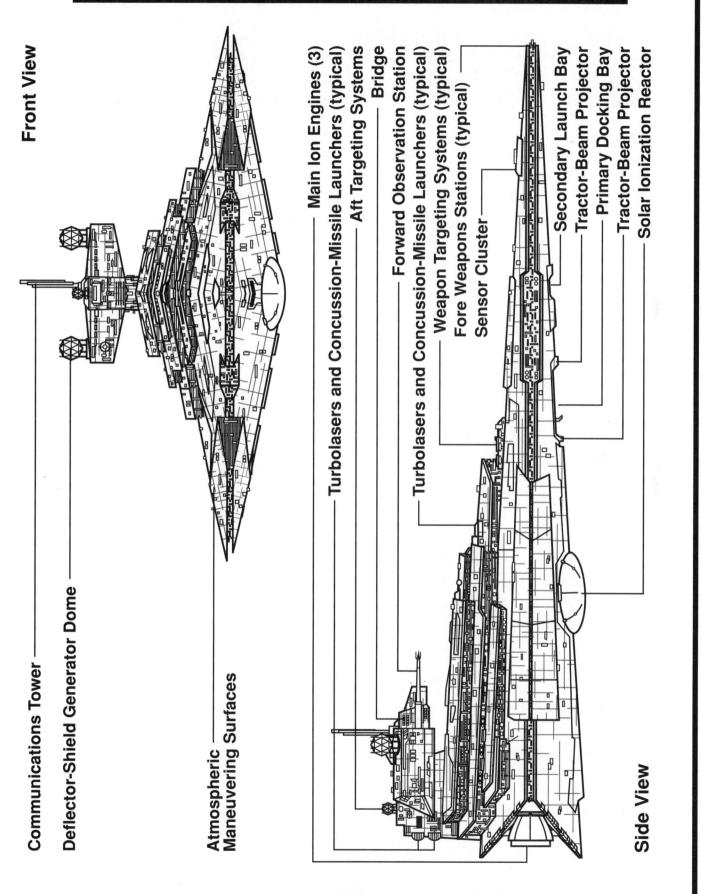

Front View

Communications Tower

Deflector-Shield Generator Dome

Atmospheric Maneuvering Surfaces

Main Ion Engines (3)

Turbolasers and Concussion-Missile Launchers (typical)

Aft Targeting Systems

Bridge

Forward Observation Station

Turbolasers and Concussion-Missile Launchers (typical)

Weapon Targeting Systems (typical)

Fore Weapons Stations (typical)

Sensor Cluster

Secondary Launch Bay

Tractor-Beam Projector

Primary Docking Bay

Tractor-Beam Projector

Solar Ionization Reactor

Side View

INCOM T-16 SKYHOPPER

INCOM CORPORATION T-16 SKYHOPPER

Incom's T-16 Skyhopper is a high-speed transorbital pleasure craft: it's the kind of vehicle that every young hot-rodder wants to have in his garage. The T-16 has been a huge success for its manufacturer, Incom Corporation, and the speeders are popular across the galaxy.

Luke Skywalker owned a T-16 Skyhopper and often raced his friends through Tatooine's Beggar's Canyon. Since his ambition was to become a fighter pilot, Luke practiced his marksmanship by "bull's-eyeing" the womp rat burrows at the end of the canyon with his stun cannons.

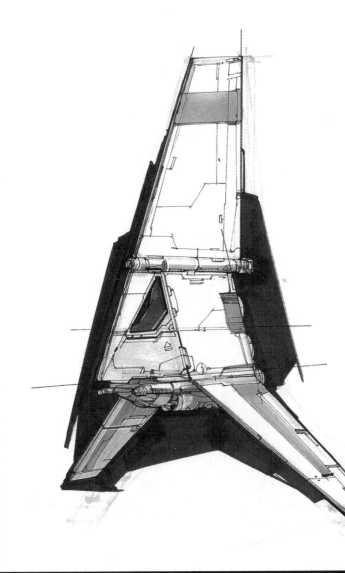

Impromptu speeder races were a great test of Luke's natural skill, as the winding canyons forced him to fly to the limit of his abilities—and sometimes beyond them. Just before he left Tatooine, Luke ripped the stabilizer off the Skyhopper while trying to maneuver through the infamous Stone Needle in Beggar's Canyon. Only luck allowed him to walk away from the accident, but the skills he picked up in those hair-raising races served him well when he maneuvered his X-wing starfighter down the Death Star's trench.

The T-16 Skyhopper has been expressly designed to be fast and easy to handle. Relying on a high-powered Incom E-16/x ion engine for thrust and two DCJ-45 repulsorlift generators for lift, the T-16 has a top speed of nearly 1,200 kilometers per hour and can reach an altitude of nearly 300 kilometers. The distinctive triwing design helps stabilize the vehicle at high speeds, although the forward stabilizer fin blocks the pilot's field of view. Advanced gyro-stabilizers help the pilot keep control, even in complex high-gee maneuvers. The ship is amazingly maneuverable, allowing it to twist through tight turns and make amazing vertical climbs.

Civilian T-16s seldom carry mounted weapons. However, optional upgrades offer four forward-firing stun cannons, or a cheaper pair of pneumatic cannons with the top pair of stun cannons stripped down to be targeting lasers. The T-16 is also a mainstay in planetary militias and police forces across the galaxy; such units are typically armed with two or four laser cannons and have heavier hull plating. The laser sighting system is used to train pilots for gunnery and bombing runs.

The bottom of the T-16 has molecular-magnetic clamps and computer interfaces that can be used to mount add-on attachments, including extra fuel slugs for added flight range, or a heavy-duty laser cannon for military duty. The T-16 depicted here has the military-grade laser attachment.

The T-16's cockpit has two sections, with room for a single pilot and one passenger. The cabin is pressurized for low orbital flight. The forward airfoil splits the windshield; this can unsettle a new pilot, but a holographic heads-up terrain display system provides complete, true-to-life detail.

Front View

Side View

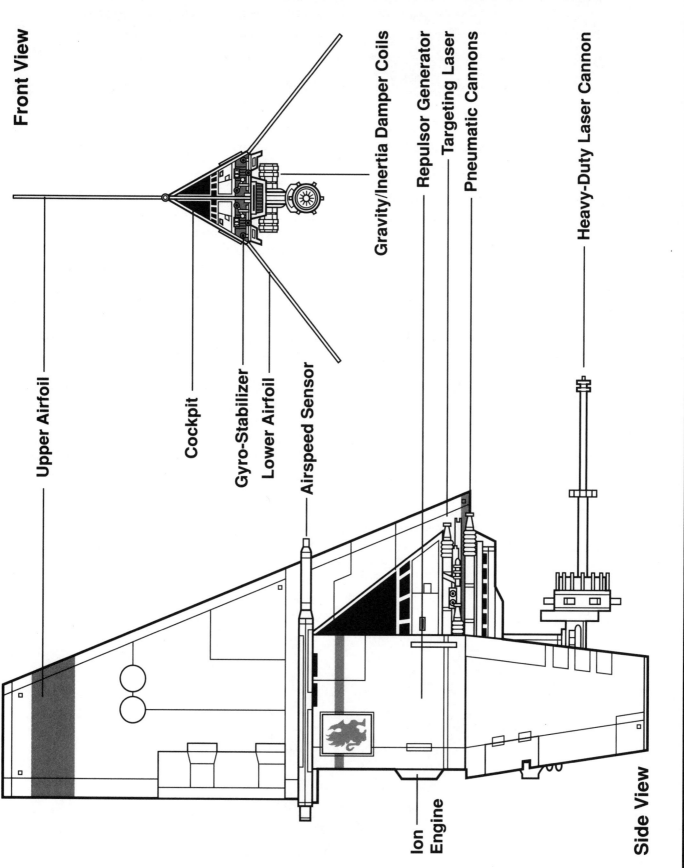

Upper Airfoil

Cockpit

Gyro-Stabilizer

Lower Airfoil

Airspeed Sensor

Gravity/Inertia Damper Coils

Repulsor Generator

Targeting Laser

Pneumatic Cannons

Heavy-Duty Laser Cannon

Ion Engine

INCOM Y-4 "RAPTOR" TRANSPORT

INCOM Y-4 TRANSPORT

Designed as a military transport shuttle, the Incom Y-4 was released to the Empire shortly before Incom Corporation was seized by decree of the Emperor. Despite good performance qualities, the ship never gained much popularity in the Imperial Navy because of the "Rebel" connotations of any Incom product—after all, Incom designers had created the X-wing fighter and then had given it to the Alliance!

Years later, as Warlord Zsinj spread the might of his own Empire, the Y-4 shuttles became popularized as the ships of "Zsinj's Raptors," the elite marine commandos Zsinj used to hold power. In common conversation, the vessel became known as the "Y-4 Raptor."

The shuttle is small—just under thirty meters long. Its main mission is to ferry troops and supplies between starships. The military version of the Y-4 can carry the equivalent of forty troops and four AT-ST scout walkers. Other vehicles, such as PX-10 ground vehicles and speeder bikes, also may be carried. Folding assault ramps allow soldiers and vehicles to depart the shuttle in mere seconds.

The Y-4 has a standard array of sublight drives, a Class Two hyperdrive, a backup hyperdrive engine, and a dedicated nav computer. The command crew numbers three, with the pilot, a chief gunnery officer on the bridge, and a second gunnery officer on the dorsal-mounted double laser cannon. The bridge has an R2 or similar astromech droid to assist in hyperspace calculations. Forward weaponry is handled by the chief gunner and includes two fire-linked laser cannons and a recessed concussion-missile launcher with a magazine of six missiles.

Zsinj's Raptors were known for quiet infiltration of planets and surgical strikes against defense grids: they required a ship that could get them onto a planet quickly and quietly. The Y-4 was perfect for their operations—it has retractable swing wings for emergency braking and increased maneuverability. A one-meter-thick heat shield and extra layers of spray-on ablative coating increase the Y-4's heat resistance.

On one Alliance mission, Han Solo used a falsified transponder code identifying the *Millennium Falcon* as one of the Y-4 transports assigned to the Raptors. The code allowed him to infiltrate the shipyards of Dathomir.

The Y-4 is available in a civilian model which lacks weaponry and armor plating. While it has less powerful engines than the military vessel, it is reliable for courier missions. While it is capable of hyperspace travel, the threat of pirates and other hazards normally forces these civilian Y-4s to carry weaponry. Warlord Zsinj used civilian Y-4s as maintenance and transport vehicles.

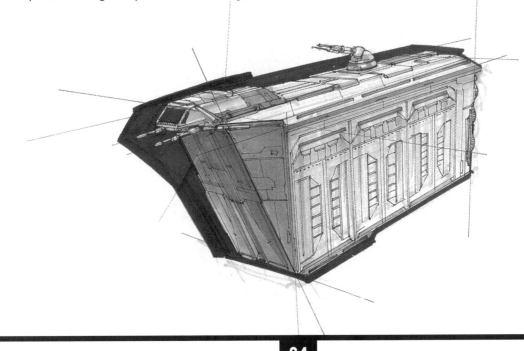

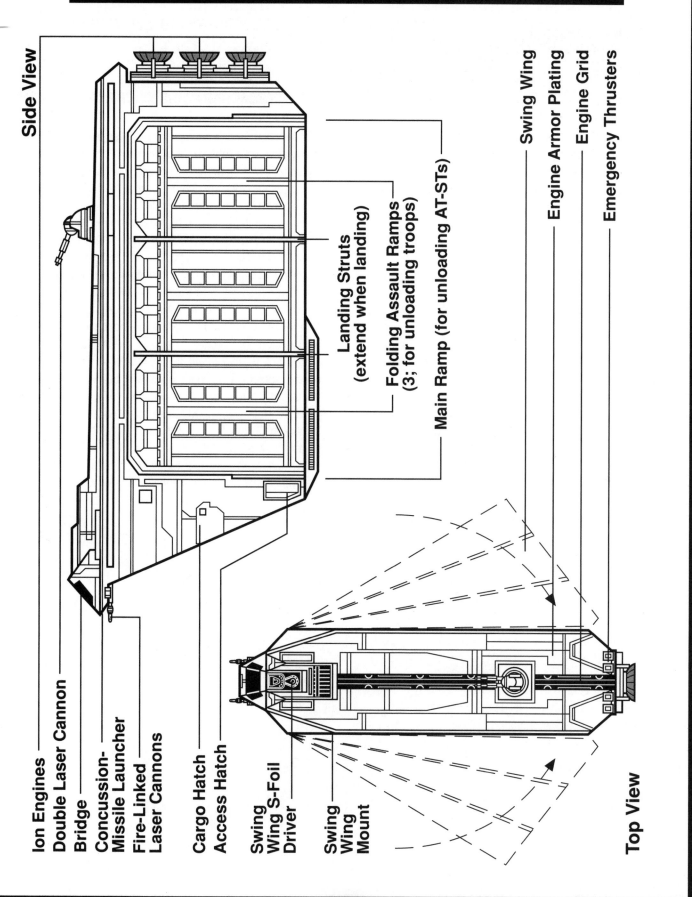

Side View

Ion Engines
Double Laser Cannon
Bridge
Concussion-Missile Launcher
Fire-Linked Laser Cannons

Cargo Hatch
Access Hatch

Swing Wing S-Foil Driver

Swing Wing Mount

Landing Struts (extend when landing)

Folding Assault Ramps (3; for unloading troops)

Main Ramp (for unloading AT-STs)

Swing Wing
Engine Armor Plating
Engine Grid
Emergency Thrusters

Top View

INTERDICTOR CRUISER

SIENAR FLEET SYSTEMS IMMOBILIZER 418

The Interdictor cruiser is a starship that served a very special purpose in the Imperial Navy's fleet. The six-hundred-meter-long star cruiser is built on a standard heavy-cruiser hull, but it carries an artificial gravity-well generator and four gravity-well projectors, which act together to simulate the tremendous effects of a stellar body in hyperspace.

When activated, the artificial gravity wells prevent nearby starships from escaping into hyperspace. Any ship already in hyperspace that crosses such a gravity well immediately drops to realspace. Cutting off the escape to hyperspace is critical—with the gravity-well projectors operating, no Rebel starship could thus escape from the Empire's cruisers and fighters.

Interdictor cruisers, also known as Immobilizer 418 cruisers, were designed by Sienar Fleet Systems, makers of both the TIE fighter and the Skipray blastboat. At first appearing to be a small Star Destroyer, the Interdictor heavy cruiser is recognizable because of the ship's four prominent globes; each globe houses a single gravity-well projector. Interdictors also have twenty quad laser cannons for short-range combat against other capital ships.

Imperial doctrine called for the Interdictors to be placed on the perimeter of a battle area. This gave Interdictor captains a clear view of any battle so they could precisely target the placement of gravity wells to prevent Rebel ships from escaping into hyperspace.

The biggest disadvantage that comes with the Interdictors is that the gravity-well generators can take more than a minute to charge up, giving quick-thinking opponents a chance to jump to hyperspace before the gravity wells can be deployed again.

The Interdictor's hull has proved to be of reliable design; it is also favored by the Imperial bureaucracy because of its close resemblance to the Imperial Star Destroyer. Designers have used the hull, which can be fitted with a wide variety of weapons, for several heavy cruiser designs. The hull and ship systems are easily converted for custom mission duties.

Interdictor cruisers figured prominently in Grand Admiral Thrawn's tactics. He used them to cut off the escape routes of Rebel starships and nearly captured Luke Skywalker by using an Interdictor to force Luke's X-wing from hyperspace to realspace. Luke escaped both the Interdictor and the Star Destroyer *Chimaera* by using a desperation move when he reversed his ship's acceleration compensators while simultaneously firing a pair of proton torpedoes to throw off the *Chimaera*'s tractor beams. While the maneuver caused significant damage to Luke's hyperdrive, the Star Destroyer's tractor beams locked on to the proton torpedoes, giving Luke the precious seconds he needed to make a microjump into hyperspace before the X-wing hyperdrive blew.

Later, Thrawn intended to use an Interdictor above Myrkr to capture Talon Karrde and his ship, the *Wild Karrde*. However, Mara Jade's sudden burst of intuition saved Karrde when she ordered the *Wild Karrde*'s crew to leave the system just before the Interdictor appeared.

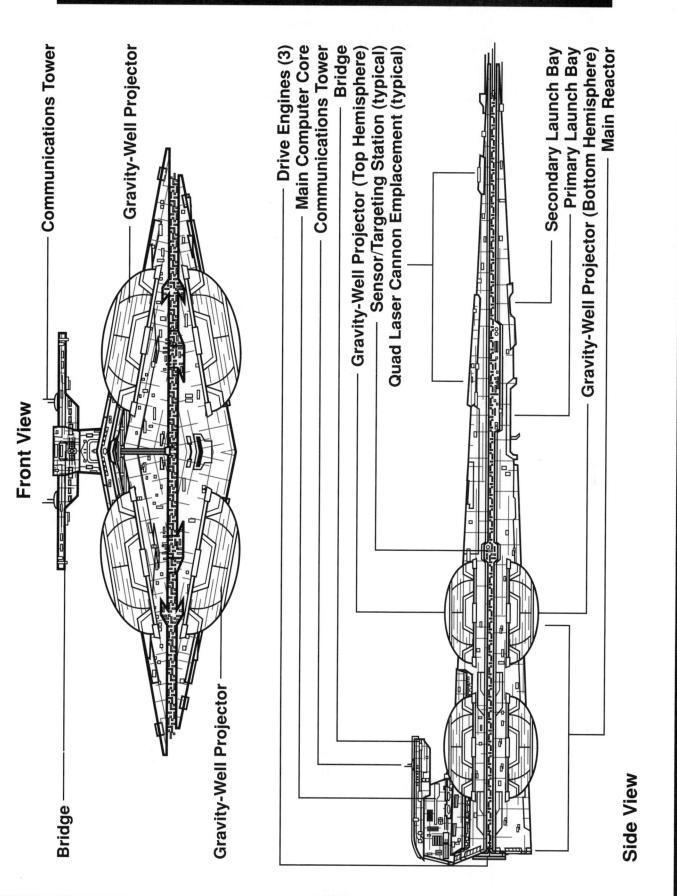

Front View

Communications Tower

Gravity-Well Projector

Bridge

Gravity-Well Projector

Drive Engines (3)

Main Computer Core

Communications Tower

Bridge

Gravity-Well Projector (Top Hemisphere)

Sensor/Targeting Station (typical)

Quad Laser Cannon Emplacement (typical)

Secondary Launch Bay

Primary Launch Bay

Gravity-Well Projector (Bottom Hemisphere)

Main Reactor

Side View

ITHULLIAN ORE HAULER

ITHULLIAN ORE HAULER

Even in a galaxy filled with wonders, the famed Ithullian ore haulers stand out. This is because the mutonium ore haulers are not "manufactured" ships. Instead, the "Nessies" (the local mining races in the Stenness Node) build their ships out of the carapaces of Ithullian colossus wasps. These ships are over a kilometer long, and their unique shape makes them unmistakable.

The Nessies began using the colossus wasps out of convenience. The wasps are native to the Stenness Node systems, a valuable mining region on the galactic frontier. They live for centuries, migrating from world to world and feeding on stellar radiation, raw materials, space slugs, and various creatures found on the asteroids.

When the creatures die, the Nessies convert them to cargo-hauling duty. The carapace hulls are naturally thick enough to repel blaster bolts, so the engineers merely need to carve and section the interior to make room for decks and ship systems such as computers, electronics, navigation computers, sensor systems, weapons, and power generators.

Any remaining space is given over to the precious mutonium ore: the wasp carapaces can carry as much cargo as the largest bulk freighters used in the Galactic Core. To save interior space, the two ion drive engines are mounted outside the hull and braced by struts. The wasp's legs have been affixed with stabilizers and maneuvering jets to provide maneuverability.

Low-power defensive blasters are mounted all along the exterior of the ship, from the head to the abdomen. The hauler's main weapons are a pair of heavy turbolasers mounted in the forward section of the thorax.

Colossus wasps follow the standard insect physiognomy, with a head, thorax, and abdomen. The head houses the command area, along with computers, sensors, and weapon-control systems. The thorax area contains the ore modules, which are the prime targets of any ore pirates who might attack these vessels. The abdomen contains additional ore bays as well as the power generators and drive-control systems. The fuel pods take up nearly half the abdomen.

While the Nessies insist that they use only colossus wasps that die of natural causes, it is well known that some mining colonies pay top price for a wasp carapace. This has led to colossus wasp poaching in the asteroid fields—although this can prove as dangerous to the poachers as to the wasps, since the giant insectoids are quite capable of defending themselves.

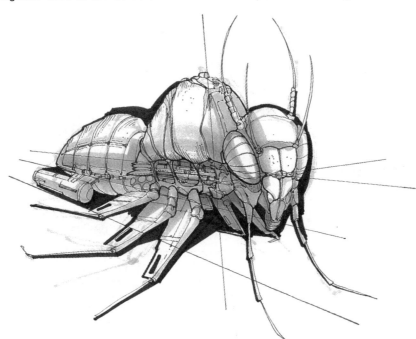

Side View

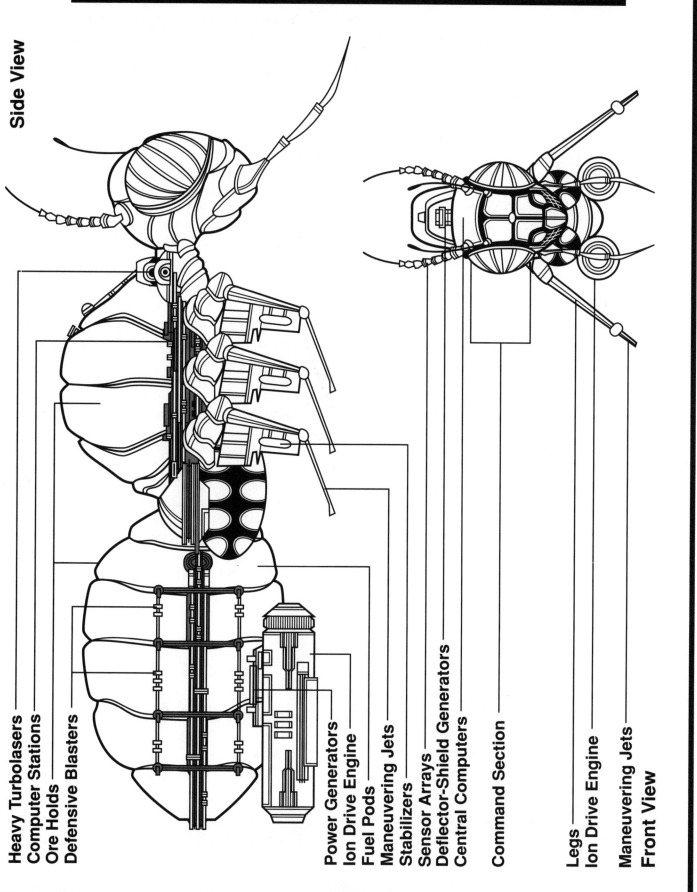

Heavy Turbolasers
Computer Stations
Ore Holds
Defensive Blasters

Power Generators
Ion Drive Engine
Fuel Pods
Maneuvering Jets
Stabilizers
Sensor Arrays
Deflector-Shield Generators
Central Computers

Command Section

Legs
Ion Drive Engine

Maneuvering Jets
Front View

JABBA THE HUTT'S SAIL BARGE

UBRIKKIAN LUXURY SAIL BARGE

Jabba's sail barge was an immense repulsorlift vehicle which the crime lord used for pleasure cruises on the desert world of Tatooine. Sail barges are recreational vehicles that are popular across the galaxy and often are used by tour companies or vacation resorts. They can travel across *any* relatively flat terrain, including sand, water, ice, and grass.

Jabba was never known for his modesty, and his customized sail barge was the finest money could buy. Whenever his sail barge anchored outside Mos Eisely's city limits, the locals knew trouble was brewing.

The sail barge's main propulsion system was a trichambered repulsorlift thrust package with a top speed of one hundred kilometers per hour. Jabba's sail barge could hover up to ten meters above the ground; when it was set in "hover" mode, the immense sails caught the wind and pulled the barge along. In this mode, the sail barge had a top speed of about thirty kilometers per hour.

The sail barge's main deck carried a heavy blaster for defense against large vehicles, while a series of antipersonnel blasters were mounted on the deck railings. Jabba also added an enhanced sensor system so he could detect enemies long before they found him—a handy tool for avoiding Imperial troops when there was questionable cargo aboard.

The passenger deck, directly below the main deck, sported a series of retractable viewports that gave Jabba and his entourage an unobstructed view of the terrain. The barge's largest room was the banquet room, where most of Jabba's entourage gathered for his decadent parties. This level also had a pantry and Jabba's private suite, and there was a kitchen to satisfy the tastes of the master criminal, who ate up to nine times a day.

The bottom deck was taken up by the sail barge's engines and maneuvering systems. Sails and steering vanes could be controlled from the control room (in the front of the barge), Jabba's private lounge, or the banquet room.

Jabba was particularly fond of staging parties involving elaborate executions during which he fed troublemakers to the Sarlacc at the Great Pit of Carkoon. In addition to pleasure cruises, Jabba often sailed from his palace out in the desert to his town house in Mos Eisely when he had business with smugglers and other criminal figures. Jabba's henchmen used the sail barge for raids against bands of Sand People and others who offended Jabba's sensibilities.

The sail barge was destroyed and Jabba was killed during the daring rescue of Han Solo at the Great Pit of Carkoon. Princess Leia Organa rigged the sail barge's laser cannon to fire directly into the deck, triggering a chain reaction which consumed the sail barge in a tremendous explosion. The wreckage has since been stripped by Jawas, while Jabba's once-mighty criminal empire has fallen into disarray.

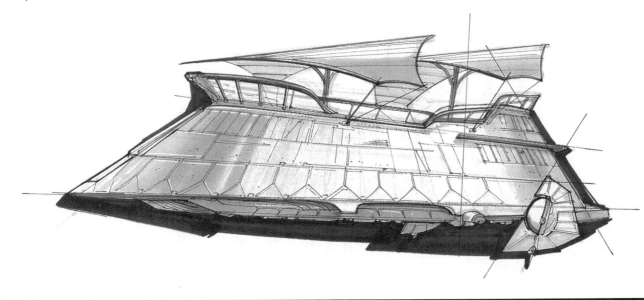

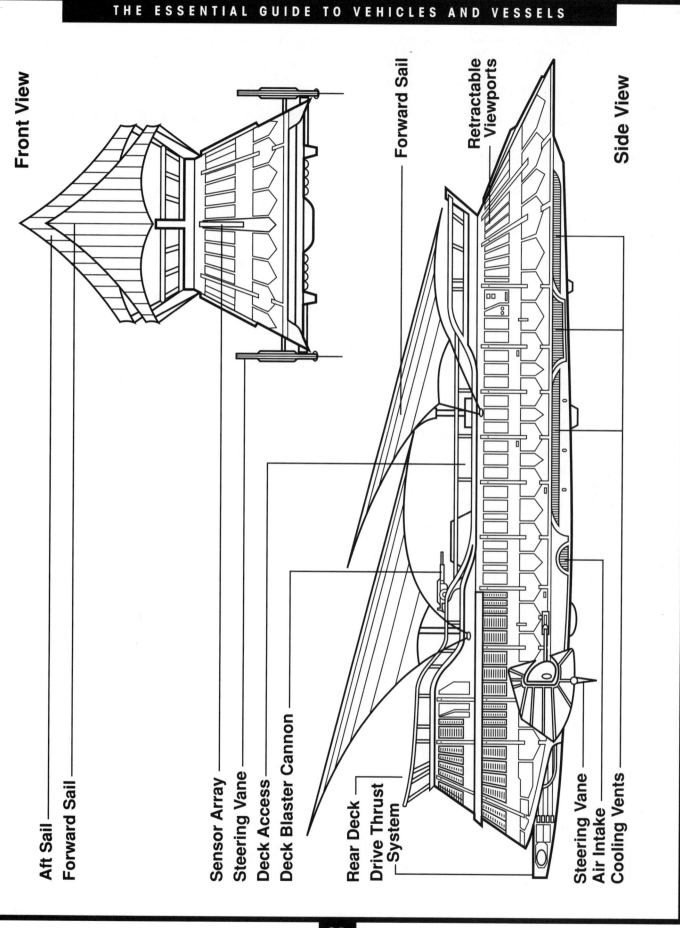

Front View

Side View

Aft Sail

Forward Sail

Sensor Array

Steering Vane

Deck Access

Deck Blaster Cannon

Rear Deck

Drive Thrust System

Forward Sail

Retractable Viewports

Steering Vane

Air Intake

Cooling Vents

JABBA THE HUTT'S SPACE CRUISER

UBRIKKIAN LUXURY SPACE YACHT

Jabba's space cruiser was a customized Ubrikkian space yacht which he used for "personal business trips" from his palace to the distant city of Mos Eisley. The infamous Hutt gangster also used it for any pressing business in the Outer Rim Territories or other areas of the galaxy. The ship was infamous both for its gaudy appearance and for the sordid goings-on known to occur within its confines.

The yacht's superstructure contained Jabba's throne room, which was dominated by a single transparisteel observation dome. Aside from hosting the many "social activities" held for Jabba's amusement, the throne room served as the sleeping quarters for many of Jabba's hired thugs and hangers-on.

Jabba's personal quarters were set immediately aft of the throne room and featured two smaller observation domes. The yacht had a galley for meal preparation, an armory, a droid labor pool, a small vehicle hangar, and numerous guest quarters—all of them with hidden listening and visual pickups for the Hutt's personal espionage and amusement. There was a small landing bay with six Z-95 Headhunter fighters, as well as a pair of small landing shuttles, had Jabba preferred to send a "greeting committee" before his grand entrance. It is rumored that there was

a holding cage built for his pet rancor in the lowest levels of the yacht.

The yacht was powered by a pair of Ubrikkian N2 ion engines supplemented by three smaller Kuat T-c40 ion engines. Sublight speed was roughly equivalent to that of the Victory Star Destroyer. Two rear vanes functioned as ailerons for atmospheric flight, while a trio of retractable rods on each side of the yacht held maneuvering jets. The yacht reached a speed of eight hundred kilometers per hour in an atmosphere, although Jabba's pilots were often instructed to set a much more leisurely pace to provide his eminence a relaxing flight—while affording those who were to be "honored" by a visit from Jabba the chance to make final preparations. A Koensayr CL-14 hyperdrive motivator slaved to a standard Ubrikkian hyperdrive unit gave the yacht a fairly slow Class Two hyperdrive rating.

The yacht's six turbolasers were discreetly mounted beneath the superstructure's ridge. The turbolasers were of Corellian design and appeared to use a very small power generator. In actuality, the weapons were fed directly from the power core in the heart of the ship. At first glance, the weapons appeared to be well within civilian legal limits—their true capabilities became apparent only after they opened fire.

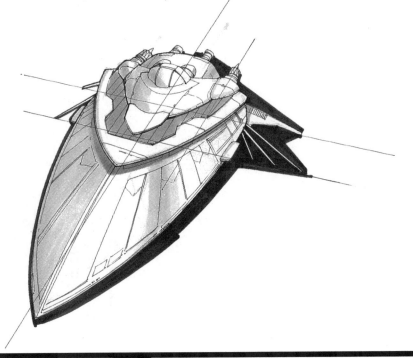

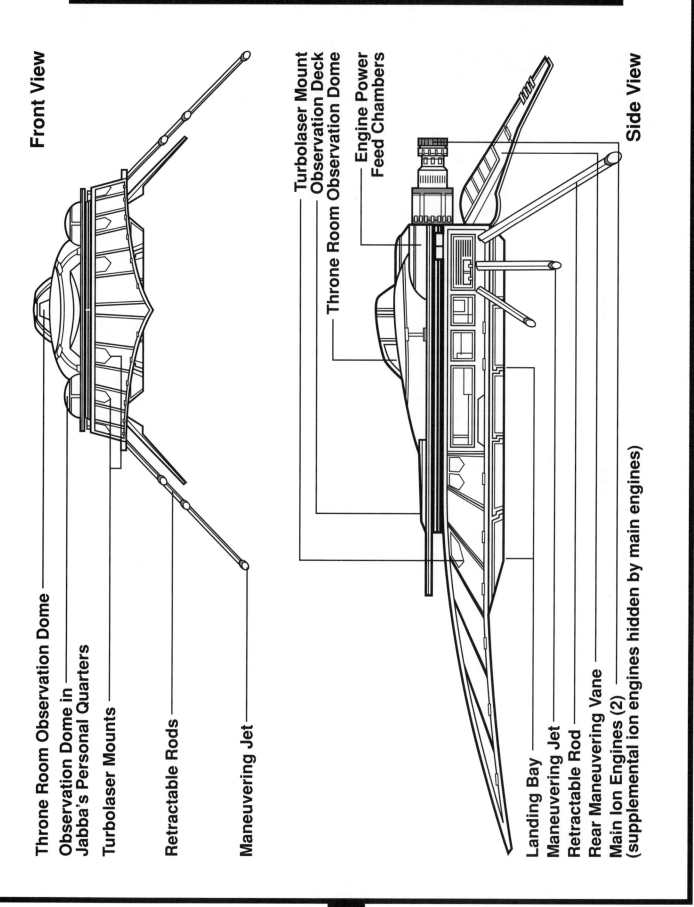

Front View

Throne Room Observation Dome

Observation Dome in Jabba's Personal Quarters

Turbolaser Mounts

Retractable Rods

Maneuvering Jet

Side View

Turbolaser Mount
Observation Deck
Throne Room Observation Dome

Engine Power
Feed Chambers

Landing Bay
Maneuvering Jet
Retractable Rod
Rear Maneuvering Vane
Main Ion Engines (2)
(supplemental ion engines hidden by main engines)

JAWA SANDCRAWLER

MODIFIED CORELLIA MINING DIGGER CRAWLER

Upon seeing a Jawa, one would hardly expect these tiny, skittish creatures to be the owners of the immense sandcrawlers which traverse the endless deserts of Tatooine. The desert scavengers eke out meager livings by combing the wastes in search of valuable minerals and salvageable or "abandoned" machinery. They store their treasures aboard their sandcrawlers, where they rebuild broken droids, getting them working just long enough to sell them to somebody else.

Sandcrawlers are steam-powered vehicles that originally were brought to Tatooine when the world was first settled as a mining colony. When mining proved to be unprofitable, the crawlers were abandoned and the Jawas quickly took them off the hands of the colonists.

Entire Jawa clans, some numbering up to several hundred individuals, live in each sandcrawler. The inside of a crawler is a winding maze of sleeping and eating alcoves, machinery, spare parts, junk, and fully functional but terrified droids. Since the Jawas don't have a ready supply of spare parts, a sandcrawler is kept running only through jury-rigged repairs, which can overload at any time.

Sandcrawlers tower nearly twenty meters high, and though plodding, they are virtually unstoppable. Immense turbines power the eight massive treads which pull the sandcrawler over steep inclines and through mountain passes. Sandcrawlers are hardy of necessity—Tatooine's massive sandstorms can topple any lesser vehicle.

The Jawas often leave the safety of their crawlers to seek out new droids which have been lost or abandoned to Tatooine's wastes, although the small aliens work in large groups whenever they leave their homes. They use makeshift ionization guns to disable the droids, then carry them back to the sandcrawler.

New droid acquisitions are taken on board either through a magnetic suction tube (originally used for loading mining ore) or by using the ore-loading ramp in the front of the vehicle.

Jawas rely on sandcrawlers for defense against their natural enemies, the Sand People and the fearsome krayt dragons. The Jawas conduct a brisk trade with Tatooine's moisture farmers, but they are always fearful that they will be endangered, and at least one Jawa colony has threatened to roll its sandcrawler right across a moisture farm. Fear of reprisal from other settlers makes this a tactic of desperation, though, and such a violent incident is out of character for the Jawa scavengers.

While they are sturdy enough to resist Tusken Raider attacks, sandcrawlers have several weak points and cannot stand up to high-power energy blasts.

No one knows exactly how many sandcrawlers wander the deserts of Tatooine. Jawa sandcrawlers seldom work in tandem, but it is known that Jawas occasionally stage "swap meets" where several crawlers gather to exchange goods and information.

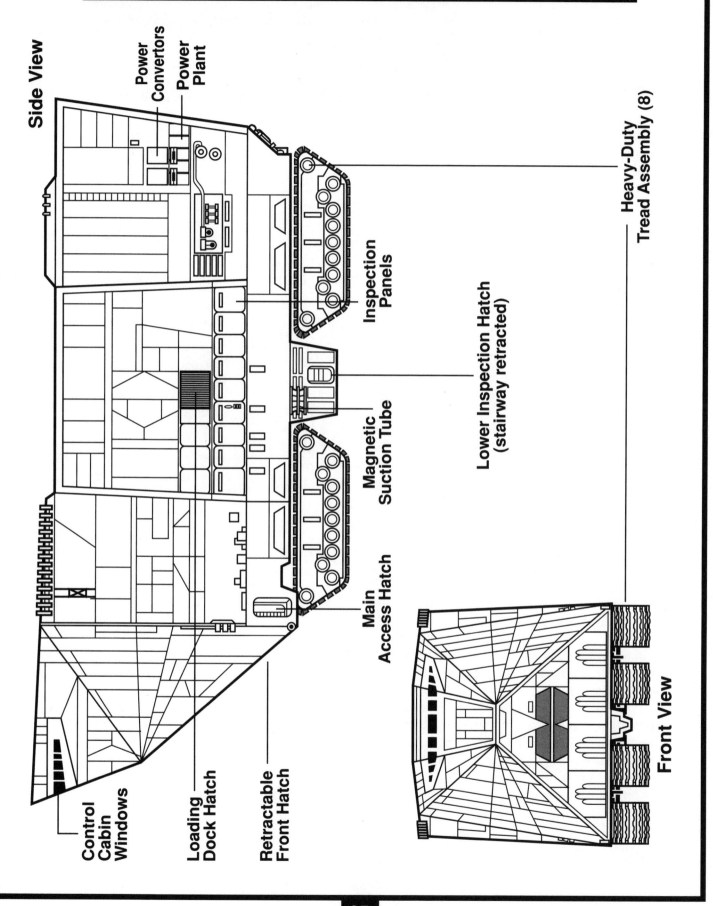

Side View

Power Convertors

Power Plant

Inspection Panels

Lower Inspection Hatch
(stairway retracted)

Magnetic Suction Tube

Main Access Hatch

Heavy-Duty Tread Assembly (8)

Control Cabin Windows

Loading Dock Hatch

Retractable Front Hatch

Front View

JUGGERNAUT

KUAT DRIVE YARDS HAVw A5 JUGGERNAUT

Juggernauts are decades-old assault vehicles that have played a prominent role in military forces dating back to the days of the Old Republic. While the juggernaut was considered state of the art when it was first developed, modern war vehicles such as AT-AT walkers have displaced it as the most powerful land combat vehicle in Imperial space.

The vehicle was first built during the waning days of the Old Republic for use by the many planetary governments that had begun building their own defense forces. Juggernauts were sold to planetary governors, corporations, and even private interests, and quite a few fell into the hands of the Hutt crime clans (and a number of other shadowy groups). Under Imperial rule, most juggernauts were commandeered by the Army and proved to be particularly useful on outlying planets where Imperial commanders could not get AT-AT walkers.

While juggernauts use ancient technology, their sheer size and thick armor plating make them as tough and dangerous as AT-AT walkers. The juggernaut is twenty-two meters long and nearly fifteen meters tall. Imperial troops have nicknamed the juggernauts "rolling slabs" because of their size and configuration.

Five sets of drive wheels propel the juggernaut to a top speed of two hundred kilometers per hour, although the primitive drive system requires the vehicle to slow to barely twenty-five kilometers per hour in order to turn. There are two drive stations, one at each end of the vehicle, so the juggernaut *can* simply reverse direction. This is of great assistance in rough terrain and urban areas, where there often is not enough room for the vehicle to turn around.

Juggernauts can transport fifty troops into battle or carry speeder bikes, light assault speeders, and other small repulsorcraft. This cargo capacity matches or exceeds that of the Imperial AT-AT walker, although the juggernaut's terrain limitations and primitive drive system make the vehicle far less attractive in the long run: a juggernaut with a damaged drive system can spend weeks in repair bays while crews wait for replacement parts.

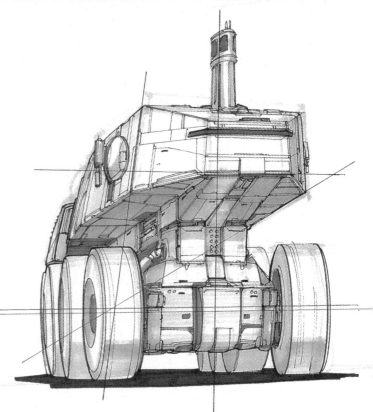

Juggernauts require a crew of two, with an additional six gunners needed for the weapons systems. A single trooper in the observation tower provides targeting information to the gunners. The juggernaut's weaponry includes a turret-mounted laser cannon and port and starboard laser cannons. These are as effective as the lasers on an AT-AT walker, although their older design limits their effective range to only two-thirds that of the walker's weapons. A medium blaster cannon is also turret-mounted and features both a longer range and better stopping power than do the chin-mounted medium blasters on the AT-AT. Two concussion-grenade launchers are mounted on independent turrets, and each draws on a magazine of ten grenades. They are used to lay down suppressing fire to protect troops and vehicles exiting a juggernaut.

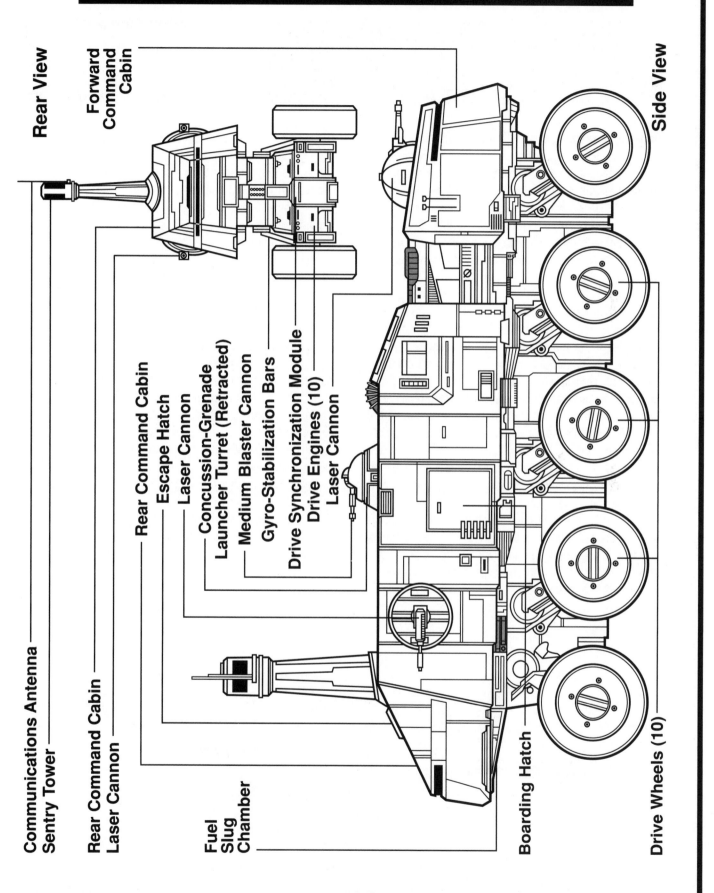

Rear View

Forward
Command
Cabin

Side View

Communications Antenna

Sentry Tower

Rear Command Cabin
Laser Cannon

Rear Command Cabin

Escape Hatch

Laser Cannon

Concussion-Grenade
Launcher Turret (Retracted)

Medium Blaster Cannon

Gyro-Stabilization Bars

Drive Synchronization Module

Drive Engines (10)

Laser Cannon

Fuel
Slug
Chamber

Boarding Hatch

Drive Wheels (10)

LADY LUCK

SoroSuub Personal Luxury Yacht 3000

The *Lady Luck* is Lando Calrissian's own modified space yacht. Lando acquired the ship from an Orthellin royal mistress at about the same time that he was setting up Nomad City, his mining operation on the sun-scorched world of Nkllon. While the famous gambler had grand plans to transform the ship into a top-flight luxury vessel, his duties on Nomad City prevented Lando from executing his fanciful designs.

The yacht is fifty meters long, with a pair of engine pods extending from the main hull. Each pod houses a sublight engine and a hyperdrive engine. Lando has always preferred finesse and misdirection to brute strength, and the *Lady Luck* reflects that philosophy. The ship appears to be an unarmed pleasure yacht, giving him a decisive advantage when dealing with smugglers, who tend to make snap judgments and base all their decisions on the initial impression. Beneath the sleek hull is an unusually sophisticated sensor system with two forward sensor arrays that allow the *Lady Luck* to detect, identify, and scan incoming vessels from an incredible distance, letting Lando know exactly what he's dealing with.

The *Lady Luck*'s only other defenses are a retractable laser cannon and a pair of shield generators, so the sensor system is a necessity. Lando intends to upgrade the weapons, hull plating, and shield generators to make the ship better suited for combat.

Calrissian has equipped the *Lady Luck* with hidden smuggler compartments and a transponder that contains three false ship identities to allow the ship to slip through spaceport customs without anyone suspecting the craft's true identity. Lando has been a longtime believer in slave-rigging his ships, and the *Lady Luck* has been equipped with a beckon call unit. When activated, the yacht's droid brain will bring the ship to the summoning unit—a datadisk-sized controller that Lando carries on his belt. The slave-rigging worked to good advantage when Lando, Luke, and Han needed a quick escape from the mining city of Ilic.

Lando has always been one to live in style, and the *Lady Luck*'s interior reflects his extravagant tastes. The observation level has an exterior deck, while the interior compartment has a small jet-stream meditation pool and several conform-couches. The main deck offers a dining area, Lando's private suite, and five visitor cabins, as well as the escape pods, the bridge, and the main control systems.

With Nkllon destroyed by Grand Admiral Thrawn's forces, Lando placed the *Lady Luck* in temporary retirement while he returned to active duty with the New Republic. He brought the *Lady Luck* back into active service for an attempt to rescue Han Solo after the Corellian's disappearance while on a diplomatic mission to Kessel.

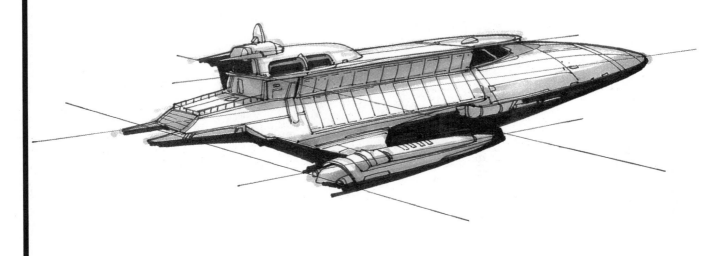

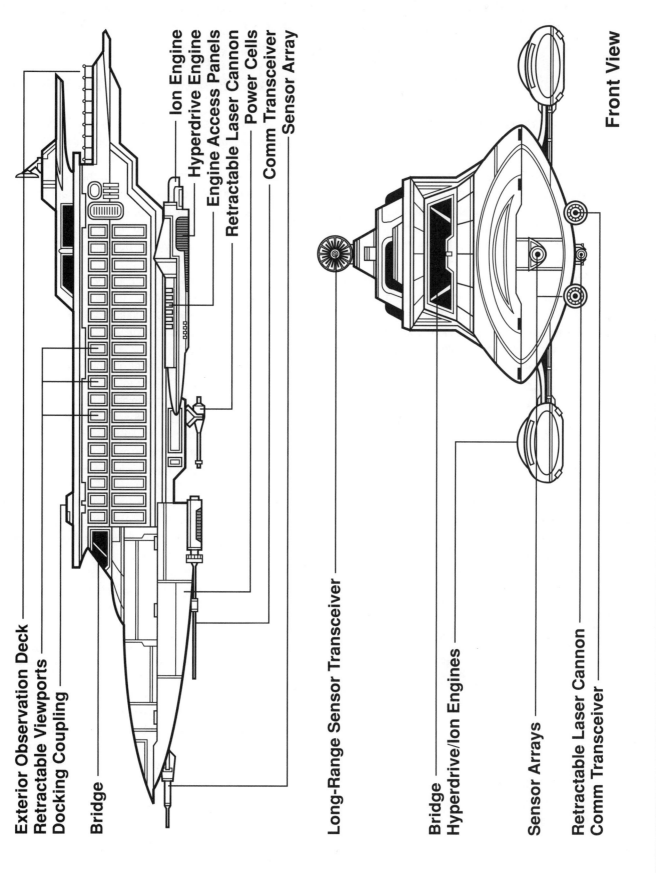

Side View

- Exterior Observation Deck
- Retractable Viewports
- Docking Coupling
- Bridge

- Ion Engine
- Hyperdrive Engine
- Engine Access Panels
- Retractable Laser Cannon
- Power Cells
- Comm Transceiver
- Sensor Array

Long-Range Sensor Transceiver

Front View

- Bridge
- Hyperdrive/Ion Engines
- Sensor Arrays
- Retractable Laser Cannon
- Comm Transceiver

SIENAR FLEET SYSTEMS *LAMBDA*-CLASS SHUTTLE

The *Lambda*-class shuttle is a cargo and passenger shuttle that was used by the Imperial fleet. The vessel has a stationary top wing and two folding bottom wings. In flight, the Lambda resembles an inverted Y, and the two lower wings fold up when the ship lands. The shuttle rests on two retractable landing legs located just inside the folding wings. A ramp telescopes from below the forward fuselage for loading and debarking.

Lambda-class shuttles were originally designed by Sienar Fleet Systems. Sienar manufactures the shuttles, while Cygnus Spaceworks is subcontracted to manufacture a more heavily armed military version of the ship. Cygnus recently has begun producing more lightly armed shuttles that are virtually identical to the Sienar model.

Lambda shuttles can carry up to twenty passengers or eighty tons of cargo. Unlike most Imperial shuttles, Lambda shuttles have hyperdrives, which allow passengers and cargo to be transferred between different fleets and systems. The Lambda has a heavily reinforced hull and multiple shield generators. The Sienar shuttle has three double blaster cannons (one is rear-mounted) and two double laser cannons. The Cygnus Spaceworks military version has ten laser cannons.

Lambda shuttles maintain a command crew of four, with the option of adding two additional officers who normally handle secured communications and power allocation. A single pilot can handle the ship, but performance suffers significantly.

Many Imperial government officials used these shuttles for personal transport owing to their combination of combatworthiness and the large interior cargo area which could be converted to passenger space. The shuttle's armament allowed the Lambda to travel without a military escort, making it difficult for Rebel raiding forces to determine whether shuttles were merely carrying cargo or transporting important Imperial officials.

The Emperor himself used a highly modified Lambda shuttle which was believed to be equipped with a cloaking device. It is known that the Emperor's top aides, military officers, and operatives, including Darth Vader and the Grand Inquisitor, had access to heavily armed Lambda shuttles. These special shuttles carried secured HoloNet transceivers, allowing instantaneous communication with Imperial City from any point in the Empire.

The Rebel Alliance used the stolen shuttle *Tydirium* to deliver a commando assault team to Endor's forest moon. Using appropriated Imperial command codes purchased from spies and a cover story claiming that they were delivering parts and technical crew, the Rebel team led by General Han Solo, Princess Leia Organa, and Luke Skywalker managed to infiltrate the Imperial base on Endor and eventually to destroy the shield protecting the unfinished second Death Star.

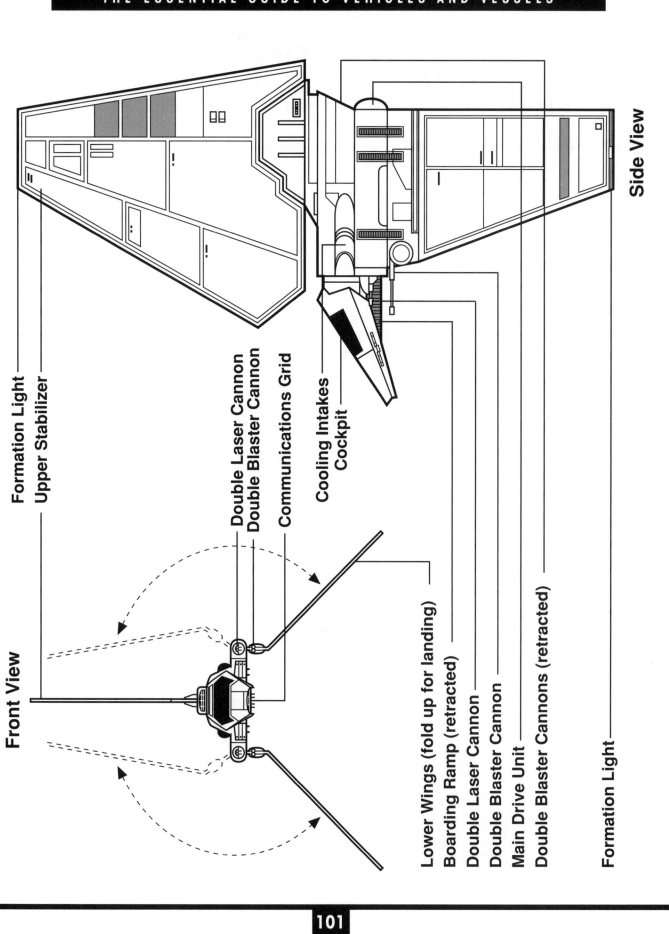

Side View

Front View

Formation Light
Upper Stabilizer

Double Laser Cannon
Double Blaster Cannon
Communications Grid

Cooling Intakes
Cockpit

Lower Wings (fold up for landing)
Boarding Ramp (retracted)
Double Laser Cannon
Double Blaster Cannon
Main Drive Unit
Double Blaster Cannons (retracted)

Formation Light

LANCER FRIGATE

KUAT DRIVE YARDS *LANCER*-CLASS FRIGATE

The Lancer frigate is a 250-meter-long capital combat starship that the Empire designed specifically to combat Rebel starfighters. The Lancer was designed by the Empire shortly after a small number of Rebel X-wing and Y-wing fighters destroyed the "invincible" Death Star battle station. While the Empire didn't face as many Rebel starfighter attacks as Imperial Navy strategists first feared, the Lancer proved its worth in its first few encounters.

The biggest problem with the Lancer is that it is expensive in relation to its actual utility. A Lancer costs as much as any other heavy combat cruiser, yet it is suitable only for repelling fighter attacks. The Empire's supply of Lancers was limited, and it proved impossible to assign the cruisers to protect every convoy. The ships were best put to use attacking Rebel starfighter bases, although the Empire's opportunities for these missions were rare since the Rebels showed an unnerving ability to operate right under the noses of the Imperials without being discovered.

The Lancer has twenty Corellian AG-2G quad laser cannons specifically calibrated for use against high-speed, maneuverable starfighters. The weapons have superior tracking and targeting capabilities and are mounted on elevated towers to provide an increased field of fire; each bank of lasers is fed by a single power generator. Backup gunners must balance power demands to keep the Lancer's weapons operating at full capacity.

Unfortunately, the Lancer has virtually no capital-scale weapons for engaging other combat or capital starships.

Another drawback is that Lancers are slow at sublight speeds, so Rebel fighters with a small lead were often able to outrun the ships. Their hull armor plating and shields are insufficient to stand up to the punishment most capital starship weapons can dish out, so Lancers proved to be targets of choice for Rebel capital ships. Each Lancer frigate has a small internal hangar bay with room for only two shuttles. Carried troops and vehicles are always kept to a minimum.

Lancers supplemented most Imperial warships, which tended to feature multiple banks of capital-scale turbolasers but few smaller weapons for dealing with starfighters. Originally the Lancers were placed on the outer perimeter of Imperial fleets to ward off fighter attacks, but Rebel capital ships found them easy pickings. The Imperial Navy then began assigning Lancer frigates to flank Star Destroyers and other large ships, where the Lancers' guns provided protection against mass starfighter attacks and the larger ships' weapons could protect the Lancers themselves from powerful Rebel cruisers.

Five years after the death of Emperor Palpatine, Grand Admiral Thrawn demonstrated his tactical genius by employing Lancer frigates as key components of Imperial raiding missions. The Lancers devastated the New Republic fighter squadrons while softening up enemy defenses so heavy Imperial cruisers could move into the opposing fleet and use their ion cannons to disable and capture lightly crewed New Republic warships.

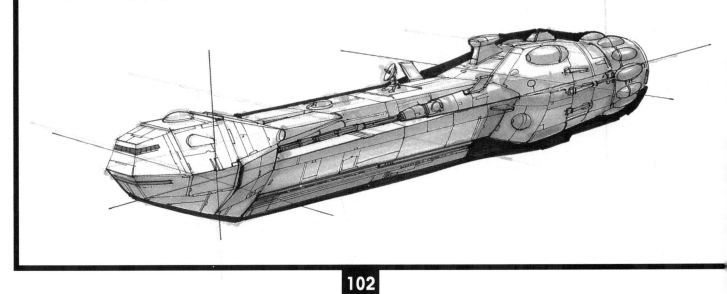

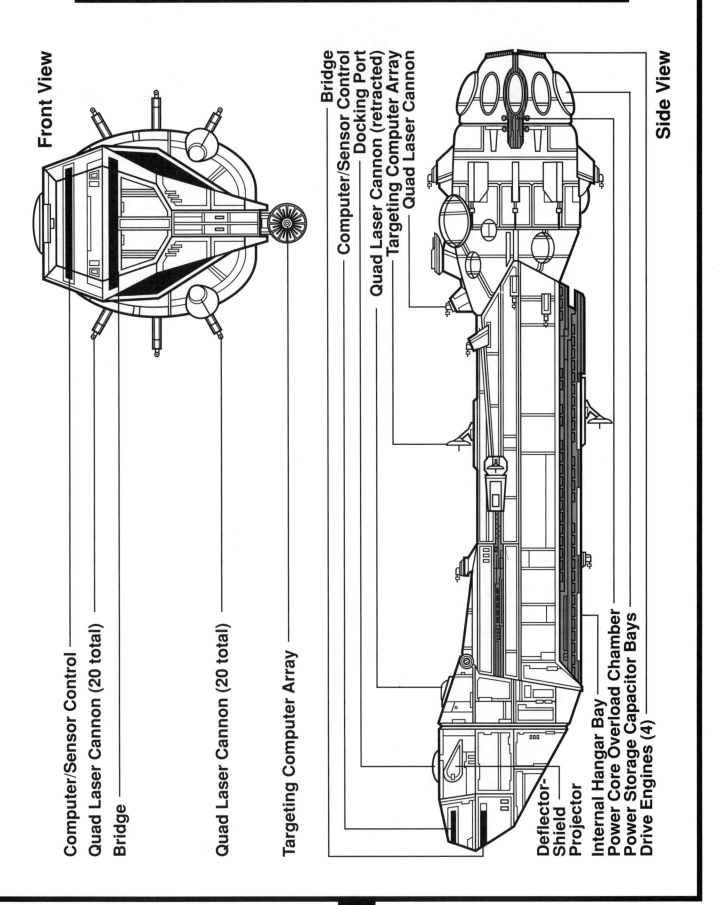

Front View

Computer/Sensor Control

Quad Laser Cannon (20 total)

Bridge

Quad Laser Cannon (20 total)

Targeting Computer Array

Side View

Bridge

Computer/Sensor Control

Docking Port

Quad Laser Cannon (retracted)

Targeting Computer Array

Quad Laser Cannon

Deflector-
Shield
Projector

Internal Hangar Bay

Power Core Overload Chamber

Power Storage Capacitor Bays

Drive Engines (4)

LARS FAMILY LANDSPEEDER

SoroSuub V-35 Courier

The Lars family's landspeeder was a typical family vehicle: it provided simple, practical transportation. Unlike Luke's once-sporty X-34, the V-35 Courier was built to be inexpensive, reliable, and thoroughly unremarkable. Although it was an older model, Owen and Luke managed to keep the heavily used SoroSuub V-35 Courier in excellent mechanical condition. With a fresh paint job and some interior work, it could have been worth a couple of thousand credits on a used speeder lot in Mos Eisley. Since Owen and Beru Lars used the speeder only about twice a month, it was often stored in the family garage, which doubled as Luke's workshop.

Uncle Owen and Aunt Beru used the vehicle for their regular errand trips to Anchorhead, the small hamlet not far from their farm. While the speeder's top cruising speed was only about one hundred kilometers per hour, that was fast enough for everyone in the family but Luke. In Anchorhead, Owen gathered supplies for the farm (he always needed parts for his moisture vaporators because of mechanical breakdown or nocturnal thieving by Jawas and other scavengers), and Beru would pick up household items and sell her excess hydroponically grown vegetables for whatever price she could get.

The Lars landspeeder would seat three. The driver sat atop the vehicle, almost directly in front of the repulsor-field generator; a rectractable windscreen provided protection from harsh weather. The unit had a simple scanner system for navigation, although Owen and Beru knew the routes around Anchorhead so well that they seldom used it.

The passenger compartment was located just beneath the cowling and was entered through folding access panels. The passenger seats folded down to reveal the large cargo compartment inside the body of the vehicle.

As is typical of many older speeders, the repulsor-field generator dominated the vehicle. The engine's accessible location made maintenance easy. Operation of the repulsor system was simple: the repulsor generator provided lift to keep the vehicle above the ground and also provided power to the turbine thrust system.

The repulsorlift generator for such a craft is open to the air for cooling purposes. While better cooling could be seen as a benefit on most planets, this particular feature is a liability on a desert world such as Tatooine, where loose sand and other particles constantly clog intake vents and ruin ion pistons. Owen Lars solved the problem in genuine moisture farmer fashion: he built homemade filtering screens for the repulsor generator and the air intakes.

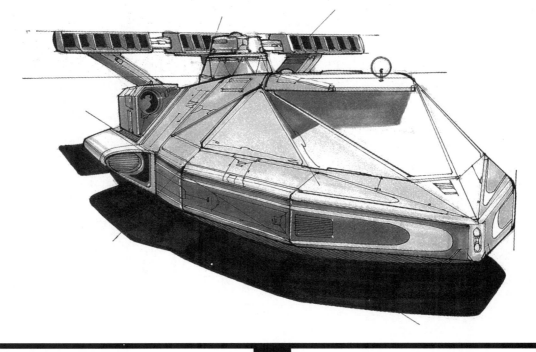

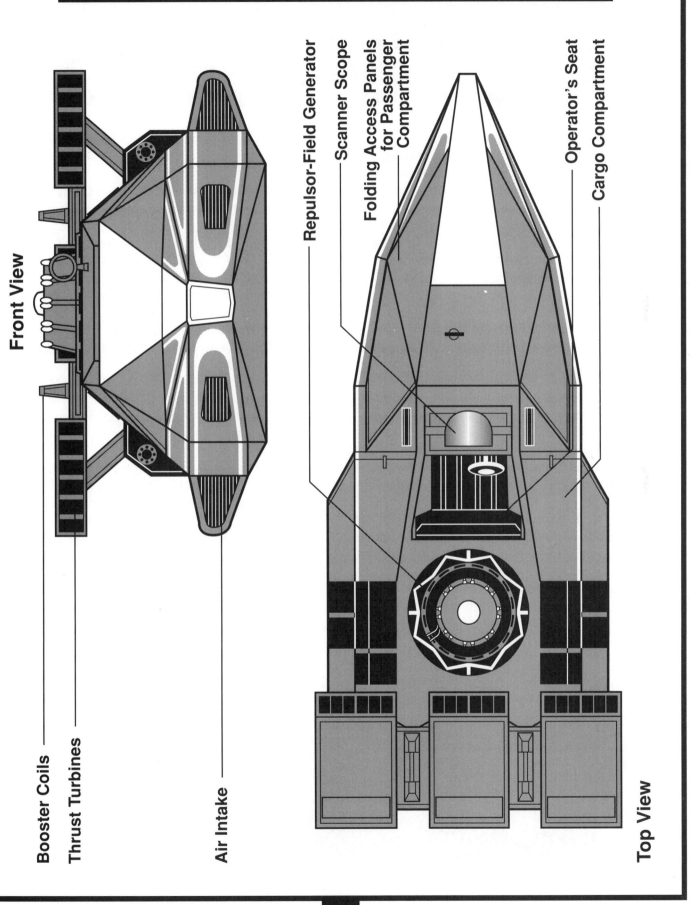

Front View

Booster Coils

Thrust Turbines

Air Intake

Repulsor-Field Generator

Scanner Scope

Folding Access Panels for Passenger Compartment

Operator's Seat

Cargo Compartment

Top View

LUKE SKYWALKER'S LANDSPEEDER

SoroSuub X-34 Landspeeder

While Luke Skywalker daydreamed about piloting Imperial fighters, his youth was spent working on his uncle's moisture farm in the desert of Tatooine. As he faced a constant regimen of repairing old moisture vaporators, Luke's greatest joy came from racing through Beggar's Canyon in his T-16 Skyhopper and from piloting his old landspeeder through the desert at speeds considered excessive by anyone's standards.

Luke argued with his uncle, Owen Lars, to get permission to buy his speeder. As Uncle Owen asked Luke to take on more and more responsibilities on the farm, Luke reasoned that he needed a way to get to all the vaporator ranges quickly. He argued that it would be practical to have a second speeder in the household. Of course, Owen knew the truth: Luke wanted a speeder for joyriding with his friends. "A waste of money" was Owen's only comment.

Finally, Aunt Beru convinced her husband to allow Luke to purchase the speeder. Owen went along to give the old brown SoroSuub X-34 a good once-over and offered his begrudging approval. Luke purchased the landspeeder for 2,400 credits.

While the landspeeder's body was scratched and dented, Luke was more concerned about whether it was at least as fast as the speeders his friends Deak and Fixer owned; after all, it wouldn't look good to let one's friends beat one in a race! It wasn't long before turbine cowlings, computer circuits, and repulsor-generator parts littered the floor of the Lars family's garage. Uncle Owen left Luke to himself, figuring that he was learning mechanical skills that would make him a better moisture farmer.

Luke's landspeeder was traditional in many respects. Its open cockpit had a retractable duraplex windscreen and seated a driver and a passenger. A pair of droids could be secured to the back panels over the repulsor-field generator. Cargo space was limited to whatever could be stashed into the passenger-side footwells.

Controls consisted of a steering wheel and foot pedals. A simple scanner, operated by the passenger or set on autoscan, provided speed, navigation, and traffic information—and allowed Luke to track down the runaway astromech droid R2-D2.

Powered by a standard repulsorlift (or "antigrav") engine, the landspeeder hovered one meter above the ground. Thrust was generated by a trio of turbine engines fed by the repulsorlift engine, with a top speed of about 250 kilometers per hour.

Every older vehicle has a few quirks, and Luke's speeder was no exception. He finished patching up the repulsion floater just a couple of days before R2-D2 and C-3PO came into his life, but the left turbine engine's convertor coil wires were constantly burning out, indicating a faulty power regulator. Still, despite the long hours for repairs, the landspeeder gave Luke something priceless: freedom and excitement.

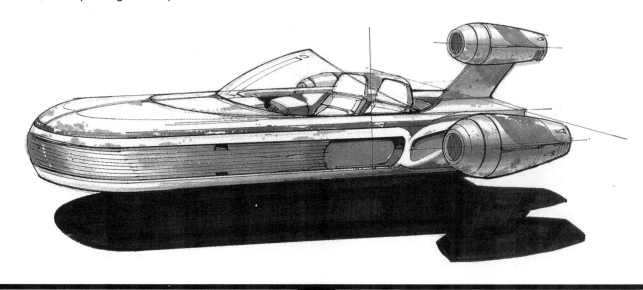

Front View

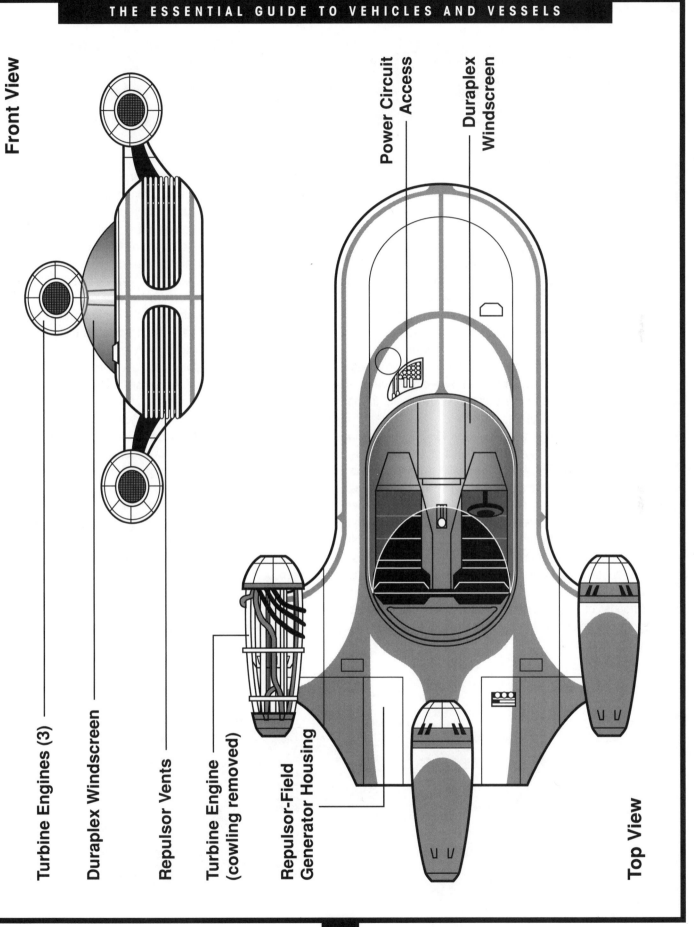

Turbine Engines (3)

Duraplex Windscreen

Repulsor Vents

Turbine Engine
(cowling removed)

Repulsor-Field
Generator Housing

Power Circuit
Access

Duraplex
Windscreen

Top View

MARAUDER CORVETTE

REPUBLIC SIENAR SYSTEMS MARAUDER-CLASS CORVETTE

Marauder corvettes are among the most common capital ships in the Corporate Sector Authority's Picket Fleet. Marauders were designed by Republic Sienar Systems, one of the Republic's prime starship designers, but Old Republic bureaucrats opted not to purchase this ship for government use. Republic Sienar Systems was going to scrap the design, but the Corporate Sector offered to purchase a fleet of the vessels. Once the ships began rolling off the assembly lines on Lianna, planetary navies and large corporations started to buy up the ships. With the implementation of the Corporate Sector Authority's aggressive armament program, the order for Marauder corvettes nearly doubled, and Republic Sienar turned a profit. And despite precautions, in recent years, some Marauders have begun falling into the hands of smugglers and pirates.

Marauder corvettes are 195-meter-long light cruisers that are aerodynamically streamlined for atmospheric combat. They have long, sleek bodies with extended airfoils and look more like oversize fighters than combat cruisers. They have a top planetary speed of 850 kilometers per hour and a sublight speed slightly faster than that of the old *Victory*-class Star Destroyer. Marauders are not powerful enough for fleet engagements against Imperial Navy vessels, but they are excellent starships for system patrol and smuggling interdiction efforts. The Authority often calls the Marauder an "assault ship" because of its effectiveness against pirate and mercenary forces, which tend to fly less advanced starships.

Standard Authority Marauders carry eight double turbolasers and three tractor-beam projectors, although they have mounting points for up to four additional turbolasers if a larger power generator is installed. The Marauders carry twelve Authority IRD fighters for assault and patrol missions. The Marauder carries two platoons of Authority Espo troopers, for a total of eighty soldiers. While these soldiers are most commonly used for boarding actions, two landing barges are carried for ground actions, as well.

In combat, Marauders often are deployed in pairs and are used to supplement the firepower of Victory Star Destroyers and Invincible heavy cruisers. Their tractor-beam projectors are particularly useful in interdiction missions because they can capture ships before their prey can escape into hyperspace.

The Corellian mercenary Han Solo had two memorable run-ins with Authority Marauders. One corvette launched an attack on an outlaw tech base, forcing Solo to lead the base's technicians into fighter combat against the Authority's IRD fighters. In this encounter, stellar anomalies foiled the Marauder's hyperradio and subspace communication, forcing the corvette to retreat to an Authority base in order to summon reinforcements. Solo and his pilots bested the Authority fighters, giving the outlaw techs an opportunity to evacuate the base.

In a second incident, another Marauder was taken over by Chewbacca and used as an evacuation vessel after Solo had engineered the destruction of the penal facility known as Stars' End.

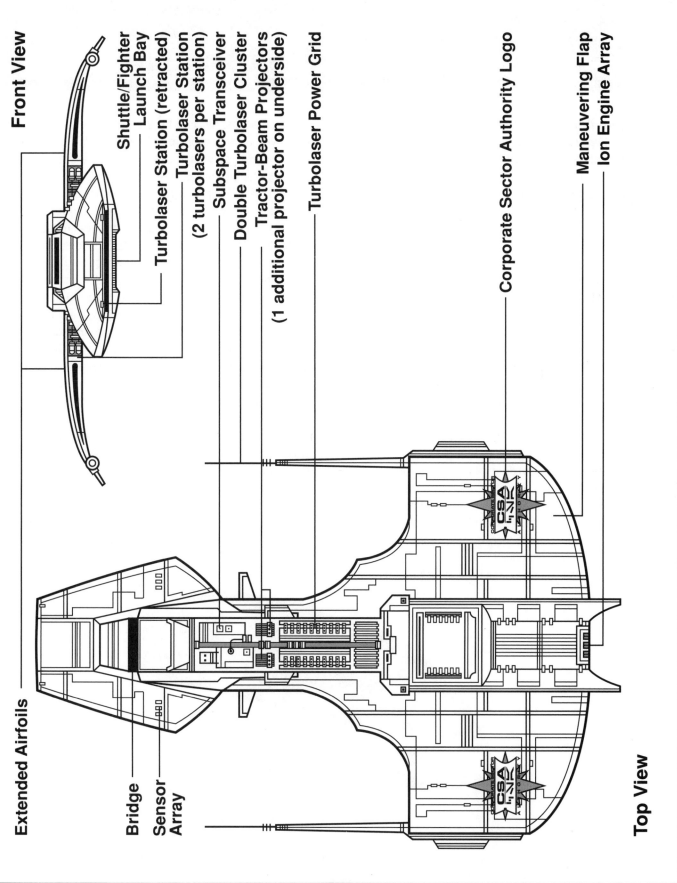

Front View

Shuttle/Fighter
Launch Bay

Turbolaser Station (retracted)

Turbolaser Station
(2 turbolasers per station)

Subspace Transceiver

Double Turbolaser Cluster

Tractor-Beam Projectors
(1 additional projector on underside)

Turbolaser Power Grid

Corporate Sector Authority Logo

Maneuvering Flap

Ion Engine Array

Extended Airfoils

Bridge

Sensor
Array

Top View

MARAUDER STARJACKER

MODIFIED BYBLOS DRIVE YARDS E-2 ASTEROID MINER

The *Marauder Starjacker* was one of two ore-raiding ships commanded by the pirate captain Finhead Stonebone. Captain Stonebone used the ships to raid Ithullian colossus wasps, and while for a time Stonebone made a handsome profit on his runs, his raids incurred the wrath of Bogga the Hutt. After being captured by Bogga's dreadnaught *Enforcer One*, Stonebone and the *Starjacker* were pressed into Bogga's service.

The *Marauder Starjacker* and her sister ship, the *Stenness Raider*, began service as standard Byblos Drive Yards E-2 asteroid-mining ships. While they appear at first glance to be small insectoid ships, the mining vessels are actually over one hundred meters long. E-2 mining ships, found throughout the galaxy, offer a simple and cheap alternative to using tractor beams to move asteroids. They have rugged claws with which to dig through solid rock and attach to an asteroid. Once they are locked in place, their thruster jets are fired to move the trapped asteroid to a specific location. An E-2 miner has plasma drills to cut through useless rock, while a central suction tube draws material up into the E-2's filtration system: valuable ores are stored in the cargo bays, while waste material is used as fuel for the E-2's thrusters. Each mining ship normally has a command crew of four, a bridge crew of ten, and over a hundred asteroid miners.

When Captain Stonebone set out to begin raiding the

colossus wasps, he knew the E-2s could be put to use. He destroyed a mining operation near the Varl system and stole two of these vessels, after which his engineers modified them for ore raiding. The plasma drills were moved to the front of the ship to serve as weapons; a trio of power generators fed each drill, and the prismatic drill crystals were modified to give the weapons a longer range. While these drills lacked the range of laser cannons, they were powerful enough to punch through the wasp carapaces.

For added speed, he replaced the motors with four Corellia StarDrive microthrusters. He reinforced the digging claws with monomolecular slicers, making the claws capable of slicing through the wasps' thick armor plating. Stonebone removed the filtering system, since he knew his ships would be drawing in only pure ore—this also increased his cargo space by a third. He removed the mining stations, giving him enough space to carry over a hundred raiders for boarding actions.

When attacking ore haulers, Stonebone's battle plan was simple: the raiding ships cut through the target wasp's hull and exposed the cargo holds to space. This created a vacuum which drew the ore modules (and wasp crew members) into the cargo bays of the raiding ships. Stonebone's raiders then entered the cargo bays to sort the loot and to "space" any ore hauler crew members not worth keeping alive.

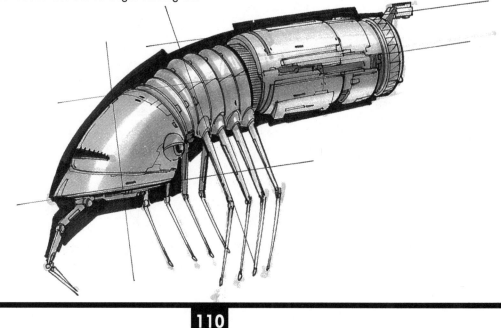

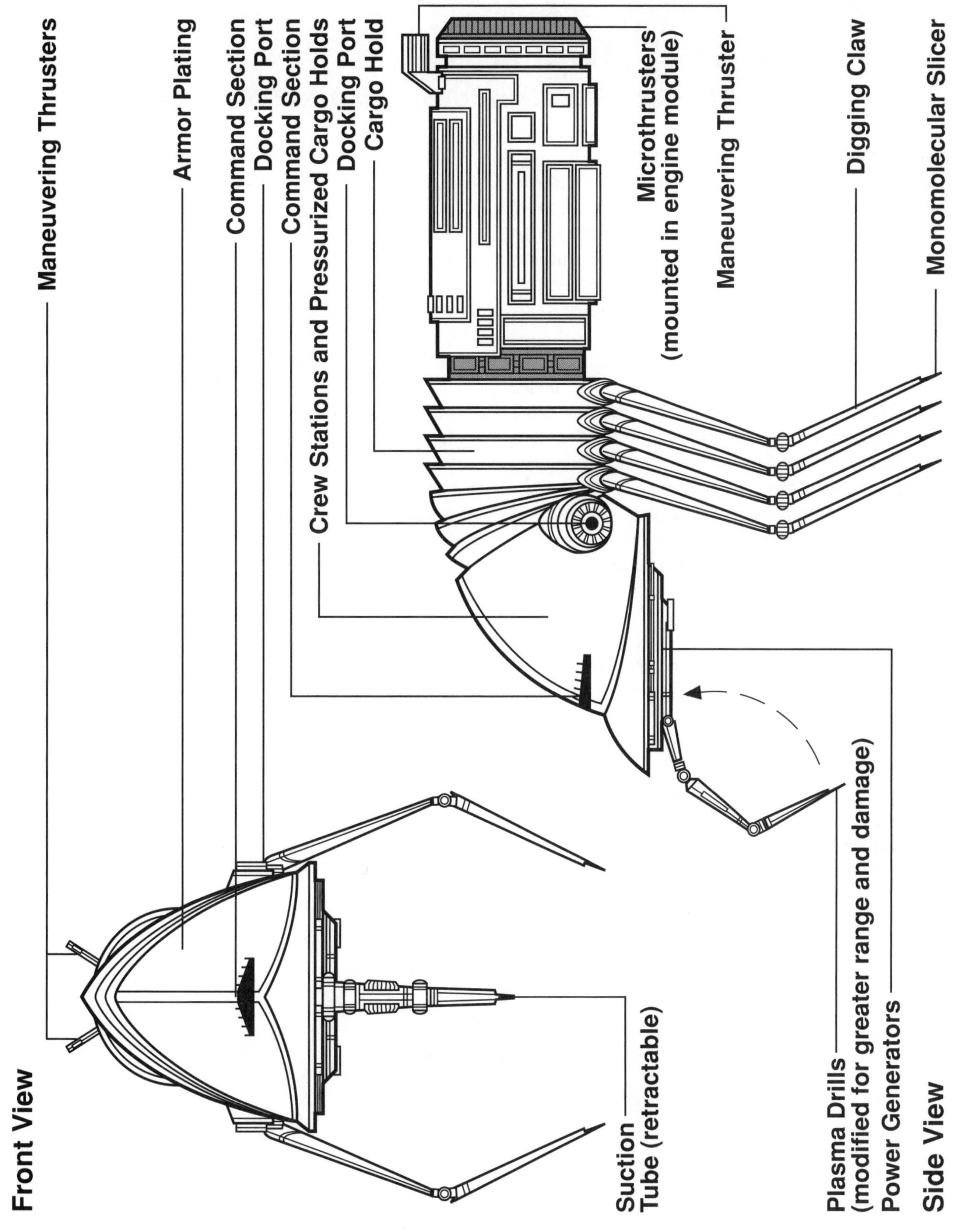

Front View

Maneuvering Thrusters

Armor Plating

Command Section

Docking Port

Command Section

Crew Stations and Pressurized Cargo Holds

Docking Port

Cargo Hold

Microthrusters
(mounted in engine module)

Maneuvering Thruster

Digging Claw

Monomolecular Slicer

Suction Tube (retractable)

Plasma Drills
(modified for greater range and damage)

Power Generators

Side View

MASTER ARCA'S SHIP

HOERSCH-KESSEL *DELAYA*-CLASS COURIER

Master Arca's courier ship, the *SunGem*, was a Hoersch-Kessel *Delaya*-class courier ship that was Arca's base of operations while he engaged in missions. Arca outfitted the ship to act as a training facility for his many Jedi students, thus enabling him to personally represent the Jedi Knights in galactic affairs while fulfilling his responsibility to his Jedi apprentices.

The *SunGem* was distinctly aerodynamic, with layers of maneuvering vanes and retractable airfoils. The airfoils were tied into a computer system that adjusted each one's angle for maximum maneuverability. The *SunGem* was equipped with twenty-one Hoersch-Kessel ion engines mounted in banks of three, with each trio of engines affixed to a servo-controlled maneuvering adjuster. The ship had incredible sublight performance for a craft of its size. In an atmosphere, the *SunGem* could reach a top speed of about 950 kilometers per hour, making it as fast as many atmospheric speeders and starfighters.

The *SunGem* had extendable hull plating sections with a dedicated defense station, allowing the pilot to control the positioning of the sections in order to stop incoming enemy fire. The panel operator worked in conjunction with the shield operator, thus creating a layered defense system.

The *SunGem* was lightly armed; Arca always preferred stealth and cunning to brute force. The main weapon was a forward proton-torpedo launcher mounted directly in front of the cockpit. The launcher carried high-yield proton torpedoes, which were far more dangerous than standard laser

cannons, although their range was still limited. The *SunGem* had enough space for twelve high-yield proton torpedoes or twenty-four standard proton torpedoes. The ship also had a pair of rotating laser cannons on the outside of the two main airfoils. These weapons were distinctive because the laser actuator and power cells were located in the center of the rotating unit and fed into two laser cannons, one on each end of the rotating spar, allowing the *SunGem* to fire in opposite directions at the same time.

The *SunGem* had a forward cockpit with pilot and gunnery stations. The central living quarters had bunks for eight beings, but most of the interior was given over to Jedi training facilities, with meditation chambers, lightsaber training areas (with remotes), and a variable gravity and atmosphere room to simulate hostile planetary conditions. Arca was particularly proud of the *SunGem*'s extensive computer library of Jedi texts.

There was almost no cargo space aboard, although Arca had managed to wedge a scouting speeder into the small storage area immediately inside the cargo air lock at the bottom of the hull. There were two escape pods at the rear of the ship.

Arca adorned the ship with his personal Jedi sigil, unmistakably marking his ship for both enemy and ally. The *SunGem* was one of the most distinctive ships in the service of the Jedi, equipped with advanced piloting computers which enabled Arca to run the vessel by himself if the need arose.

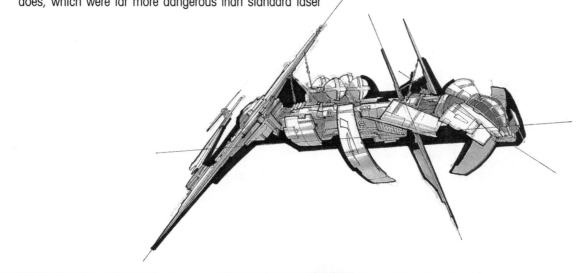

Side View

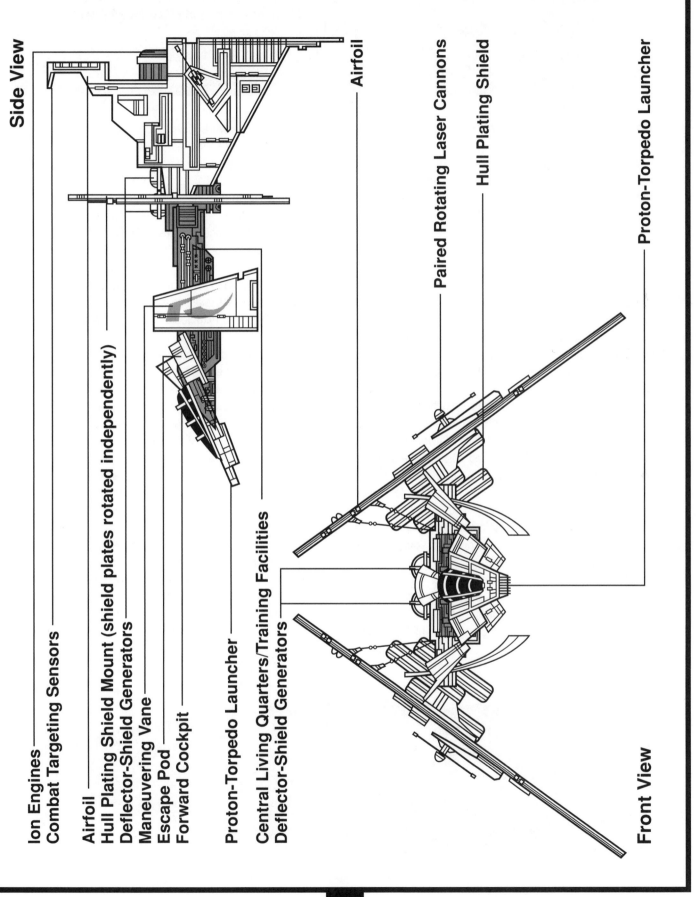

Ion Engines
Combat Targeting Sensors

Airfoil
Hull Plating Shield Mount (shield plates rotated independently)
Deflector-Shield Generators
Maneuvering Vane
Escape Pod
Forward Cockpit

Proton-Torpedo Launcher

Central Living Quarters/Training Facilities
Deflector-Shield Generators

Airfoil

Paired Rotating Laser Cannons

Hull Plating Shield

Proton-Torpedo Launcher

Front View

MILLENNIUM FALCON

MODIFIED CORELLIAN ENGINEERING CORPORATION YT-1300 TRANSPORT

"What a piece of junk!" Luke Skywalker couldn't hold in his reaction upon first seeing the *Millennium Falcon*, the battered freighter that was somehow to transport him, Obi-Wan Kenobi, and the droids R2-D2 and C-3PO from Tatooine to the planet Alderaan. Luke doubted that the ship would be able to lift off from Docking Bay 94, much less make it halfway across the galaxy.

Of course, the *Falcon*'s dilapidated appearance was part of spice smuggler Han Solo's game plan. The best way to avoid "Imperial entanglements" was to give nosy Imperial Customs inspectors nothing to suspect in the first place. The *Falcon* appeared to be no different from the thousands of other Corellian Engineering YT-1300 light freighters plying the star routes of the Empire.

However, Han Solo, First Mate Chewbacca, and the *Millennium Falcon* have always been famous in smuggler circles. Just before hiring on to take Skywalker, Kenobi, and the droids, Solo was smuggling spice for the gangster known as Jabba the Hutt. Unfortunately, Solo's famed "smuggler's luck" failed him, and he was forced to jettison the cargo of spice when he was boarded by an Imperial Customs cruiser. Solo's inability to reimburse Jabba for the lost cargo led the Hutt to post a significant bounty on the young Corellian's head.

Beneath the *Falcon*'s battered exterior hides a fast, tough smuggling vessel. It has a Class 0.5 hyperdrive, which is nearly twice as fast as the fastest Imperial warships. It is fitted with a top-of-the-line (and highly illegal)

sensor suite system to detect incoming Imperial ships long before those craft notice the "lowly freighter." And Solo has shielded smuggling compartments hidden throughout the ship's interior.

When combat is necessary, the *Falcon* is ready. It sports a deflector-shield system "liberated" from the Imperial maintenance facilities at Myomar. Two quad laser cannons are enough to stop TIE starfighters and pirate ships, while concussion missiles provide short-range punch. Solo is an expert at the quick getaway: the ship has a remarkably short start-up sequence of about three minutes and sports a retractable repeating blaster for covering fire.

Solo's modifications push the ship far past the manufacturer's original specifications, but both the sublight drives and the hyperdrives are as finicky as they are fast, and Solo frequently has to crawl around inside the hull making last-minute repairs to get the ship flying. The *Falcon*'s three droid brains often predict that the ship won't fly—but somehow Solo and Chewbacca manage to get the *Falcon* through countless scrapes, from evading irate Imperial Customs ships to dodging vengeful pirate corvettes.

Han Solo won the *Falcon* from a young gambler named Lando Calrissian in a high-stakes sabacc game several years before the Battle of Yavin. Lando himself had won the ship just as he was beginning his "career" as a gambler, and even back then the ship had a questionable past. Neither Solo nor Calrissian has ever bothered to trace the ship's history, figuring that some things are better left unknown.

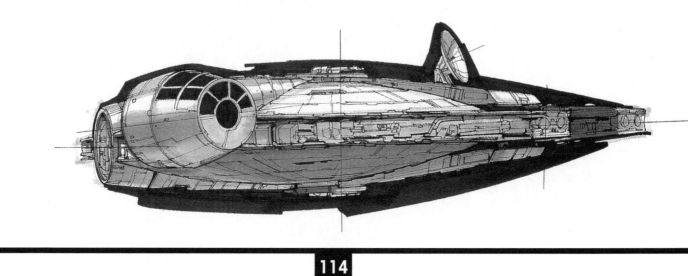

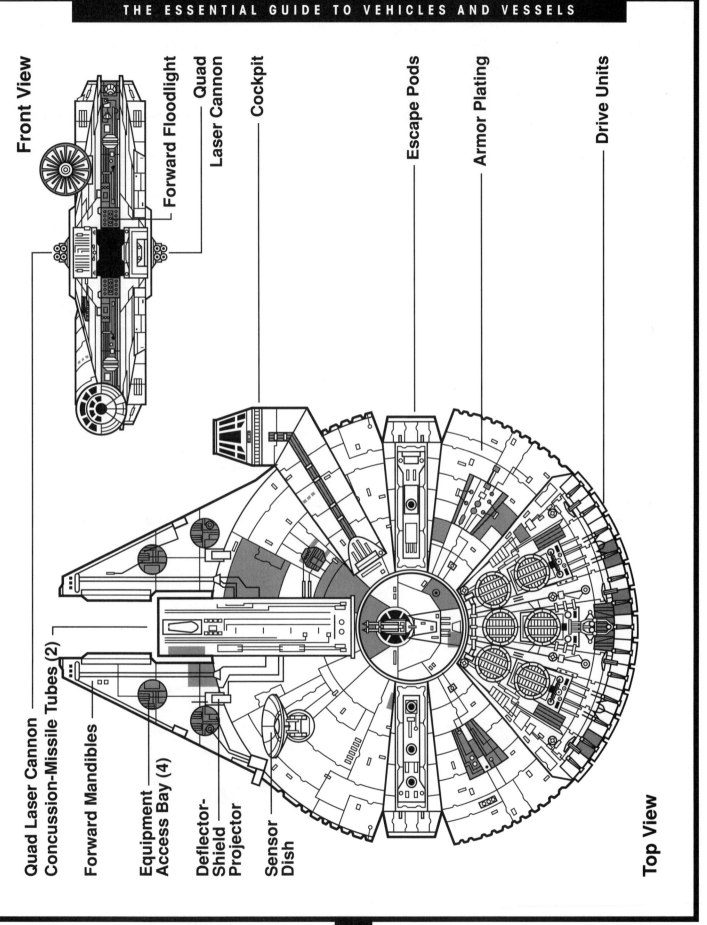

Front View

Forward Floodlight

Quad
Laser Cannon

Cockpit

Escape Pods

Armor Plating

Drive Units

Quad Laser Cannon
Concussion-Missile Tubes (2)

Forward Mandibles

Equipment
Access Bay (4)

Deflector-
Shield
Projector

Sensor
Dish

Top View

MON CAL CRUISER

MON CALAMARI MC80 STAR CRUISER

The Mon Calamari Star Cruisers are the main cruisers in the New Republic's battle fleet. They are durable ships that are as fast and almost as tough as the larger Imperial Star Destroyers. It must be noted that even Imperial Navy commanders have reluctantly admitted that the Mon Cals are superior space combatants.

The Mon Cal cruisers were originally civilian ships designed for pleasure cruises and colonization efforts. However, when an Imperial ship found the Mon Calamari homeworld, the Empire's invasion forces were dispatched immediately. After forcing the Empire from Calamari, the Mon Cals converted their ships to military duty by adding thick hull plating and numerous weapon emplacements. The Mon Cals became totally committed to the Alliance's cause and built huge shipyards in orbit around Calamari.

Each Mon Cal cruiser is unique in design; to the Mon Cals, their ships are as much works of art as weapons of war. While this individualized design bewilders most technicians, the Mon Cals find it a logical approach. Mon Cal ships are notoriously difficult to repair, but they are so durable that they are seldom damaged in combat. Notable Mon Cal ships include the round, blimp-shaped *Headquarters Frigate* (also known as *Home One*) and the winged *Medical Frigate*.

Home One served as Admiral Ackbar's command vessel for the attack on the second Death Star and went on to excel in a number of other pivotal battles against Imperial forces. An exceptionally well armed vessel, it carries an incredible ten squadrons of starfighters, for a total of 120 fighters. Its weaponry includes twenty-nine turbolasers, thirty-six ion cannons, and multiple tractor-beam projectors and shield generators. Mon Cal ships have unusually powerful shields—extra shield redundancies allow the Mon Cals to quickly replace damaged shield arrays even while in combat, and this made it much more difficult for Imperial guns to wear down a Star Cruiser's defenses.

Even standard Mon Cal MC80 cruisers maintain three squadrons of starfighters (thirty-six fighters), forty-eight turbolasers, twenty ion cannons, and six tractor-beam projectors. A number of more powerful cruisers, including the MC80a, MC80B, and MC90, are being built.

While beings of all species serve aboard Mon Cal cruisers, the command sections are geared specifically for the Mon Cals' unique aquatic anatomy. Controls are affected not only through computer keyboards but by making specific movements in the command chairs—while natural to the Mon Cals, these movements are often difficult for other species to perform. Bridge display monitors are geared to the Mon Cals' vision spectrum—to humans, these holo-displays seem warped and distorted.

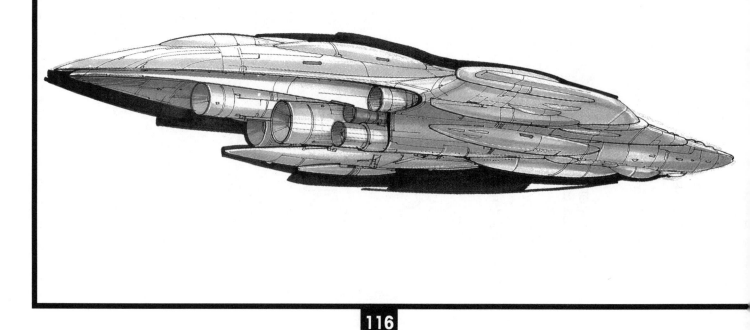

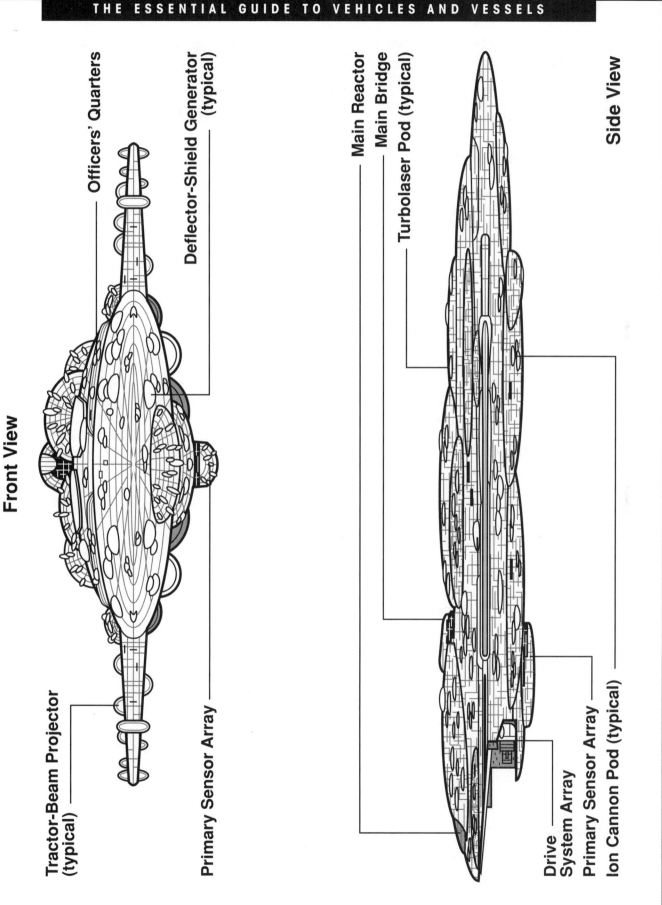

Front View

Officers' Quarters

Deflector-Shield Generator (typical)

Tractor-Beam Projector (typical)

Primary Sensor Array

Side View

Main Reactor

Main Bridge

Turbolaser Pod (typical)

Drive System Array

Primary Sensor Array

Ion Cannon Pod (typical)

MON REMONDA

MON CALAMARI MC80B STAR CRUISER

With the defeat of the Empire at Endor, the Rebel Alliance, renamed the New Republic, had to alter its combat strategy, switching from harassing Imperial bases to taking and holding territory. Smaller ships, such as Corellian gunships and Nebulon-B escort frigates, were no longer sufficient; the New Republic needed heavy combat cruisers such as the Mon Calamari MC80 Star Cruisers used at the Battle of Endor.

So the Mon Calamari began working on the MC90 line of star cruisers approximately six months after the Battle of Endor. A year later the *Mon Remonda*, an interim Mon Cal Star Cruiser classified as an MC80B, was delivered to the New Republic. The MC90 cruisers would not be ready for nearly another four years, but in the interim the MC80B cruisers led the New Republic's spirited effort to unite the galaxy.

The *Mon Remonda* was immediately put to use as the flagship of a New Republic fleet sent to repel the offensive launched by rogue Imperial Warlord Zsinj. The expedition was commanded by General Han Solo, and after five months Solo returned victorious to Coruscant. Zsinj's Super Star Destroyer *Iron Fist* had been destroyed, and his forces had been pushed back to their original territory.

The *Mon Remonda* was approximately 1,200 meters long and used the organic form characteristic of Mon Calamari starships. The most significant upgrade on the MC80B line was a more heavily reinforced hull and multi-ple backup shield generators. This reinforcement gave the MC80B line a decisive edge in extended battles, where the Mon Cal cruiser could take a severe beating but had time to blast through the more limited shielding found on Imperial warships.

The MC80B's forty-eight turbolasers are linked in banks of twelve, while the twenty ion cannons are linked in banks of four, allowing intense fire to be brought to bear against a single target. The *Mon Remonda* carried four squadrons of fighters, for a total of forty-eight fighters, including one A-wing squadron, two X-wing squadrons, and a single B-wing squadron; later MC80B cruisers were to be refitted to carry up to eight squadrons of fighters.

While the new MC90 cruisers were being built with an eye toward accommodating other species, the *Mon Remonda* retained many of the MC80's original components and was specifically designed for the Mon Calamari physiology. Holographic displays and monitors were configured for the Mon Cals' visual range, while some controls were keyed to crew seats and were activated by certain movements that were perfectly natural for Mon Calamari . . . and almost impossible for humans.

The *Mon Remonda* was destroyed by the World Devastator *Silencer-7* at the Second Battle of Calamari during the campaign of the resurrected Emperor Palpatine. While all hands were lost, the crew destroyed an Imperial Star Destroyer and several support vessels, saving thousands of civilian Mon Calamari and Quarren lives.

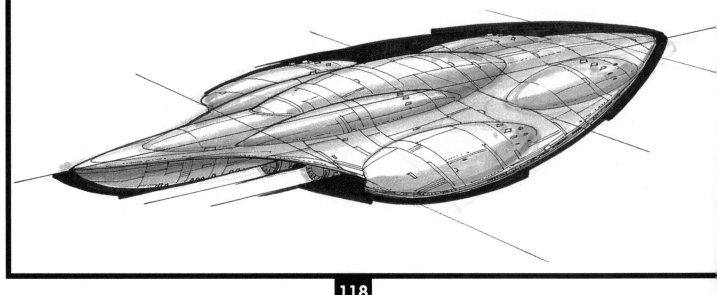

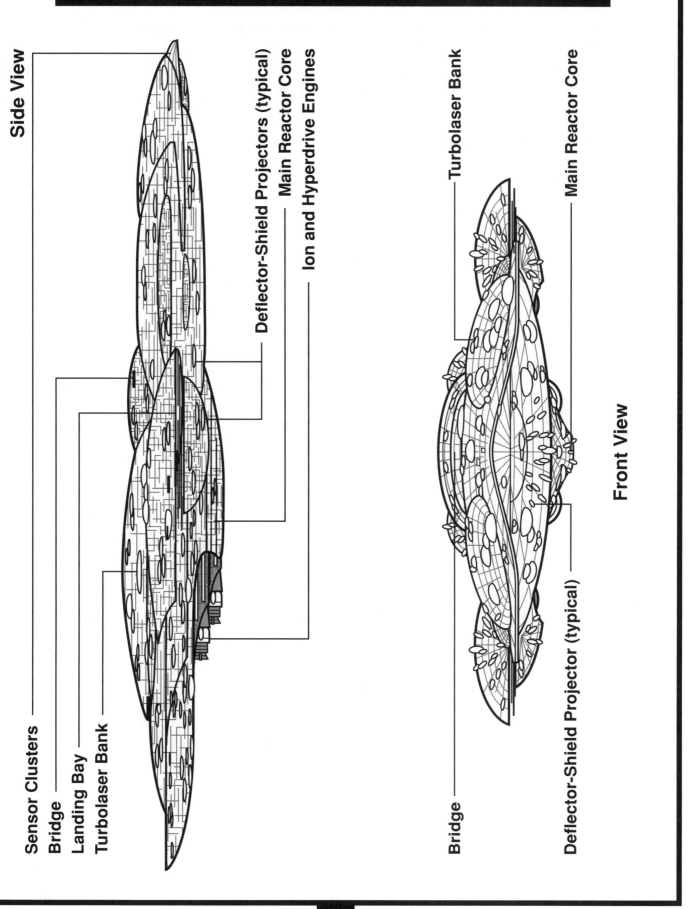

Side View

Sensor Clusters

Bridge

Landing Bay

Turbolaser Bank

Deflector-Shield Projectors (typical)

Main Reactor Core

Ion and Hyperdrive Engines

Turbolaser Bank

Bridge

Main Reactor Core

Deflector-Shield Projector (typical)

Front View

MT-AT TRANSPORT

CARIDAN MOUNTAIN TERRAIN ARMORED TRANSPORT

The Mountain Terrain Armored Transport (MT-AT) was a late-model Imperial walker designed at the Empire's testing and manufacturing grounds on Carida. These eight-legged machines were designed specifically for sheer inclines, with independently articulated legs and clawed footpads to allow the walkers to secure themselves to sheer rock faces. The transports were first used when Caridan Ambassador Furgan ordered an attack on a New Republic facility on the world of Anoth.

The MT-AT consists of a central drive pod housing the engine and drive motors that run the eight legs. A platform attached to the bottom of the drive pod holds both the forward pilot compartment and a rear cargo pod. This platform can spin 180 degrees, allowing instantaneous changes of direction. The vehicle has exceptional stability.

The forward command pod has sufficient operating space for a pilot and a gunner, while the aft cargo pod is used to carry repeating blasters and supplies for use by ground troops. The aft pod is elevated during movement but lowers to the ground and retracts its protective shell in order to unload cargo. Each leg has an independently rotating double laser cannon with an advanced computer interface to assist the gunnery officer. The MT-AT's driver has two laser cannons that can be used to shoot down attacking starfighters.

MT-ATs can be deployed to a planetary surface through standard transports, landing barges, and drop ships. For the mission to Anoth, MT-ATs used an experimental thermal-resistant cocoon. Each such cocoon encases a single walker in a fluid gel that secures the walker for the fiery descent to the planet. A droid brain controls the cocoon's direction and speed, activating emergency braking thrusters shortly before impact. Upon impact, the cocoon's bistate gel hardens and absorbs the kinetic energy from the outside surface of the cocoon, all the while protecting the walker inside. Once the impact energy has been bled away, the cocoon breaks open, enabling the MT-AT walker to move into battle.

Caridan Ambassador Furgan used eight MT-AT walkers for the attack on Anoth. The Anoth sanctuary's defenses destroyed half the walkers, while two more were destroyed through the efforts of New Republic operatives who arrived on the scene shortly after the invasion had been launched. The final two were destroyed when the Mon Calamari named Terpfen used one of the walkers to push Furgan's walker over the edge of a cliff; Furgan died, but Terpfen was rescued by Admiral Ackbar.

With the destruction of Carida by the Sun Crusher, the only known MT-AT manufacturing facility was destroyed, but it is safe to assume that Imperial warships evacuating the planet managed to bring the design plans with them. New Republic strategists believe that the Imperials may be developing a larger MT-AT model to transport larger numbers of troops into battle.

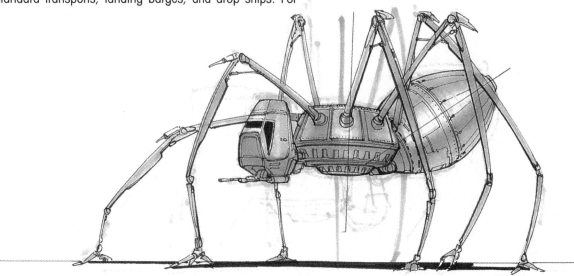

Front View
(MT-AT in space cocoon pod)

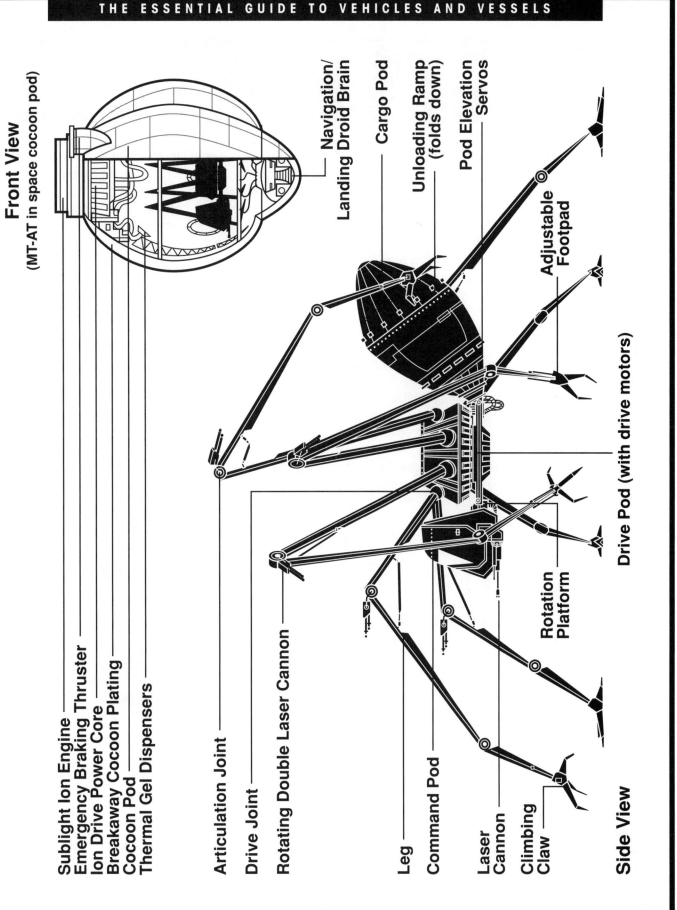

Navigation/
Landing Droid Brain

Cargo Pod

Unloading Ramp
(folds down)

Pod Elevation
Servos

Adjustable
Footpad

Drive Pod (with drive motors)

Rotation
Platform

Climbing
Claw

Laser
Cannon

Command Pod

Leg

Rotating Double Laser Cannon

Drive Joint

Articulation Joint

Thermal Gel Dispensers
Cocoon Pod
Breakaway Cocoon Plating
Ion Drive Power Core
Emergency Braking Thruster
Sublight Ion Engine

Side View

NEBULON RANGER

CORELLIA STARDRIVE *CORUSCANT*-CLASS HEAVY COURIER

The *Nebulon Ranger* was the courier ship of the Jedi Knight Ulic Qel-Droma, his brother Cay, and the Twi'lek Jedi Tott Doneeta. These famed Jedi Knights were key players in the great Sith War, which occurred 4,000 years before the rise of the Empire and the collapse of the Old Republic.

The *Nebulon Ranger* was a large, multisectioned ship. The *Ranger* had two main series of engine arrays mounted on a right-angle starframe. This design element provided an easy way to separate the engines and give the ship greater maneuverability without the need for bulky maneuvering jets.

The *Ranger* had retractable wings which could be extended for atmospheric flight but retracted for landing. The main wing was heavily armored and contained the ship's fuel tanks, which fed directly into the six AlderaanMotors power generators and engine arrays. The wing also held the *Ranger*'s round air lock (for deep space docking) and a sensor array pylon. While the pylon was more easily damaged in combat, it gave the *Ranger*'s sensors far greater range and sensitivity than could a unit flush with the hull.

The *Ranger* featured a series of eight shield generators, providing full protection around the hull. Because of their immense power drain, the shields were raised only in combat. This made the *Ranger* vulnerable to attack, as the beast-riders of Onderon showed when they downed the *Ranger* with a single seeker torpedo.

The *Ranger* packed a forward-firing pulse cannon with enough power to slice through the shields of any pirate ship. There was a retractable, rotating laser cannon on each wingtip as well as a more powerful rotating laser cannon at the base of the second engine array. Each forward mandible held a pair of linked proton-torpedo launchers, with a magazine of six torpedoes in each mandible. Each mandible also had a single short-range concussion-sphere launcher with a magazine of eight concussion spheres. The laser cannons and missile weapons were controlled from a dedicated gunnery station in the cockpit, although the pilot could also choose to handle these weapons.

The cockpit was nestled between the forward mandibles

and opened back to the living and cargo sections in the center of the ship. The main boarding ramp (bottom side) and emergency escape hatch (top side) were found in the "neck" behind the cockpit. Three escape pods were forward-mounted below the pulse cannon.

The *Ranger* had a cargo bay that was sectioned off into compartments with variable life support, gravity, and atmosphere controls. The modular wall sections could also be removed for larger cargoes, such as courier vehicles. A drop bay at the bottom of the ship (between the engines) allowed such vehicles to be deployed within seconds. Ulic and Cay were known to keep short-range airspeeders in the cargo bay to surprise attackers.

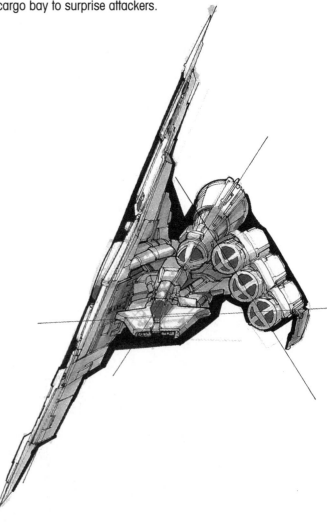

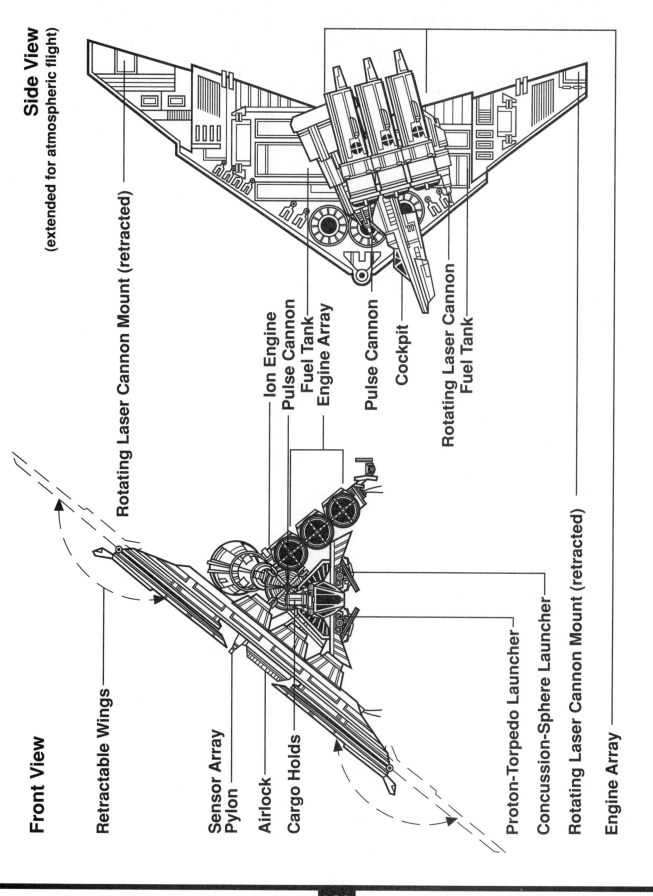

Side View
(extended for atmospheric flight)

Rotating Laser Cannon Mount (retracted)

Ion Engine
Pulse Cannon
Fuel Tank
Engine Array

Pulse Cannon

Cockpit

Rotating Laser Cannon
Fuel Tank

Front View

Retractable Wings

Sensor Array
Pylon

Airlock

Cargo Holds

Proton-Torpedo Launcher

Concussion-Sphere Launcher

Rotating Laser Cannon Mount (retracted)

Engine Array

PRINCE XIZOR'S *VIRAGO*

MANDALMOTORS STARVIPER

Prince Xizor, of the mysterious Falleen species, rules the criminal organization Black Sun. The wealthy and influential Prince owns an immense castle on Coruscant, capital of the Empire. From his castle, mere kilometers from Emperor Palpatine's palace, he controls the most powerful crime syndicate in the galaxy.

Among Xizor's many starships, his favorite is the heavily modified fighter *Virago*. The ship is both a personal transport and assault vessel. The *Virago* is Prince Xizor's vehicle of choice when he must leave the protection of his castle or skyhook, *Falleen's Fist*.

Xizor has extravagant tastes, and nothing less than the best is good enough for him. Rather than purchase a "common" space yacht or fighter, Xizor contracted the entire MandalMotors design team to create a unique ship.

The design team produced the *StarViper*-class vessel, a heavy assault starfighter with incredible speed, armor, and weaponry. This performance came at a very high cost, but after a few moments contemplating "his" prize, Xizor announced that he was . . . *satisfied*.

The MandalMotors designers opted to make the StarViper a "mobile platform" ship. To enhance performance, the wings and thrust nacelles move in such a way that, to the casual observer, the ship appears to be "alive" as its wings constantly fold and adjust in flight.

The *Virago* can match the new TIE interceptor for speed and maneuverability despite its far greater mass. The rear-mounted Quadex IGt engines provide forward thrust, while maneuverability is enhanced by a pair of Koensayr N2-f microthrusters mounted on the tip of each wing. The in-flight computer control system individually adjusts each microthruster.

In combat, the *Virago*'s four wings fold out fully to give the maneuvering thrusters maximum effect. The wings also hold reserve fuel tanks and are extremely well armored—even concentrated fire from an X-wing doesn't stand much chance of puncturing the armor plating. The rear of the vessel is not significantly armored, but a trio of Torplex shield generators provide ample protection. A single shield generator is forward-mounted to supplement the forward armor plating.

The *Virago*'s wings fold flush against the engines and pilot compartment for standard space flight. While the expanding wing arrangement is excellent for space combat, it severely hampers atmospheric flight, and the wings must remain retracted during planetary landings.

The main weapons are a pair of Taim & Bak Ht-12 double heavy laser cannons. Each cannon is mounted on a forward-extending arm which can rotate 180 degrees to provide fire to fore, aft, and either port or starboard facings. An advanced Carbanti St2x targeting computer and sighting laser system gives the pilot tracking information even in the middle of complex maneuvers. When the wings are retracted, the laser weapons are restricted to forward fire. Supplementing the laser cannons are two forward-firing Borstel proton-torpedo launchers, each with a magazine of three torpedoes.

As might be expected, a ship this powerful consumes an inordinate amount of energy. No fewer than four separate power generators (one in each wing spar) keep the StarViper going. Each generator supplies its nearest wing and provides a quarter of the thrust for the main engines.

MandalMotors produces additional vessels based on the StarViper design. While virtually identical in appearance, they are far less powerful.

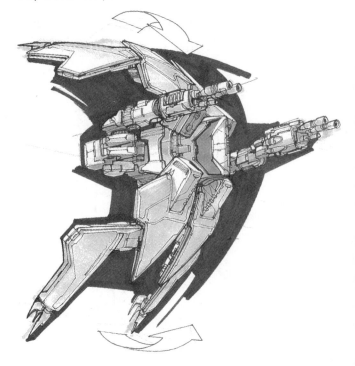

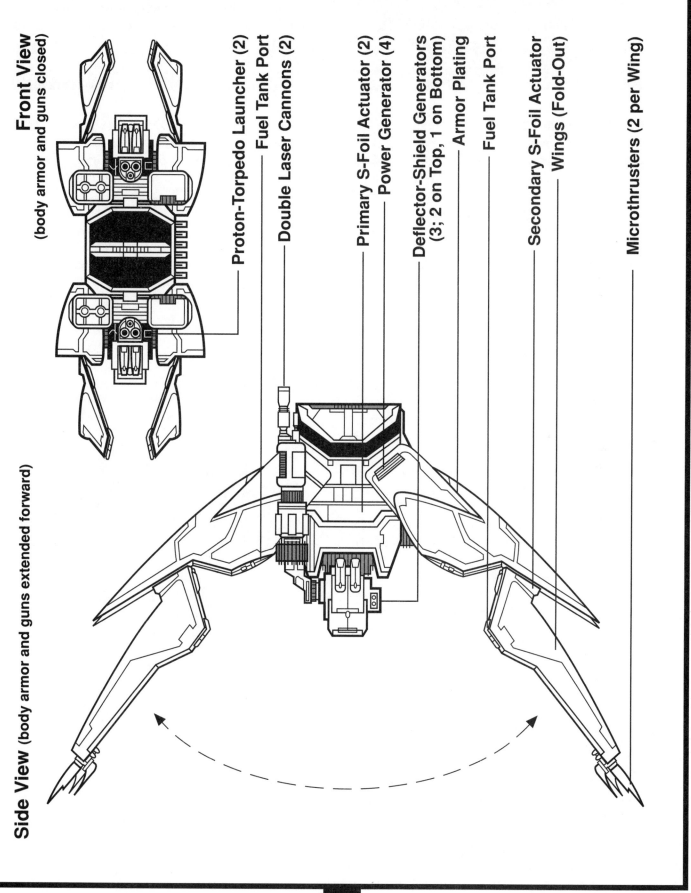

Front View
(body armor and guns closed)

Side View (body armor and guns extended forward)

Proton-Torpedo Launcher (2)

Fuel Tank Port

Double Laser Cannons (2)

Primary S-Foil Actuator (2)

Power Generator (4)

Deflector-Shield Generators
(3; 2 on Top, 1 on Bottom)

Armor Plating

Fuel Tank Port

Secondary S-Foil Actuator

Wings (Fold-Out)

Microthrusters (2 per Wing)

PROBOT

Arakyd Viper Probe Droid

Imperial probe droids, or probots, were used extensively by Lord Vader's squadron in the search for the main Rebel base after the Battle of Yavin. Vader ordered thousands of probots to be sent out to unexplored or uninhabited systems in the hope that one might uncover the Rebels; indeed, a probot discovered the Alliance base on Hoth.

The probots Vader used were Arakyd Viper units, one of the top military probe droids manufactured in the Empire. These probots have two main components. The first is an exterior hyperdrive pod, which transports the probot inside across thousands of light-years to its destination. These pods are one-use-only, meaning that each probot is sent on a one-way trip. After deployment, probots are left behind to continue observation.

Upon arriving at the destination world, the pod streaks in to the planet's surface, applying emergency braking thrusters. Observers often mistake arriving pods for meteorites. After impact, the pod opens to release the probe droid.

Probots are very intelligent droids. Equipped with repulsorlift and thruster units, they can move across planetary surfaces at about forty kilometers per hour. They are cunning and incessantly curious: if there is anything to be found on a world, a probot *will* find it. They are armed with a blaster, although they are programmed to avoid conflict and to self-destruct if discovered by enemies.

Probots have extremely sensitive sensor arrays that are used to detect signs of habitation, with acoustic, electromagnetic, motive, seismic, and olfactory sensors. Optical cameras, zoom imagers, infrared scopes, magnetic imagers, radar and sonar transceivers, and radiation meters all combine to give the probot a detailed view of the world around it. Four manipulator arms and a high-torque grasping arm allow the probot to take samples from the planet, while protected and retractable ultrasensitive sensor probes extrude from the arms for detailed close scans.

Of course, Vader's plan worked, and a probot discovered the Hoth base. Having picked up Alliance communications, the probot discovered a Rebel monitoring post. After destroying the post, the probot traced its communications vectors, discovering the main Rebel base. It informed the Imperial fleet with its instantaneous omnisignal unicode,

which can reach across the galaxy by using restricted Imperial HoloNet communication frequencies. These communicators are extremely expensive, but they allowed the probots to inform the Imperial fleet of potential Rebel activities with no delay.

The probot on Hoth made detailed observations of the Rebel base, reporting the location of shield generators, artillery emplacements, and troop deployments, thus giving the Empire excellent intelligence before the assault. While Han Solo and Chewbacca destroyed the probot, the probe droid succeeded in its mission of leading the Empire to the Rebels.

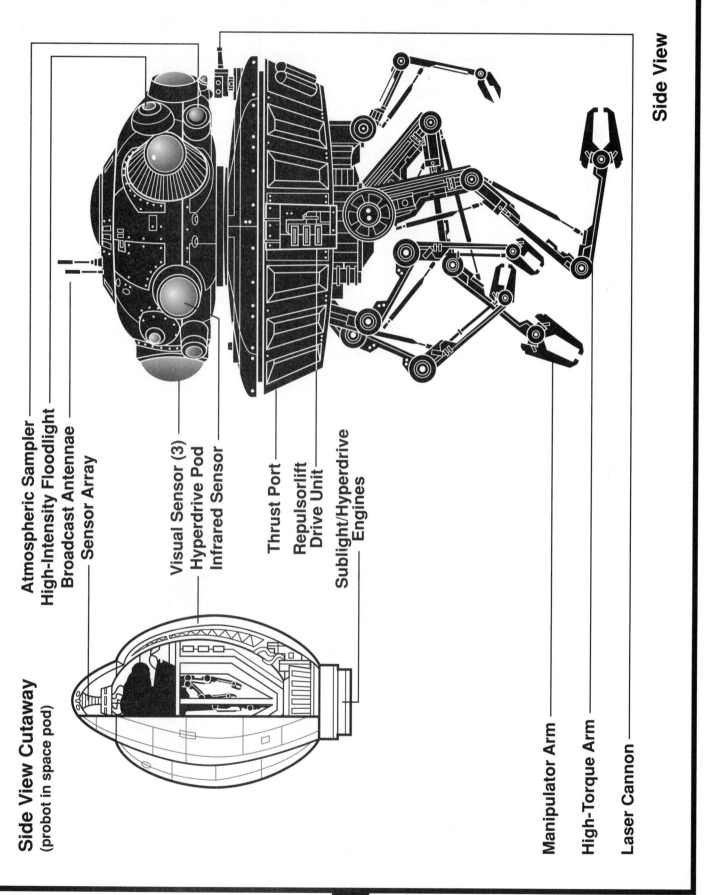

Side View

Side View Cutaway
(probot in space pod)

Atmospheric Sampler
High-Intensity Floodlight
Broadcast Antennae
Sensor Array

Visual Sensor (3)
Hyperdrive Pod
Infrared Sensor

Thrust Port
Repulsorlift
Drive Unit
Sublight/Hyperdrive
Engines

Manipulator Arm
High-Torque Arm
Laser Cannon

STAR WARS

REBEL BLOCKADE RUNNER

CORELLIAN ENGINEERING CORPORATION CORVETTE

The famous "Rebel Blockade Runner" in actuality was a single ship named the *Tantive IV*. A Corellian corvette, the ship was registered as a consular vessel with the Royal House of Alderaan's diplomatic corps. It was destroyed shortly after being captured by the Imperial Star Destroyer *Devastator* over the desert world of Tatooine.

In an elaborate ruse perpetrated by Lord Darth Vader, all personnel aboard were reported killed in a deep-space disaster. In truth, only Senator Leia Organa escaped execution, although she was held as a prisoner aboard the Empire's Death Star battle station.

The *Tantive IV* was commanded by Captain Antilles and was used frequently by Organa for her covert espionage activities on behalf of the Rebel Alliance. The *Tantive IV*'s diplomatic status gave the ship free reign in an era when increasingly aggressive Imperial Navy captains clamped down on any ship suspected of Rebel activity.

The *Tantive IV* played a vital role in the Rebel Alliance victory against the first Death Star. After intercepting secret Rebel codes while on a "relief mission" to Ralltiir (which was under Imperial martial law), Princess Leia learned about the construction of the Death Star over the distant prison world of Despayre. Leia later received the technical readouts to the Death Star from Rebels over Toprawa and then raced to distant Tatooine with the hope of finding the reclusive General Obi-Wan Kenobi and convincing him to help lead the Rebel Alliance. However, a double agent apparently hid a tracking beacon aboard the Blockade Runner, and the Star Destroyer *Devastator* emerged in Tatooine system space immediately behind the ship. Opening up with its turbolasers, the *Devastator* quickly disabled the *Tantive IV* and Imperial stormtroopers boarded the ship, rounding up all personnel for questioning.

Fortunately for the Rebel Alliance, Leia hid the battle station plans in the astromech droid R2-D2, which, with its companion C-3PO, used an emergency escape pod to blast down to Tatooine's surface and continue the search for Obi-Wan Kenobi.

The *Tantive IV* was armed with six Taim & Bak H9 turbolaser cannons, and had heavily reinforced shields, but it was no match for the Imperial Star Destroyer *Devastator*.

The Corellian corvette is a common multipurpose vessel. It has a modular design and can be configured for cargo transport, passenger liner service, or even military duty. The corvette is so common among legitimate shipping, passenger, and government interests that many pirate and Rebel Alliance groups have taken to using it for their own purposes, frustrating the efforts of the Imperial Navy to control the spread of the Rebellion.

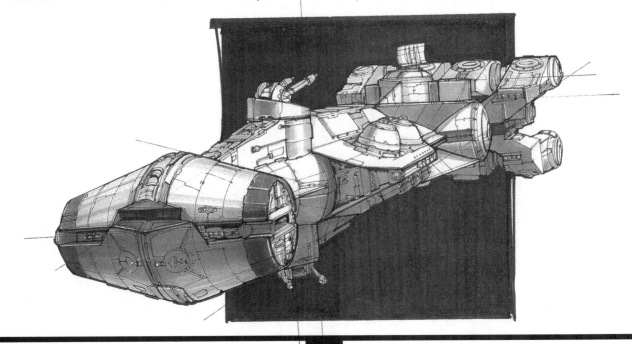

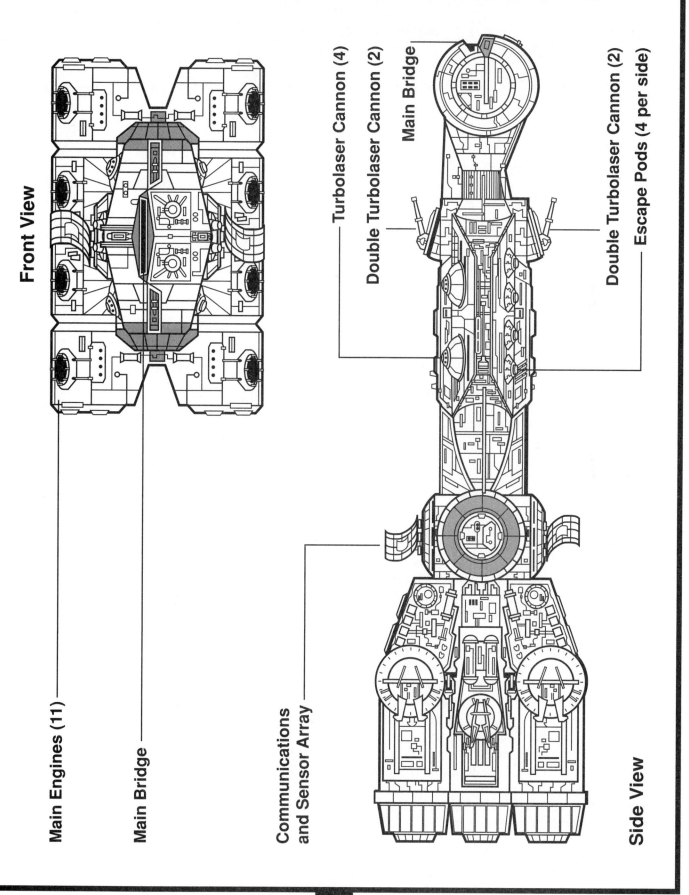

Front View

Main Engines (11)

Main Bridge

Turbolaser Cannon (4)

Double Turbolaser Cannon (2)

Main Bridge

Double Turbolaser Cannon (2)

Escape Pods (4 per side)

Communications and Sensor Array

Side View

REBEL CRUISER

KUAT DRIVE YARDS NEBULON-B FRIGATE

The Rebel fleet used many different types of combat cruisers, including the Nebulon-B escort frigate. After his confrontation with Darth Vader on Cloud City, Luke Skywalker was treated aboard a Nebulon-B converted for medical duty.

The Nebulon-B escort frigate is three hundred meters long and was originally designed by the Empire for use *against* Rebel starfighters, which had scored several victories against poorly defended Imperial cargo convoys (much to the embarrassment of Imperial Navy commanders). The Alliance acquired several Nebulon-B frigates when a number of the vessels were captured by Rebel forces, and when crews defected to the Alliance. These escort frigates proved to be key starships in the Alliance's fleet, especially in the early stages of the war against the Empire. As larger cruisers came into the Rebel fleet, the Alliance converted several of the Nebulon-B ships into medical frigates, command ships, long-range reconnaissance ships, and search and rescue frigates.

Standard Nebulon-B frigates are equipped with twelve turbolaser batteries (for use against capital ships) and twelve laser cannons (for starfighters). Nebulon-Bs often are equipped with a pair of tractor-beam projectors. Each ship can carry two squadrons of twelve fighters in interior landing bays, and these ships have several docking fixtures for light and medium freighters. Many Nebulon-Bs include sophisticated sensors and deep-space, multifrequency antennas, allowing them to function as long-range scouts or relay battle information to a command vessel. In many cases, a shorthanded Rebel task force used a Nebulon-B as a command ship, with Corellian corvettes and gunships acting as supplementary capital ships.

Though Nebulon-B frigates are medium-size combat ships, they pack more weaponry than does any other vessel in their class except *Carrack*-class light cruisers, and the Nebulon-B's contingent of fighters make it the superior vessel. While the ship is slow and unwieldy, the Rebel Alliance mastered the art of using the Nebulon-B as a base ship for strike missions against vulnerable Imperial targets. Often, the escort frigate didn't even have to enter the battle zone.

The Alliance's medical frigate, a converted Nebulon-B, has treatment facilities for over seven hundred patients. With complete modern medical materials, including fifteen bacta tanks, the ship's patient survival rate is nearly 98 percent. To make room for the medical facilities, the ship's weaponry is generally reduced to six turbolasers and eight laser cannons. Most of the interior hangar bay space is lost, and the medical frigate carries no fighters, instead relying on other ships for protection.

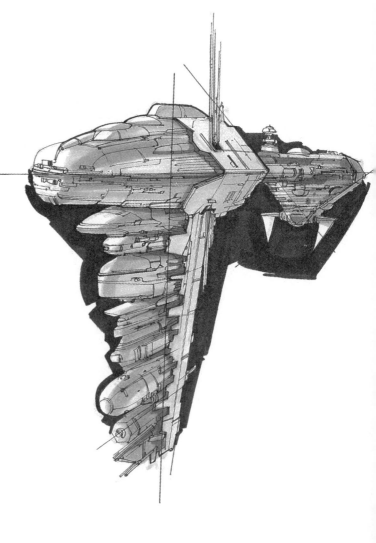

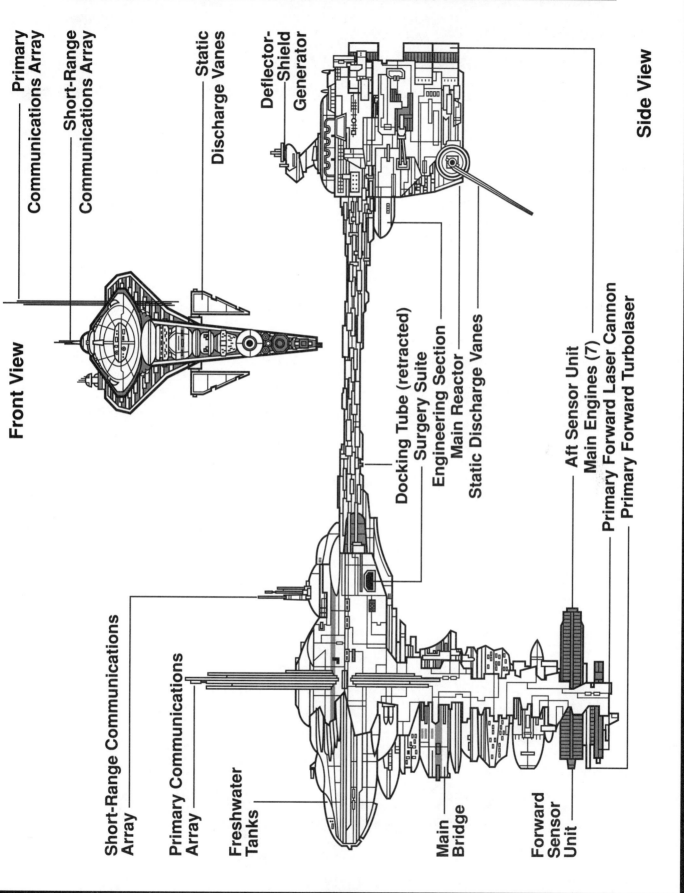

Front View

Primary Communications Array

Short-Range Communications Array

Static Discharge Vanes

Deflector-Shield Generator

Side View

Docking Tube (retracted)

Surgery Suite

Engineering Section

Main Reactor

Static Discharge Vanes

Aft Sensor Unit

Main Engines (7)

Primary Forward Laser Cannon

Primary Forward Turbolaser

Short-Range Communications Array

Primary Communications Array

Freshwater Tanks

Main Bridge

Forward Sensor Unit

REBEL SNOWSPEEDER

MODIFIED INCOM T-47 "SNOWSPEEDER"

When Imperial AT-AT walkers assaulted the Rebels on the ice planet of Hoth, the Alliance's defense rested on a dozen highly modified airspeeders, nicknamed "snowspeeders," and the brave pilots and gunners who manned them. While the Rebel pilots stood no chance against the walkers, Rogue Squadron's snowspeeders delayed the Imperials long enough to allow the Alliance's leaders to escape.

Snowspeeders are heavily modified Incom T-47 airspeeders. Designed for low atmospheric duty, they are powered by a pair of repulsorlift drive units (on either side of the canopy) and high-powered afterburners. The drive units' circuity is left exposed (located beneath the laser cannon power convertors) to allow Rebel technicians easy access for repair and maintenance. Mechanical braking flaps located above each repulsor engine assist in maneuvers. Snowspeeders can reach speeds in excess of a thousand kilometers per hour, with an effective combat speed of about six hundred kilometers per hour. They lack shields but are small, compact, and fast: they are hard to target and rely on this maneuverability for survival.

For combat duty, snowspeeders are fitted with heavy armor plating and twin laser cannons (one on each side of the cockpit). The harpoon gun with its tow cable is a standard tool on most T-47s and normally is used for retrieving and hauling repulsor-assisted cargo barges.

A snowspeeder seats a pilot and a gunner, who sit back-to-back. Computerized targeting systems allow the gunner to target the forward laser cannons, although the pilot can choose to handle them.

The Rebel Alliance pioneered an innovative combat maneuver for the Battle of Hoth. Suspecting that the Empire would use walkers against the Rebels, Rogue Squadron Commander Luke Skywalker and Alliance tactician Beryl Chiffonage devised the harpoon and tow cable approach by which a single tow cable, wrapped several times around a walker's legs, could trip and disable the massive Imperial war machine. Since walker armor proved impervious to the snowspeeders' laser cannons, this tactic, first demonstrated by Alliance pilot Wedge Antilles, proved the only reliable way for small airspeeders to topple Imperial walkers.

The Alliance's technicians faced difficulties adapting the vehicles to the cold of Hoth. Additional repulsor-coil heaters had to be added to prevent the motors from freezing, and deicing nozzles had to be mounted beneath the mechanical braking and turning flaps.

The Rebel Alliance used these speeders in many terrains, although specific modifications for extreme environments were necessary. Today these speeders may be nicknamed, among other things, "sandspeeders," "skyspeeders," or "swampspeeders," depending on where they are deployed. Aside from straight combat duty, the Alliance uses speeders for patrol and reconnaisance duties and cargo hauling.

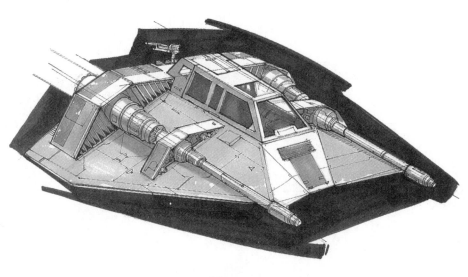

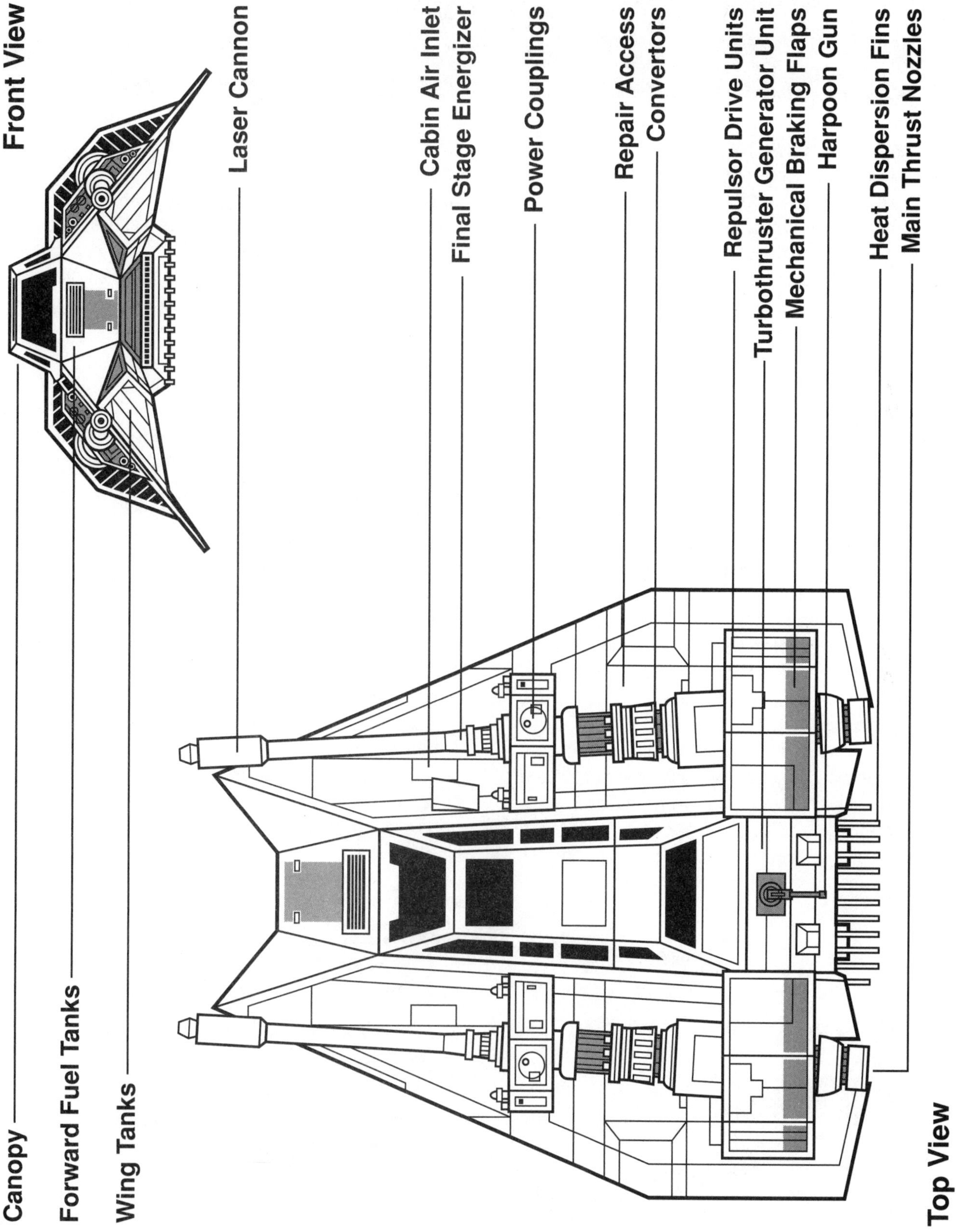

Front View

Canopy

Forward Fuel Tanks

Wing Tanks

Laser Cannon

Cabin Air Inlet

Final Stage Energizer

Power Couplings

Repair Access

Convertors

Repulsor Drive Units

Turbothruster Generator Unit

Mechanical Braking Flaps

Harpoon Gun

Heat Dispersion Fins

Main Thrust Nozzles

Top View

REBEL TRANSPORT

GALLOFREE YARDS MEDIUM TRANSPORT

The Rebellion's transports proved to be a vital tool in the Galactic Civil War against the Empire. An army without food, ammunition, and other supplies cannot fight; these transports got war matériel to the Alliance's soldiers. The Alliance used a number of different transport ships to keep its army ready for combat.

Often the Alliance got transports by converting old passenger liners, small freighters, and other elderly ships most companies would have considered "useless": to the Alliance, those outdated ships were as precious as X-wing fighters!

Transports normally worked in convoys, and their most visible effort was the evacuation of Echo Base on the ice planet of Hoth. With only a pair of X-wings and a few suppressing shots from the planet-based ion cannon for protection, these lightly armed cargo ships blasted past the Imperial blockade and saved the Rebel Alliance's main computers and core equipment.

The vehicles used on Hoth were Gallofree Yards Medium Transports. With a cargo capacity of 19,000 metric tons, these vessels can haul an immense amount of equipment, considering that they are only ninety meters long.

The Gallofree transport's outer hull is little more than a thick shell; the interior is open. Modular cargo pods speed loading and unloading procedures. When the ship is full, an invisible magnetic shield locks the cargo modules in place and keeps the vacuum of space out. Typical cargoes include medicine, food, fuel, spare parts, weapons, and raw materials. A few of these ships were converted for fuel tanker duty for long-range Rebel fighter missions. These transports also can be adapted for passenger or troop transport duty by adding sealed passenger pods.

The command crew of seven (including one gunner) operates from a small, cramped pod mounted above the ship's rounded hull. The transport's deflector-shield generator is part of the pod, so the pod is not as exposed as it first appears to be.

These ships have hyperdrives for rapid transport to different systems as well as standard sublight ion drives. They also have repulsorlift drive units for landing directly on a planet. Retractable landing gear and a loading ramp are on the underside of the vessel.

The Gallofree transports are not combat vessels and make every effort to avoid enemy ships. They rely on sensitive sensors to detect incoming vessels; advanced countermeasures systems hide them from probing enemy scans. They have minimal armament, typically consisting of four twin laser cannons, but it is not uncommon to find that a transport's weapons have been stripped and installed on combat starships. In these cases, the transports must rely on starfighters for protection.

While the Alliance purchased these ships at greatly reduced prices, Alliance technicians maintain that they were ripped off. The Gallofree transports have always been prone to breakdown and tend to spend as much time in repair bays as in space.

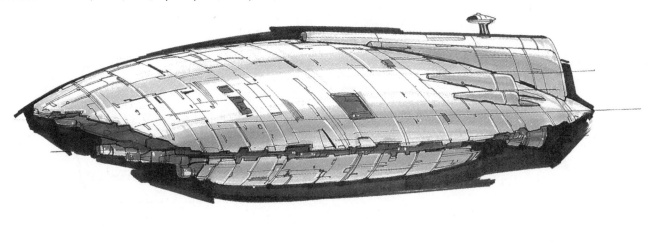

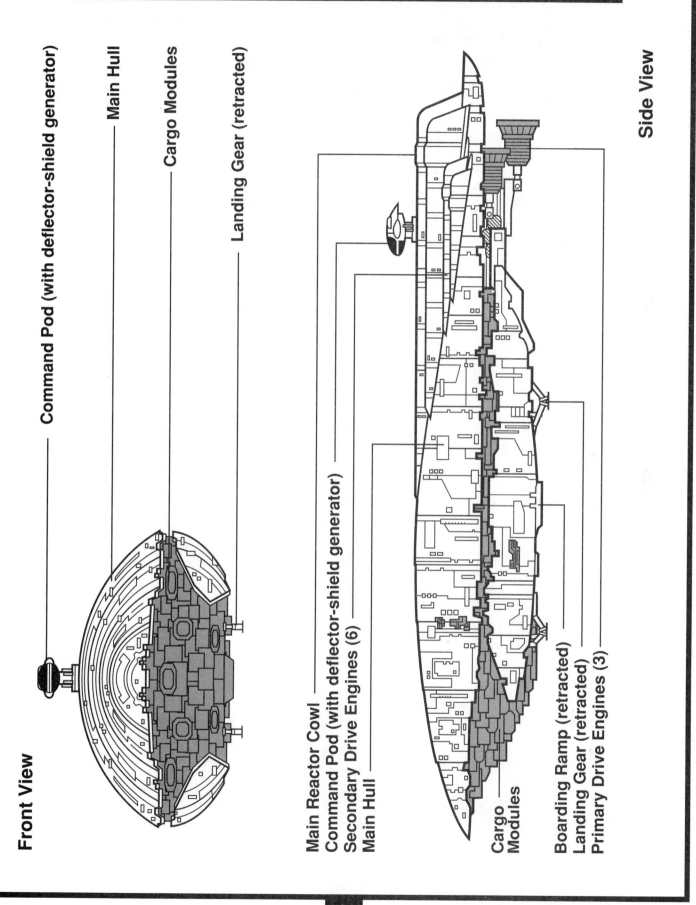

Front View

Side View

Command Pod (with deflector-shield generator)

Main Hull

Cargo Modules

Landing Gear (retracted)

Main Reactor Cowl
Command Pod (with deflector-shield generator)
Secondary Drive Engines (6)
Main Hull

Cargo Modules

Boarding Ramp (retracted)
Landing Gear (retracted)
Primary Drive Engines (3)

SCIMITAR ASSAULT BOMBER

SIENAR FLEET SYSTEMS SCIMITAR ASSAULT BOMBER

Scimitar assault bombers are the newest generation of Imperial bombers and were ordered into production when Grand Admiral Thrawn returned to seize control of the Empire's remnants. The ship is a dedicated atmospheric and space bomber with superior performance compared with the standard TIE bomber. It was designed with the assistance of the elite "Scimitar" bomber assault wing, the most decorated active Imperial bomber wing.

The bomber has a single pod with two elongated solar array wings. Unlike most Imperial vessels, the Scimitar is a two-man ship. The pilot and bomber compartment is in the forward section of the pod and can be quickly ejected from the main hull in the event of a critical hit by enemy gunners. This compartment extends ahead of the wings, giving the pilot and bomber superior visibility compared with the TIE bomber.

The navigation and targeting systems, the power generator, and the twin repulsorlift engines are housed in the middle of the pod. The repulsor thrusters are placed in the Scimitar's wing struts for greater maneuverability. The rear portion of the pod contains the bomb bay and the sublight ion engine.

The Scimitar differs significantly from the standard TIE bomber in that it has only a single ion engine and a pair of interlocked repulsorlift engines. In space, it is significantly faster than a TIE bomber. In an atmosphere, its cruising speed is equivalent to a standard TIE bomber at 850 kilometers per hour, but it uses the repulsorlift units to boost its dive-bombing speeds above 1,000 kilometers per hour.

This makes the Scimitar as fast as most combat airspeeders, although this incredible power output severely limits the ship's effective flight range. The repulsorlift also greatly enhances maneuverability, compensating for the hull's poor aerodynamics.

Sienar Fleet Systems released the Scimitar Mark II shortly before Grand Admiral Thrawn's death. The Mark II's most significant difference was improved ion and repulsorlift engine output, boosting the normal atmospheric cruising speed to 1,150 kilometers per hour, with a dive-bombing speed of 1,250 kilometers per hour.

The Scimitar assault bomber was developed with a reinforced hull, allowing it to take far more damage in combat than a TIE bomber could. In keeping with Grand Admiral Thrawn's military policies, the bomber has shields.

The bomb bay has room for sixteen concussion missiles, each with an effective range of nine kilometers. Each warhead is powerful enough to destroy city buildings, reinforced bunkers, heavy repulsorlift speeders, or even AT-AT walkers. While the concussion missile load is the standard weapon complement, proton grenades and free-falling thermal detonators also can be loaded into the Scimitar's bomb bays. The linked forward laser cannons have superior computer targeting for strafing runs against enemy troops and other ground targets.

The Scimitar assault bomber quickly proved its worth against the New Republic. A full wing of bombers (seventy-two ships) led the assault on Mrisst, one of Thrawn's feints before his final assault on Coruscant.

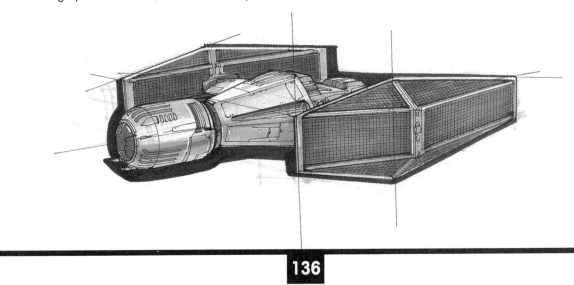

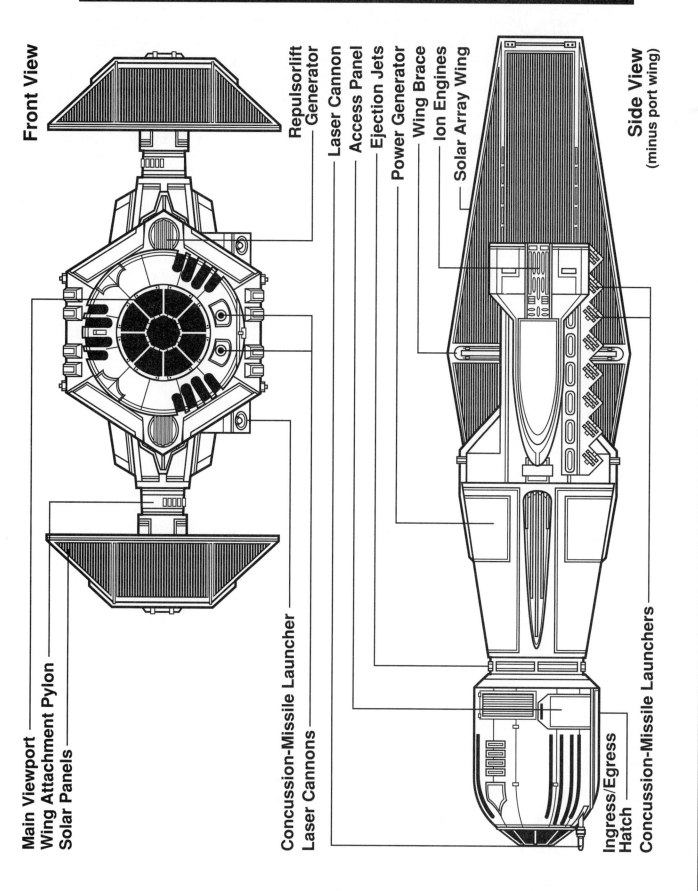

Front View

Repulsorlift Generator
Laser Cannon
Access Panel
Ejection Jets
Power Generator
Wing Brace
Ion Engines
Solar Array Wing

Main Viewport
Wing Attachment Pylon
Solar Panels

Concussion-Missile Launcher
Laser Cannons

Side View
(minus port wing)

Ingress/Egress Hatch
Concussion-Missile Launchers

SHIELDSHIP

REPUBLIC ENGINEERING CORPORATION HEAT-RESISTANT ESCORT VEHICLE

Shieldships are unique escort vessels that protect ships traveling to the planet Nkllon in the Athega system. These vessels are necessary to block the searing rays of Athega's superhot star, which can destroy ships that carry only standard shielding.

Nkllon is so hot that it is habitable only on the dark, or "night," side. However, its mineral resources are too valuable to pass up, especially for someone like Lando Calrissian, who's willing to bet on the longest odds if the payoff is right. Lando's payoff was handsome indeed—once Nomad City was up and running, it was pulling in nearly 10 million credits per year.

The shieldships were built to Lando's specifications by the Republic Engineering Corporation, which was formed shortly after the New Republic seized power in the Galactic Core. The shieldships have proved extraordinarily difficult to pilot and need constant maintenance. The cooling gear must be replaced after every trip in-system, requiring substantial downtime for each vessel. Lando purchased twelve of the shieldships, allowing for up to three visits to Nkllon per day once normal maintenance was taken into account.

The ships appear to be giant umbrellas; the shields are giant cones approximately eight hundred meters across. The face of the shieldship has thick armor plating honeycombed with coolant chambers to keep the outer surface from being burned off. The back has immense tubes and fins to vent the intense heat. The shadow behind the shield is the protected area for incoming starships. Trailing behind the shield is a four-hundred-meter pylon with a drive tug which provides sublight and hyperdrive thrust.

The vehicles operate from a central depot on the outer rim of the Athega system, and use a sophisticated slaving system to tie their navigation computers into the computers of any ships they are escorting. Normally, the shieldship simply takes control of the escorted vessel and jumps into the heart of the system, bringing the other vessel along for the ride. In this manner, the journey from the outer depot to Nkllon takes only one hour.

Ships without slave circuits must be escorted to Nkllon by utilizing sublight drives; even a slight miscalculation on the hyperspace jump into the system would leave the visiting ship unprotected, resulting in its destruction. The sublight journey into the system takes ten hours.

The success of the Nkllon mining operation and its strong New Republic affiliations made it a prime target for Grand Admiral Thrawn's forces. Thrawn's second attack on Nomad City destroyed its drive units and long-range communications; the Star Destroyers attacking the outer depot disabled all but one of the shieldships. Only the timely assistance of Senator Garm Bel Iblis allowed the evacuation of Nomad City before it was melted by Athega's sun. No additional shieldships have yet been built.

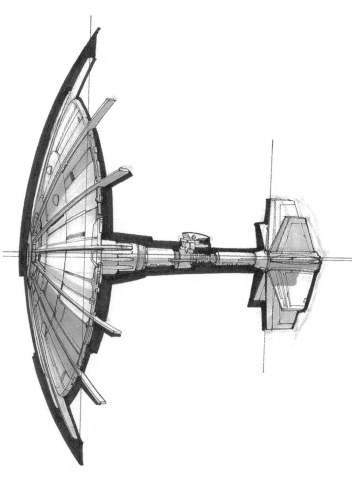

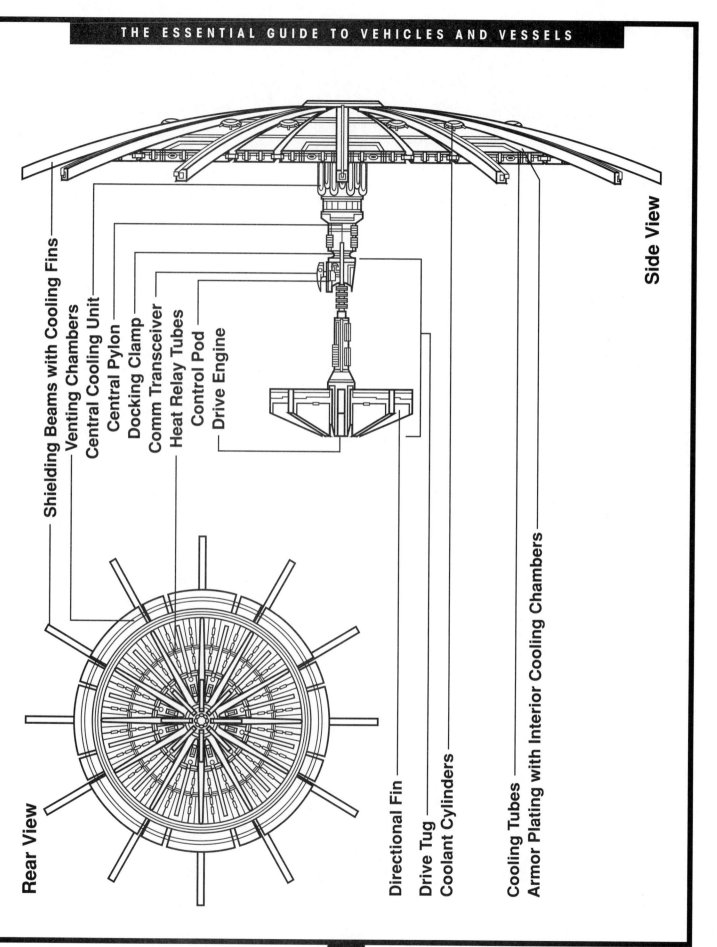

Side View

Rear View

Shielding Beams with Cooling Fins
Venting Chambers
Central Cooling Unit
Central Pylon
Docking Clamp
Comm Transceiver
Heat Relay Tubes
Control Pod
Drive Engine

Directional Fin
Drive Tug
Coolant Cylinders
Cooling Tubes
Armor Plating with Interior Cooling Chambers

SHRIWIRR

SSI-RUUVI SHREE-CLASS BATTLE CRUISER

The *Shriwirr* was the lead attack cruiser for the reptilian Ssi-ruuvi assault force that attacked the remote Imperial planet Bakura shortly after the Battle of Endor and the death of the Emperor.

The *Shriwirr* is a *Shree*-class heavy cruiser and is fitted with a large entenchment lab and dozens of weapon emplacements. It is approximately nine hundred meters long, and its weapons include the Ssi-ruuvi equivalent of twenty-four heavy turbolasers, twenty-four ion cannons, twelve concussion-missile launchers, and twelve tractor-beam projectors. The *Shriwirr* also has five hundred battle droids, the Ssi-ruuvi equivalent of starfighters.

Members of the Ssi-ruuk species place a high priority on capturing enemy ships; destroying them is considered a needless waste. To that end, the *Shriwirr* normally uses its ion cannons to disable opposing craft, while tractor beams reel the ships into the Ssi-ruuvi cruiser's massive landing bays. The Ssi-ruuk use a process they call "entenchment" to draw the life forces out of prisoners—energies which are then used to power Ssi-ruuvi computers and droids, including fighter battle droids.

The interior decks of the *Shriwirr* have five-meter-tall ceilings to accommodate the immense Ssi-ruuk form. There are countless crawlways and access tunnels for the smaller P'w'ecks, a conquered servant species responsible for maintenance and day-to-day operations aboard the cruiser. The Ssi-ruuk have a series of stun traps throughout the ship to prevent P'w'ecks from entering sensitive areas and sabotaging equipment; these stun traps are lethal to humans.

The Ssi-ruuk lack sophisticated artificial gravity systems and use conductive nets to stabilize gravity and repel energy surges.

The *Shriwirr* cruiser had a single entenchment lab deep inside the ship. When the Ssi-ruuk learned that they might be able to adapt the Force abilities of Luke Skywalker in order to be able to entech humans from light-years away, they immediately began building another thirty labs aboard the ship.

In addition to the *Shriwirr*, the Bakura invasion fleet included four four-hundred-meter-long *Wurrif*-class light cruisers, twenty *Fw'Sen*-class P'w'eck picket ships, a single *Sh'ner*-class planetary assault carrier (with twelve *D'kee*-class P'w'eck landing ships), a *Lwhekk*-class manufacturing ship, and a force of over 1,300 battle droids. This preliminary invasion force, led by Admiral Ivpikkis, easily overwhelmed the small protective force at Bakura. Only the timely arrival of the Rebel task force, under the command of Luke Skywalker, prevented this border system from falling to the Ssi-ruuk.

Ultimately, the *Shriwirr* was single-handedly captured by Skywalker. Having been captured by the Ssi-ruuk, Luke managed to break out of the main entenchment lab and disable the engineering control station. The Ssi-ruuk evacuated the ship rather than face Skywalker's Force abilities in battle. The Rebel Alliance refitted the ship for combat duty, renaming it the *Sibwarra*, although the techs tended to call the ship the *Flutie*, after their derisive nickname for the Ssi-ruuk.

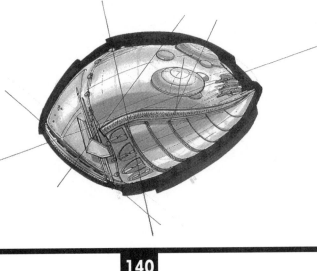

Front View

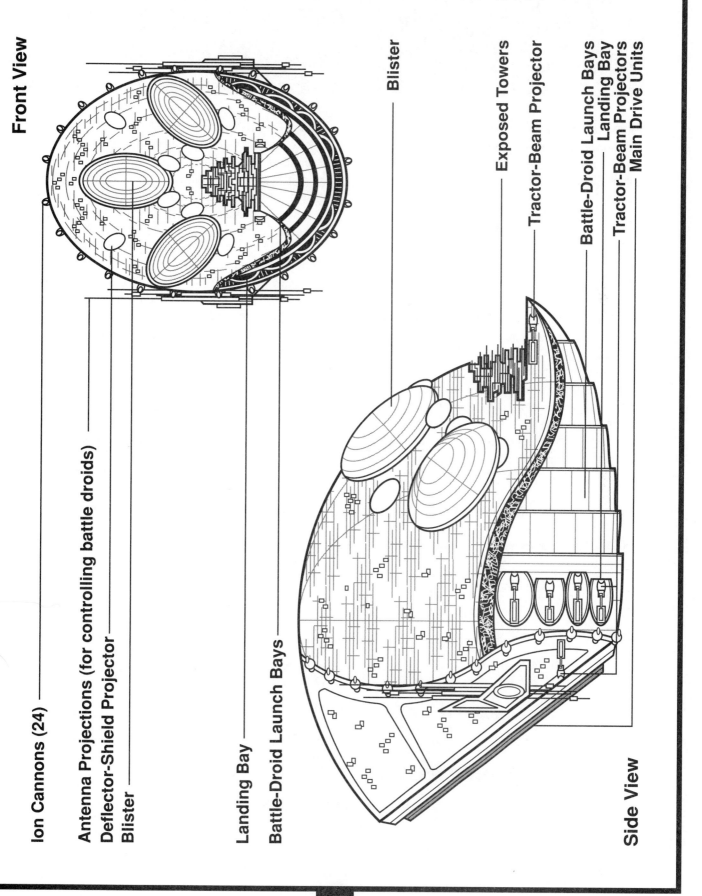

Ion Cannons (24)

Antenna Projections (for controlling battle droids)
Deflector-Shield Projector
Blister

Landing Bay

Battle-Droid Launch Bays

Blister

Exposed Towers
Tractor-Beam Projector

Battle-Droid Launch Bays
Landing Bay
Tractor-Beam Projectors
Main Drive Units

Side View

SKIPRAY BLASTBOAT

SIENAR FLEET SYSTEMS GAT-12H SKIPRAY BLASTBOAT

Blastboats are assault gunships that were used by the Empire. They are larger and far more powerful than starfighters but are small enough to be carried aboard capital ships. The most prominent line of blastboat is the Sienar Fleet Systems GAT series, which includes the 12h, the 12i, and the 12j models.

The 12h was released shortly before the destruction of the first Death Star, while the 12j upgrade was released only weeks after the death of Emperor Palpatine. Its most significant additions were larger ammunition bays for the proton-torpedo and concussion-missile launchers, increasing the capacity to twelve torpedoes and eighteen missiles, respectively.

When the Empire chose not to purchase the GAT-12h Skipray in large quantities, Sienar Fleet Systems began to sell the ships on the open market, so many can be found in corporate, mercenary, pirate, and smuggler fleets. Talon Karrde's smuggling fleet on Myrkr included two Skipray blastboats, although both ships were destroyed after Luke Skywalker and Mara Jade crashed them in the heart of Myrkr's dense forests.

The ships are only twenty-five meters long yet have an incredible weapon array, including three capital ship medium ion cannons, a proton-torpedo launcher, two laser can-

nons, and a concussion-missile launcher. The ion cannons give the Skipray a reasonable chance of disabling larger combat ships. The hull plating is so heavy that most starfighter lasers would have a tough time penetrating the armor, making the ship impervious to all but the most powerful fighter weapons.

The Skipray's ventral and dorsal stabilizer fins assist the ship's atmospheric flight and rotate 180 degrees to a horizontal landing configuration. Blastboats are more maneuverable in an atmosphere than in a vacuum, and have a top atmospheric speed of over 1,200 kilometers per hour; they are as fast as the Alliance's X-wing fighters in space. Skiprays are equipped with hyperdrives and a nav computer that can store four sets of astrogation coordinates, allowing them to operate independently of larger base ships.

The Skipray normally carries a crew of four: the pilot, the copilot and sensor officer, and two gunnery officers. In an emergency, the vessel can be flown by a single person. Blastboats are used for system patrol duty, point defense, or fire support for larger capital ships. They are normally deployed in pairs so that the ships can cover each other. Imperial commanders knew that they could send these ships into the middle of a battle and expect them to come back.

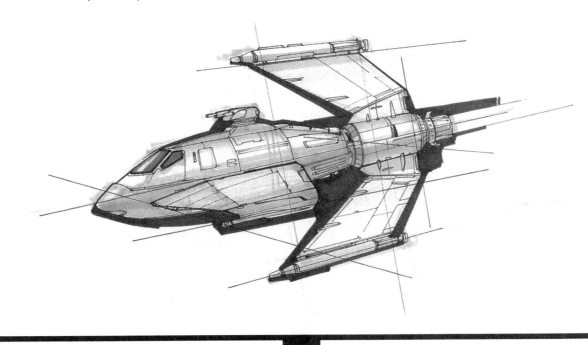

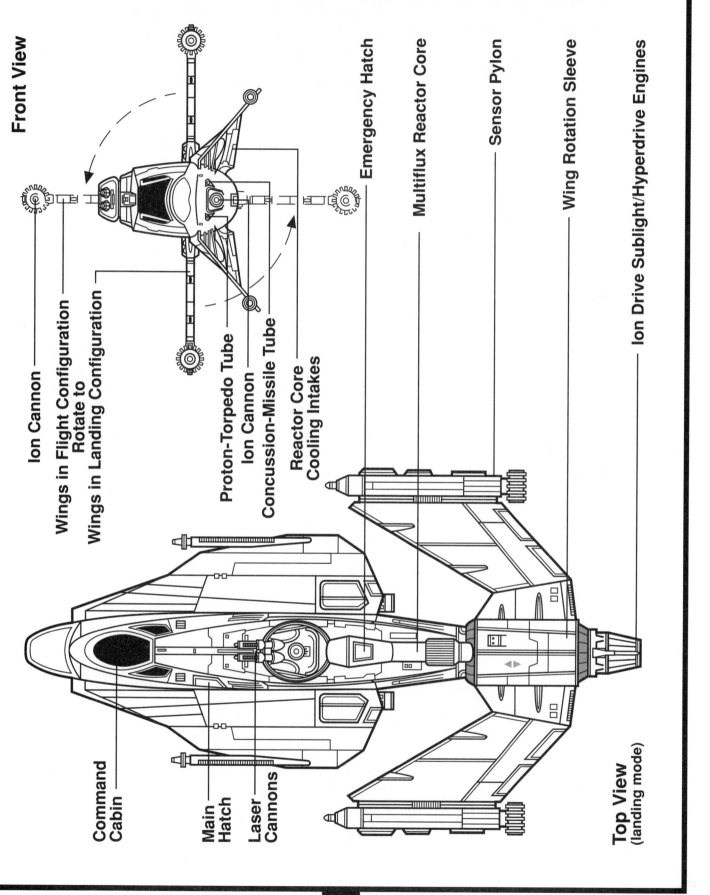

Front View

Ion Cannon

Wings in Flight Configuration
Rotate to
Wings in Landing Configuration

Proton-Torpedo Tube
Ion Cannon
Concussion-Missile Tube

Reactor Core
Cooling Intakes

Emergency Hatch

Multiflux Reactor Core

Sensor Pylon

Wing Rotation Sleeve

Ion Drive Sublight/Hyperdrive Engines

Command
Cabin

Main
Hatch

Laser
Cannons

Top View
(landing mode)

SLAVE I

MODIFIED KUAT SYSTEMS ENGINEERING *FIRESPRAY*-CLASS PATROL AND ATTACK SHIP

Slave I is Boba Fett's unique starship. It is quite similar to its owner: obviously dangerous and with many deadly surprises for those who would dare challenge it.

Slave I is a highly modified *Firespray*-class patrol and attack ship originally designed for planetary law enforcement and interdiction duty. Fett has rebuilt this outdated vessel to be the perfect bounty-hunting ship. It has several hidden weapon systems, a dedicated sensor masking and tracking system, interior prisoner cages, reinforced armor plating, and powerful shield generators, all of which enable Fett to fend off assailants and disable the craft of his quarry.

The ship has an unusual aspect: it lands with its engines down, and in flight, it flies effectively "standing up." Two-thirds of *Slave I*'s interior is dedicated to the powerful Kuat Engineering Systems F-31 drive engines and the four Kuat X-F-16 power generators, giving *Slave I* the speed of an Alliance Y-wing fighter.

The interior sections are cramped, containing only enough room for Fett's living quarters, his equipment locker, and the six prisoner cages, which include a contraband Force cage to contain Force-using individuals.

The bottom rear section of the hull has fully rotating twin blaster cannons. *Slave I* also conceals a forward-firing concussion-missile launcher and ion cannon as well as a turret-mounted tractor-beam projector and a pair of proton torpedo launchers that are also on a turret. Combatants normally are so intent on avoiding the blaster cannons that they blunder right into the hidden torpedo launchers' field of fire.

In addition to combat-grade shields and sensors, *Slave I* has an illegal sensor masking and jamming system that allows it to slip through sensor grids undetected. This system, thought to be an Imperial Navy military secret, was somehow acquired by Fett and has given him a decisive advantage on many hunts. He can use the system to sneak onto worlds undetected, much to the dismay of his targets and planetary law-enforcement agents.

Slave I has dummy proton torpedoes mounted with homing beacons and S-thread trackers. By tagging a ship with one of these dummy beacons, Fett can use his contraband HoloNet transceiver to track ships through hyperspace. In other words, once he has found you, it is almost impossible to dodge the infamous Boba Fett.

After Fett's apparent death, *Slave I* was captured by Rebel Alliance forces and held in impound on the planet Grakouine. Fett managed to get the ship back without alerting the New Republic that he was alive. In his most recent encounter with Han Solo, Boba Fett used *Slave I* to chase down the *Millennium Falcon* on the smugglers' moon of Nar Shaddaa, but once again Solo evaded capture by his old foe.

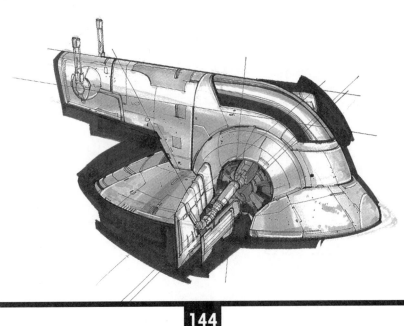

Front View

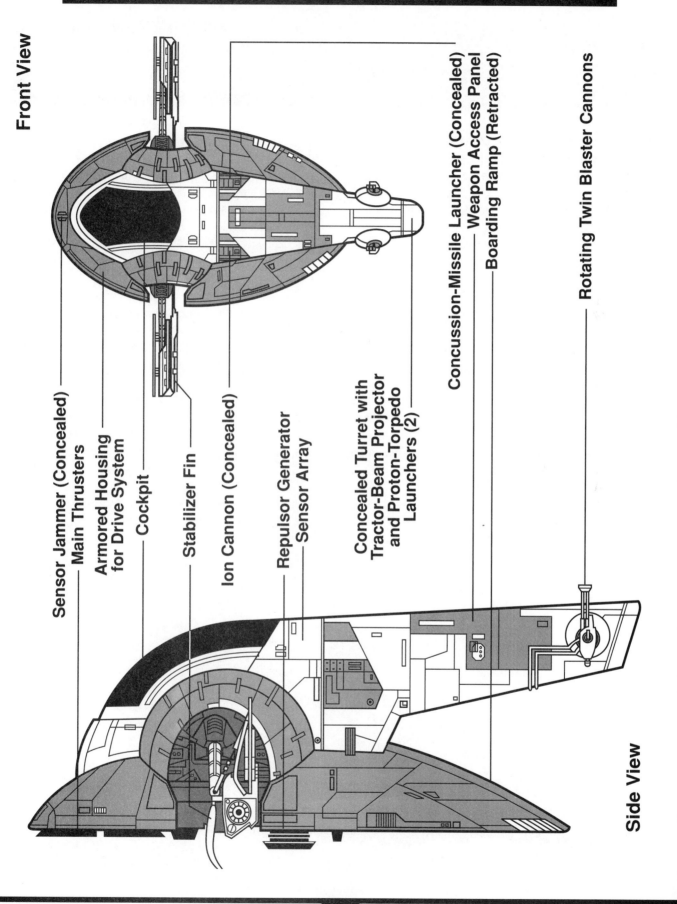

Side View

Sensor Jammer (Concealed)
Main Thrusters

Armored Housing
for Drive System

Cockpit

Stabilizer Fin

Ion Cannon (Concealed)

Repulsor Generator

Sensor Array

Concealed Turret with
Tractor-Beam Projector
and Proton-Torpedo
Launchers (2)

Concussion-Missile Launcher (Concealed)

Weapon Access Panel

Boarding Ramp (Retracted)

Rotating Twin Blaster Cannons

SLAVE II

MandalMotors Pursuer Enforcement Ship

After escaping from the jaws of the Sarlacc on Tatooine, bounty hunter Boba Fett vowed revenge on Han Solo. Solo would pay—and so would the Hutt crime clans, if Solo was delivered to them. As Fett recovered from the encounter, he set into motion a plan.

Slave I was in impound, but a new ship would help Fett keep a low profile until he actually confronted Solo. Fett picked out a MandalMotors *Pursuer*-class patrol ship that was popular with Mandalorian police units because it was tough enough to handle pirates but had enough cargo space for standard policing duties. Using a false identity, Fett purchased the *Slave II* and began modifying this new prize for his hunt for Solo.

Slave II is essentially a heavy patrol craft with a superior hull and powerful Torplex military-grade shield generators. Dual Tion Mil/Sci Mil-StarIV engines propel the ship, while three Corellian Engineering x41 maneuvering thrusters are mounted in the port-side stabilizer brace. The three thrusters can be individually directed and provide excellent performance, especially for a heavy patrol ship.

For weaponry, *Slave II* has forward-firing twin blaster cannons and an ion cannon turret. Fett, always a suspicious type, has a rear-firing proton-torpedo launcher with a magazine of six torpedoes—an unwelcome surprise for anyone who has decided to follow too closely. Like *Slave I*, *Slave II* has a sophisticated sensor array system, although the ship at present lacks the stealth systems of *Slave I*.

Rumors have suggested that Boba Fett placed five force field–enclosed prisoner cages aboard *Slave II*. Knowing that his prime target's best friend is a Wookiee, Fett probably also installed molecularly reinforced cell walls and gravitic restraints in his cells.

Fett encountered Solo on the smugglers' moon of Nar Shaddaa, and the Corellian and his companions barely escaped. *Slave II* jumped into hot pursuit of the fleeing *Millennium Falcon* (which had been secreted aboard Salla Zen's *Starlight Intruder*). By cross-checking the *Intruder*'s hyperspace vector, Fett was able to track Solo to the new Imperial capital of Byss. *Slave II* was severely damaged over Byss when Fett, attempting to follow the *Falcon* down to the planet's surface, smashed into the planetary shield. The stabilizer bar was ripped off in the crash, and the ship was disabled. All things considered, Fett got off lightly—if *Slave II*'s shields had been down, the shield would have incinerated the ship. Rather than get the ship repaired, Fett has placed *Slave II* in drydock while retrieving *Slave I* to continue his pursuit of Han Solo.

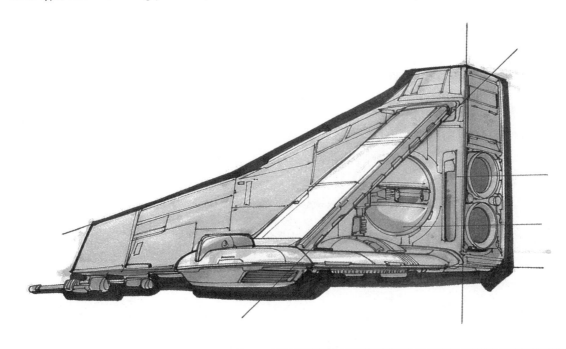

Top View

Front View

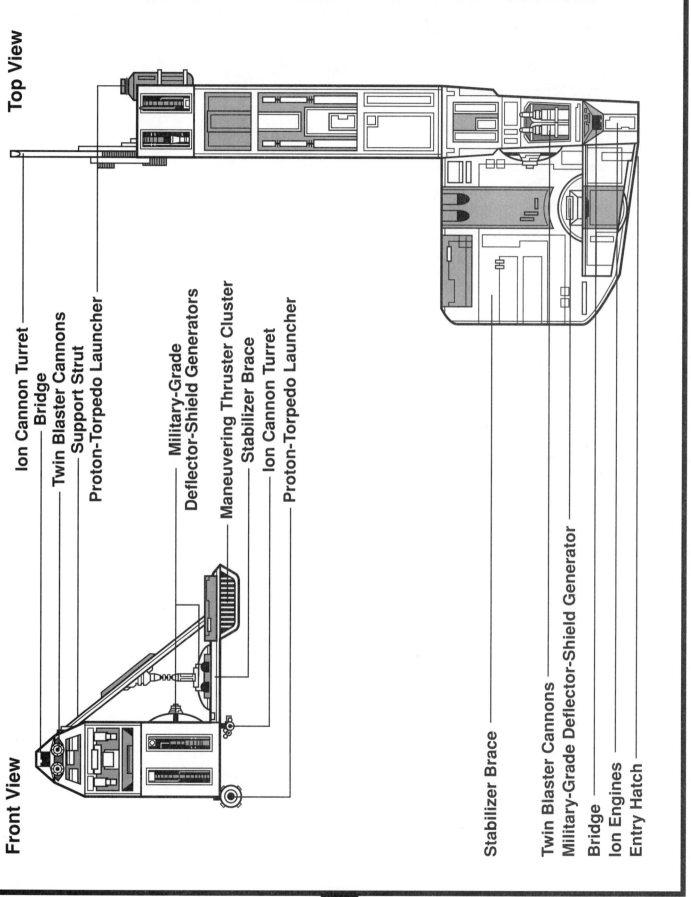

Ion Cannon Turret
Bridge
Twin Blaster Cannons
Support Strut
Proton-Torpedo Launcher

Military-Grade
Deflector-Shield Generators

Maneuvering Thruster Cluster
Stabilizer Brace
Ion Cannon Turret
Proton-Torpedo Launcher

Stabilizer Brace

Twin Blaster Cannons
Military-Grade Deflector-Shield Generator
Bridge
Ion Engines
Entry Hatch

SPEEDER BIKE

ARATECH 74-Z MILITARY SPEEDER BIKE

Speeder bikes are small repulsorlift vehicles that are popular throughout the galaxy as personal transports and recreational vehicles. They are so effective that the Empire's scout troops often used them for military purposes.

Speeder bikes make excellent ground reconnaissance craft. They can reach speeds up to five hundred kilometers per hour and are more maneuverable than both landspeeders and airspeeders, allowing them to travel through terrain that would stop those vehicles. Most speeder bikes have a low flight ceiling of about twenty-five meters above ground level.

While they had access to several speeder bike models, the Empire's scout troopers preferred the Aratech 74-Z bikes for both speed and reliability. The Aratech 74-Z can run for thousands of kilometers without any significant maintenance, allowing biker scouts to operate unsupported for weeks at a time. These speeder bikes have armor plating and a single blaster cannon.

Aratech 74-Zs have two outriggers with four forward steering vanes. Maneuver controls are located in the hand grips, while altitude controls are built into the foot pedals. Speed normally is controlled through the foot pedals. Communications, sensors, and weaponry controls are set in a panel in front of the saddle, while a small cargo compartment is found beneath the seat. A biker scout may reset the control configuration through this panel: some biker scouts prefer to run the accelerator controls through the hand grips.

The forward undercarriage of the speeder bike houses the maneuvering control units (linked to the directional vanes) and the blaster cannon. The rear of the speeder bike is taken up entirely by the power cell and repulsorlift engine.

While the Aratech 74-Z was the most popular Imperial speeder bike, the Empire used several other versions for patrol duty, including the Aratech 64-Y Swift 3 Repulsorlift Sled, the Ikas-Adno Starhawk, and the Mobquet TrailMaker III.

Imperial biker scouts normally worked in units called lances. Each lance had four standard speeder bike scouts and a sergeant commander; a lance generally split into two elements for field operations. Imperial biker scouts could explore and survey far more territory per man than could those using almost any other type of vehicle, and these troops operated with unusual autonomy.

Speeder troops were normally used for scouting and exploration and were ordered to avoid combat so they could report to base command. Biker scouts were also used to spy on Rebel bases before a ground assault. Biker scouts were also trained for urban patrol duty, where the maneuverability and speed of their bikes made them a great asset in searches for entrenched Rebel urban assault forces.

Speeder bikes were part of the Empire's efforts to patrol the forests on Endor, but a Rebel commando team led by Han Solo and Princess Leia managed to eliminate a perimeter-scouting lance, giving the Rebels a clear path to the Empire's shield-generator base.

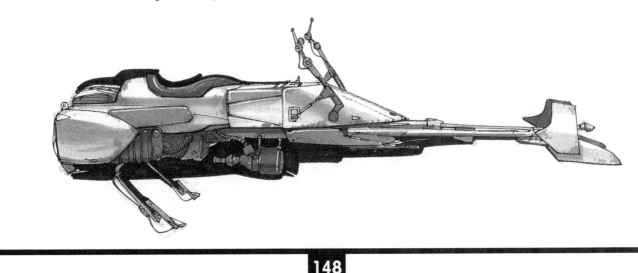

Top View

Side View

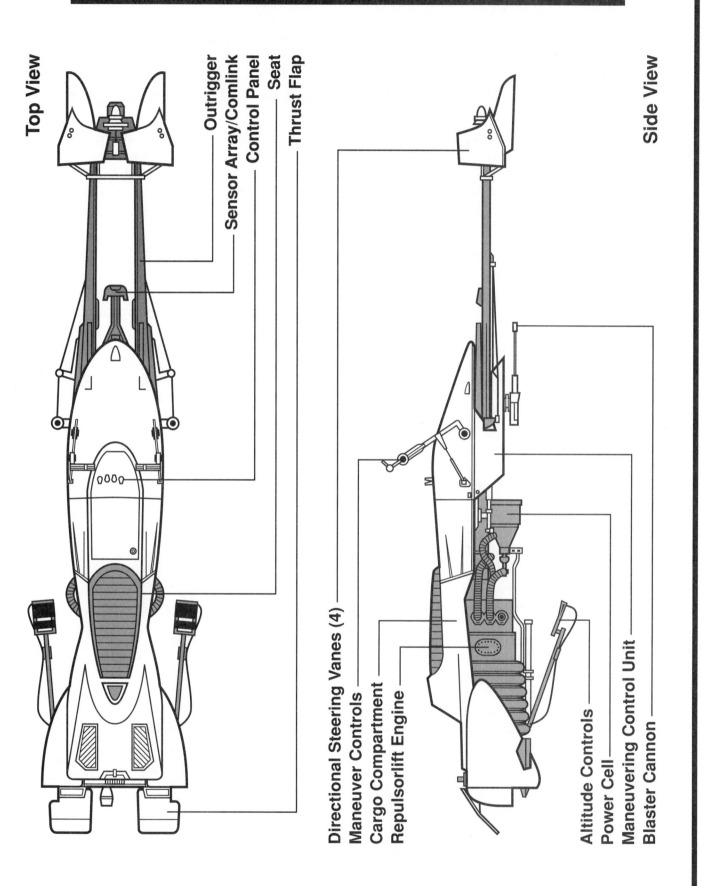

- Outrigger
- Sensor Array/Comlink
- Control Panel
- Seat
- Thrust Flap

- Directional Steering Vanes (4)
- Maneuver Controls
- Cargo Compartment
- Repulsorlift Engine

- Altitude Controls
- Power Cell
- Maneuvering Control Unit
- Blaster Cannon

SSI-RUUVI BATTLE DROID

SSI-RUUVI *SWARM*-CLASS BATTLE DROID

Ssi-ruuvi battle droids are small drone ships powered by the enteched life forces of captured prisoners. The space droids are pyramid-shaped and roughly two meters across, making them significantly smaller than any starfighter in Imperial space. Since only the *life essence* of a being is trapped in the fighter, there is no need for a cockpit or life support system.

These droids are the main assault fighters of the Ssi-ruuvi fleet. The ship known as the *Shriwirr* carried five hundred battle droids, while each *Wurrif*-class cruiser carried two hundred droids. Their high speed, maneuverability, and small target area make them deadly in combat. They have shields as heavy as those of many starfighters and can take an incredible amount of punishment relative to their size.

A battle droid's interior contains power generators for the weapons and shields, battery coils to house the enteched life forces (two per droid), the sensor system, and the drive unit. The droids are powered by heavy fusionables, making them more primitive than Imperial ships. The ships leave a significant radiation trail and are easily tracked by sensors. Radioactive remnants from destroyed Ssi-ruuvi battle droids can, in sufficient quantities, overwhelm even capital ship shields.

Ssi-ruuvi battle droids achieve their maneuverability by mounting a separate engine thruster on each side of the fighter. Each thruster can be angled independently, allowing for turns and maneuvers that far exceed the capabilities of Imperial or Rebel starfighters.

Around each thruster is a sophisticated sensor array, supplemented by a sensor antenna on each corner of the ship. The sensor data are used for targeting and also are fed back to the commanding Ssi-ruuvi cruiser. Thus, the Ssi-ruuk can make informed decisions at every stage of the battle, and subspace communication systems allow for instant changes of strategy regardless of distance.

The faces of the battle droids have what appear to be etchings: they are in fact microfilament grids which can capture part of the energy of incoming blasts and siphon that energy back into the battle droid's main generator.

Ssi-ruuvi battle droids have a laser cannon placed on each corner of the vessel. The cannons have 360-degree rotation, giving them a wide field of fire. The life forces trapped within the battle droid find it difficult to target more than one fighter at a time, but the rotating laser cannons allow the battle droids the flexibility to fire in any direction, even directly behind the ship.

Battle droids are remotely controlled by Ssi-ruuvi command cruisers. The cruiser's droid operators deliver instructions, forcing the trapped life energies to obey commands. One life force handles the shield generators, while the other takes care of sensors, flight control, and weaponry. Using the Force, Luke Skywalker proved that the life forces still retained a will of their own and in essence were trapped in torment until such time as their energies had been exhausted.

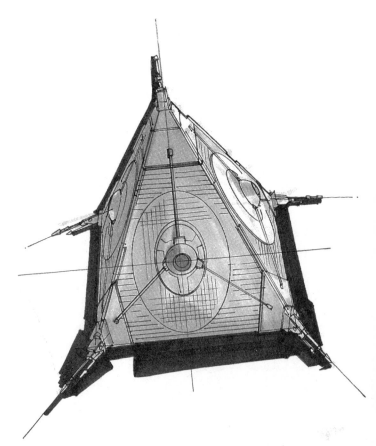

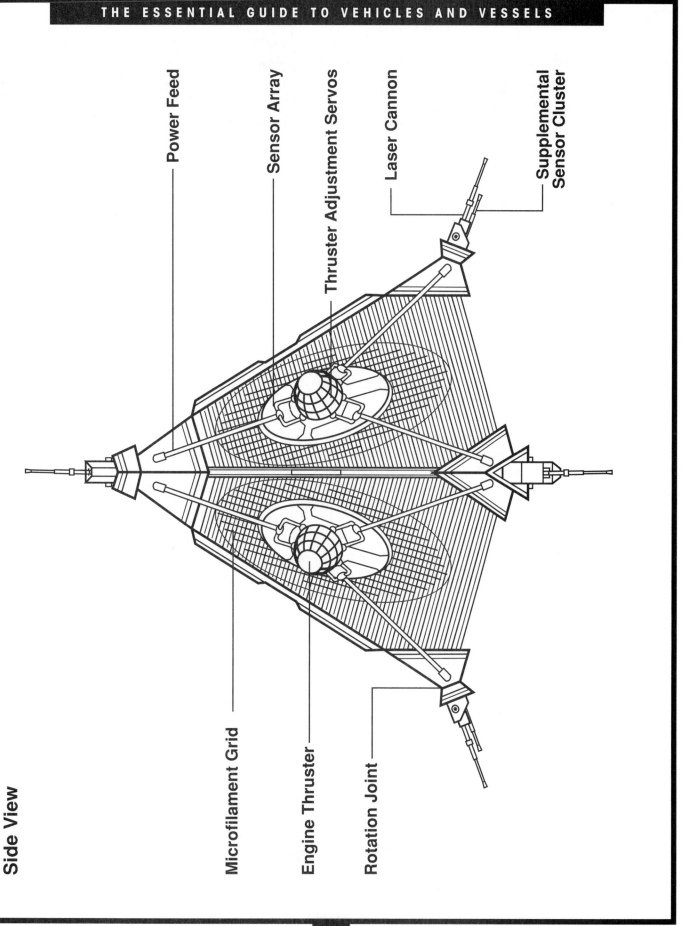

Side View

Power Feed

Sensor Array

Thruster Adjustment Servos

Laser Cannon

Supplemental Sensor Cluster

Microfilament Grid

Engine Thruster

Rotation Joint

SSI-RUUVI PICKET SHIP

SSI-RUUVI *FW'SEN*-CLASS PICKET SHIP

The Ssi-ruuvi invasion force at Bakura included twenty light Fw'Sen picket ships. Such small combat ships are utilized to supplement the larger Ssi-ruuvi cruisers and disable enemy vessels so that their crews may be captured and enteched. They are also used to guard the perimeters of Ssi-ruuvi fleets, and they escort *Sh'ner*-class planetary assault carriers when the carriers are deploying their P'w'eck troop landers.

Fw'Sen picket ships are just under fifty meters long and are crewed only by the Ssi-ruuvi P'w'eck servants. The ships are extremely fragile—even the *Millennium Falcon*'s quad laser cannons were powerful enough to destroy one of these vessels, once its shields were disabled. The Ssi-ruuk designers decided to rely on shield generators instead of thick hull plating, so the Fw'Sen gunships need an incredible amount of energy (which is supplied by the consumption of heavy fusionables and supplemented by enteched life force energy). This makes P'w'eck crews dependent on their masters for survival, giving the Ssi-ruuk yet another tool for controlling the sometimes rebellious creatures.

These Fw'Sen gunships, like the large Ssi-ruuvi cruisers, rely on ion cannons instead of lasers, since capturing ships is far more important than destroying them. A ring of six ion cannons is built around the hull's vertical centerline, and the weapons can be linked for sustained fire on any target.

A pair of standard laser cannons are mounted near the front of the ship and are quite capable of dealing with small freighters and fighters. Fw'Sen picket ships have no space battle droids aboard, so they are often deployed in groups to guard each other's flanks.

Fw'Sen gunships have crews of thirteen P'w'ecks and about half a dozen enteched servant droids. While this arrangement has meant that performance can suffer, the lack of Ssi-ruuk aboard allows the ships to be considered "disposable" for dangerous missions. Ssi-ruuvi commanders have shown a clear preference for sending these ships on suicide missions.

While the P'w'ecks can pilot the ships, Ssi-ruuvi commanders often choose to control the ships remotely, from their main cruisers, and allow the P'w'ecks access only to the weapons systems. The ship's crew members are fitted with neural inhibitors, which the Ssi-ruuk can activate remotely to stun and disable any P'w'ecks who refuse to follow orders.

Five of the twenty deployed Fw'Sen picket ships were destroyed in the original attack on Bakura, while many more were destroyed after the Rebel Alliance relief fleet arrived in-system. The Rebel Alliance and the Bakurans captured several of the small cruisers and began refitting them for use in their respective fleets. However, the technicians had a great deal of trouble, because the vessels have insufficient shielding to protect the crew from radiation.

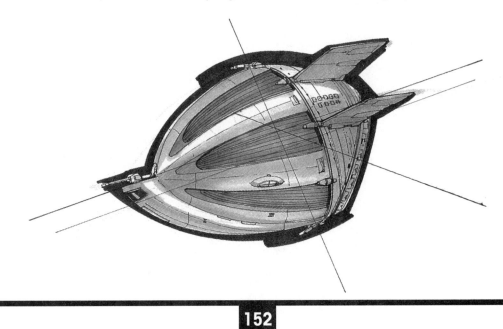

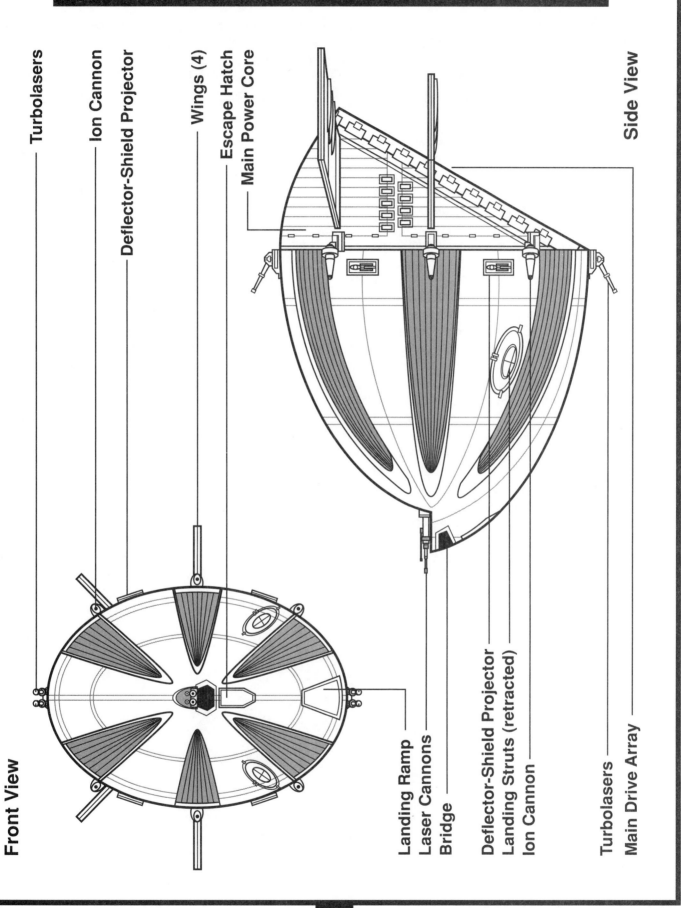

Turbolasers

Ion Cannon

Deflector-Shield Projector

Wings (4)

Escape Hatch

Main Power Core

Side View

Front View

Landing Ramp
Laser Cannons
Bridge

Deflector-Shield Projector
Landing Struts (retracted)
Ion Cannon

Turbolasers
Main Drive Array

SSI-RUUVI ASSAULT CARRIER

SSI-RUUVI *SH'NER*-CLASS PLANETARY ASSAULT CARRIER

Ssi-ruuvi *Sh'ner*-class planetary assault carriers are essential to any Ssi-ruuk invasion force. Almost as large as the Ssi-ruuvi *Shree*-class battle cruisers, Sh'ner carriers are ovoid ships nearly 750 meters long. The Bakura invasion fleet had only one of these carriers, but it is not known how many additional Sh'ner cruisers remained in reserve with the main Ssi-ruuvi battle fleet. The carrier assigned to Bakura retreated back to the main Ssi-ruuvi battle fleet after Luke Skywalker captured the *Shriwirr* battle cruiser.

Sh'ner carriers normally are held in reserve until the target world's forces have been significantly weakened. Even after they have been deployed, Sh'ner carriers remain in the heart of the Ssi-ruuvi fleet and are protected by Fw'Sen picket ships and Wurrif light cruisers. Sh'ner cruiser ships are slow and underpowered and are closer to transports than to combat ships. They have weak shields, making them easy targets for any enemy vessels that can close to point-blank range. Sh'ner cruisers have minimal weaponry, each with only six ion cannons and two tractor-beam projectors.

A Sh'ner cruiser has six launch bays for the D'kee landing ships, with a dozen secondary landing bays designated for captured enemy vessels. These secondary bays are equipped with stun traps, microtractor-beam generators, and heavy gravity-conductive nets to immobilize and imprison enemy soldiers. The interior of each Sh'ner cruiser has nearly a dozen entechment labs for rapidly processing

prisoners; giant batteries store the enteched life energies until they are needed.

The crew is surprisingly small, with only about sixty Ssi-ruuk aboard to form the command crew and run the entechment labs. About five hundred P'w'ecks and three hundred enteched droids are also kept aboard as assistants and for manual labor. Because of the large percentage of P'w'ecks aboard, security stun traps can be found in almost every corridor and room, and all can be activated from the bridge or the main engineering section; also, each P'w'eck is fitted with a neural inhibitor to ensure loyalty.

A Sh'ner carrier maintains a dozen *D'kee*-class P'w'eck landing ships, each armed with one hundred paralysis canisters. The canisters are dropped over major population centers and explode at an altitude of 3,000 meters, spreading Ssi-ruuvi paralysis toxins over an area of nearly nine square kilometers. These small landing ships can devastate a city with only two or three bombing runs. The paralysis toxin is effective upon contact with the skin or when inhaled; its effects last up to eight hours and neutralize all voluntary nerve activity, leaving victims fully alert but unable to move.

With target cities effectively neutralized, the D'kee landing ships descend to gather entechment subjects. Each landing ship can carry nearly 10,000 prisoners in confinement pens. Like the Fw'Sen picket ships, the D'kee landing craft are remotely controlled by the Sh'ner cruiser through high-density subspace transmissions.

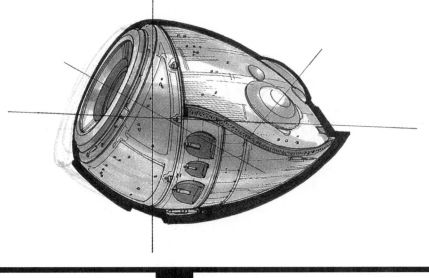

Front View

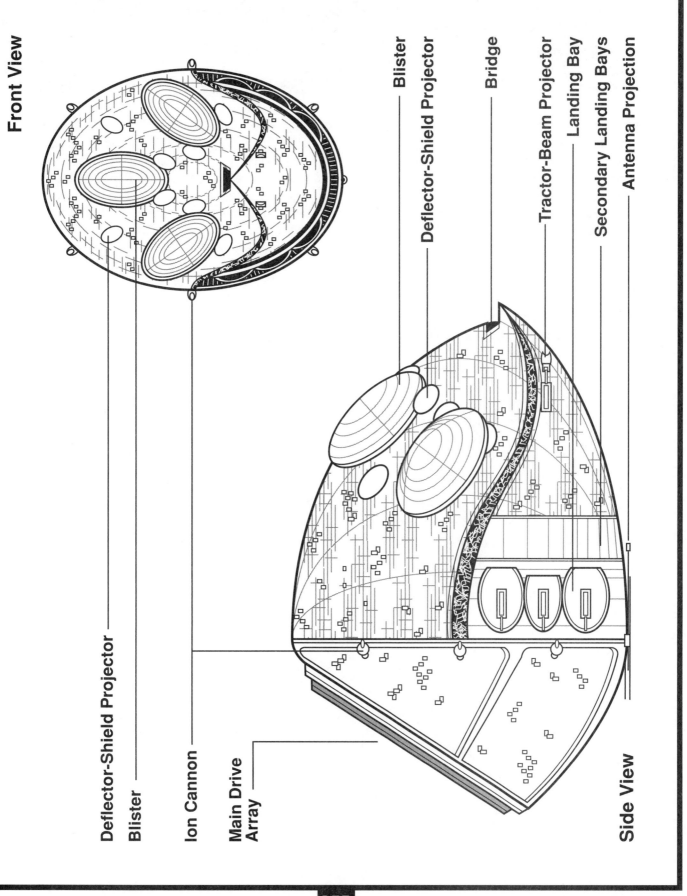

Blister

Deflector-Shield Projector

Bridge

Tractor-Beam Projector

Landing Bay

Secondary Landing Bays

Antenna Projection

Deflector-Shield Projector

Blister

Ion Cannon

Main Drive Array

Side View

STAR HOME

CUSTOMIZED LUXURY TRANSPORT

The *Star Home* is a unique transport vessel reserved for the exclusive use of the Hapan Queen Mother. The ornate vehicle is over four millennia old and was designed to replicate the Queen Mother's ruling castle on Hapes. The ship is essentially a giant castle on a huge chunk of black basalt, and despite appearances, the *Star Home* is quite spaceworthy.

The castle contains the Queen Mother's quarters and hearing room as well as dining halls, meeting rooms, and quarters for all Queen Mother Ta'a Chume's guests and confidants. Every interior corridor and room is covered in dark stone to perpetuate the illusion of the occupant's being in an ancient Hapan castle instead of aboard a starship. The castle features a number of towers, each capped with a crystal dome that allows an unobstructed view of space, while stunning spires and lush gardens dot the upper "courtyard" levels. A private hangar bay is maintained at the lowest level of the castle and is reserved for use by Queen Mother Ta'a Chume's personal guests.

To the matriarchal Hapan people, the *Star Home* represents wealth, power, and the supreme authority of the Queen Mother. The wind-sculpted basalt was carved from the surface of Hapes itself, while the stone for the castle was quarried from the moons orbiting Hapes. The crystal for the domes comes from Selab, while each of the other sixty-one inhabited worlds of the Hapes Cluster contributed stone, woodwork, gems, or other ornamentation for the interior. Each year the governor of each world presents the most treasured artifact from his or her planet to be stored forever in the galleries and vaults of the *Star Home*. Honored visitors can view treasures of the Hapan people dating back over four millennia, including the first great epic poems of the Hapan privateers, the incredible sonic-crystal sculptures of Gallinore, and the latest works of the great Duinuogwuin scientist Mont'Kar'oh from the technology world of Charubah.

The ship's systems are housed in the basalt base, which has been hollowed out and reinforced by a unique molecular shielding system. The castle and basalt alone are fragile, so the shielding system provides the *Star Home*'s only protection.

Nearly a third of the base's interior is taken up by the six massive power generators needed to power the drives and keep the shield generators going. Twenty-four sublight engines drive the vessel through realspace, while four hyperdrive engines are slaved to a single motivator to propel the bizarre craft into hyperspace. The *Star Home*'s weapons include twenty turbolasers, twenty laser cannons, and six tractor-beam projectors. Interior hangar bays house five squadrons of fighters, for a total of sixty fighters, as well as numerous transports and shuttles.

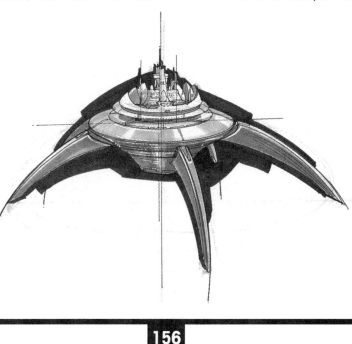

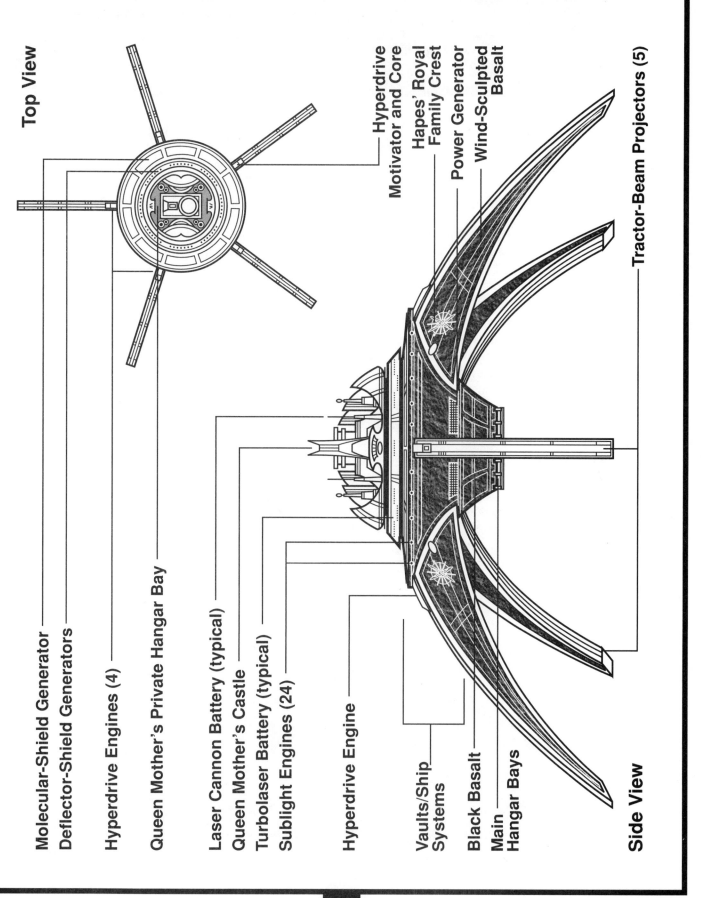

Top View

Side View

Molecular-Shield Generator
Deflector-Shield Generators
Hyperdrive Engines (4)
Queen Mother's Private Hangar Bay
Laser Cannon Battery (typical)
Queen Mother's Castle
Turbolaser Battery (typical)
Sublight Engines (24)
Hyperdrive Engine
Vaults/Ship Systems
Black Basalt
Main Hangar Bays

Hyperdrive Motivator and Core
Hapes' Royal Family Crest
Power Generator
Wind-Sculpted Basalt
Tractor-Beam Projectors (5)

STARLIGHT INTRUDER

MODIFIED MOBQUET MEDIUM TRANSPORT

The *Starlight Intruder* is Salla Zend's cobbled-together medium freighter. Salla built the *Intruder* for hot-rod smuggling runs, but as Palpatine's new Empire opened up the Deep Galactic Core, Salla found added reason to get the ship finished.

Salla built a ship that she claims can outrun any smuggling ship in space, and the *Intruder* is specced for Imperial military runs. Salla's mouth still waters at the thought of all those free-flowing credits the Imperials were once doling out for runs into the Core.

The *Starlight Intruder* is based on an old Mobquet medium transport hull, but there's a lot hidden under that battered surface. The ship can carry seven times the cargo of standard light freighters. Salla has added hull bracing and armor plating and has replaced the standard Mobquet drives with four military-grade Damorian RX7 ion engines for fast getaways. For extra maneuverability, she's added four maneuvering jets to the bottom of the hull and has equipped the *Intruder* with a pair of medium turbolaser turrets and four heavy-duty Novaplex DuR-4 shield generators.

When Han Solo showed up asking for a favor—transport to Byss—the *Intruder* was in pieces and still needed a hyperdrive. The one Salla planned on installing was a nightmare of patchwork engineering: an old Koensayr CL-14 hyperdrive motivator fitted onto a pair of Rendili StarDrive hyperdrives. While no Imperial safety inspector would ever approve the rig, Salla was sure it would hit at least Class 0.75 speed. That would make the *Intruder* just slightly slower than the *Millennium Falcon*'s Class 0.5 speed—and she was willing to bet money that Solo had exaggerated the speed of the *Falcon*.

Because the *Intruder* was unfinished, Solo offered to lend a hand. Chewbacca helped Salla install a hyperdrive from an old Hutt chariot while Han Solo and Leia Organa Solo set out to get some advanced Koensayr W-0 power couplings, since standard power couplings would be instantly blown out by the souped-up power generator Salla had fitted into the *Intruder*.

Salla ended up using the *Starlight Intruder* on Byss, but not as she'd ever intended. Solo talked her into using it to smuggle his rickety old crate, the *Millennium Falcon*. As usual, Solo attracted trouble like a magnet . . . and as usual, Salla paid the price: Byss security impounded the *Intruder* until she and Shug Ninx were able to break into the impound yards and blast away with it. Of course, Salla brought even more trouble on herself by rescuing New Republic forces stranded on the Imperial capital world, but it'll probably be a while before any authorities catch up with her.

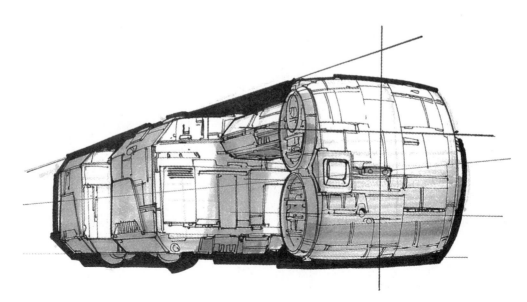

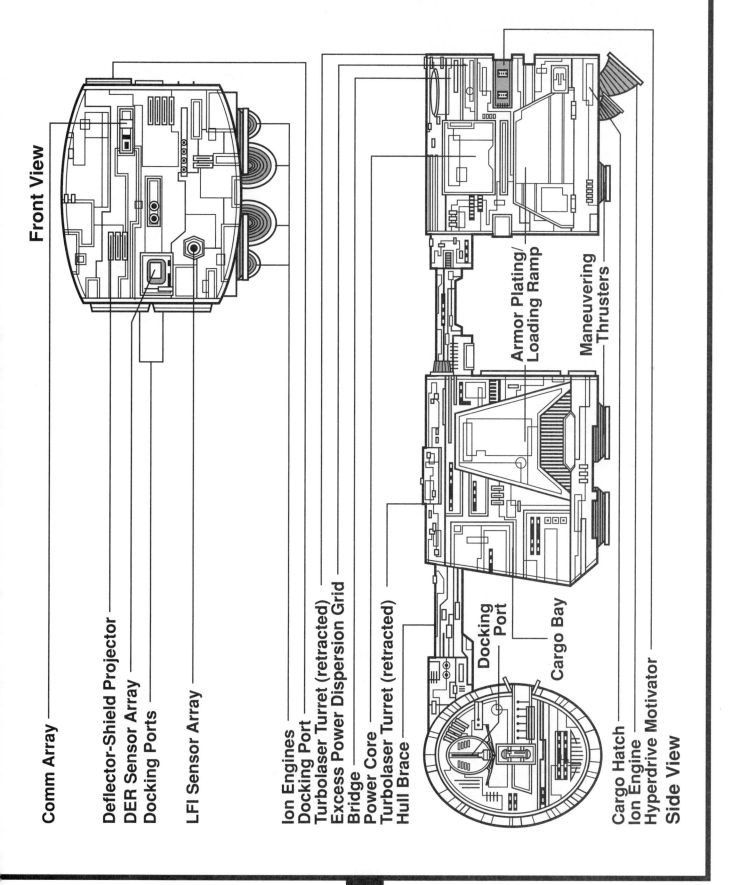

Front View

Comm Array

Deflector-Shield Projector
DER Sensor Array
Docking Ports

LFI Sensor Array

Ion Engines
Docking Port
Turbolaser Turret (retracted)
Excess Power Dispersion Grid
Bridge
Power Core
Turbolaser Turret (retracted)
Hull Brace

Docking Port

Cargo Bay

Armor Plating/
Loading Ramp

Maneuvering
Thrusters

Cargo Hatch
Ion Engine
Hyperdrive Motivator
Side View

STORM

CUSTOM-MODIFIED HAPAN CLUSTER MIY'TIL FIGHTER

Prince Isolder, crown prince to the Hapan throne, personally designed his starfighter. Isolder began with the basic hull of the Hapan Miy'til fighter, but more than half a million credits of refinements have turned *Storm* into a fighter that can stand against any short-range ship in the Hapan Cluster. It is thought that the Hapan military plans to incorporate some of *Storm's* elements, including a limited turbogenerator, into the next generation of Miy'til fighters.

The basic hull is short and sleek, with the fighter coming in at just over seven meters long. This required the Hapan engineers to miniaturize as many components as possible to get them to fit inside the hull. The ship has a prototype R2-Series5 astromech droid that was received as a gift from Princess Leia during the initial negotiations with the Hapans. The R2(S5) is a perfect mate for *Storm's* computer and weapon systems, which are too advanced for compatibility with regular R2 astromech units.

Storm is equipped with four banks of Nordoxicon 38 anticoncussion-field generators. Immediately in front of the canopy sits the sensor and communication scrambler, very similar to the sensor jammer mounted on the A-wing fighter. It allows Isolder to block all communications from enemy fighters and prevents enemy scanners from acquiring a target lock.

The nose holds a set of triple-linked laser cannons and a miniconcussion-missile launcher with a bay of ten missiles. The missiles are custom-built, featuring a sophisticated tracking system that can overcome *Storm's* jamming system. Each wing contains an ion cannon, and there are twin thermal-detonator bombing tubes for pinpoint bombing—*Storm* carries sixteen thermal detonators.

The ship has a transparisteel bubble canopy for excellent visibility in all directions. The four Incom 6X4 fusial thrust engines have been rebuilt with modified Tykannin Class-4 power converters to give the ship the sublight speed of a TIE interceptor. Each engine has an oversize Cygnus turbo generator for short bursts that propel the ship to speeds one-third faster than that of the Republic A-wing fighter. As a result of the dangerous nature of the generators, *Storm* is equipped with an emergency shutdown system for critically overloaded engines.

Storm was a common sight in battles in the Hapan Cluster, since Prince Isolder often chose to lead his fighters into battle, and the ship crash-landed on the planet Dathomir during a rescue attempt involving Princess Leia. *Storm* was recovered and rebuilt after the Battle of Dathomir, but even so, the Hapans have refused to share their technological breakthroughs with the New Republic's technicians.

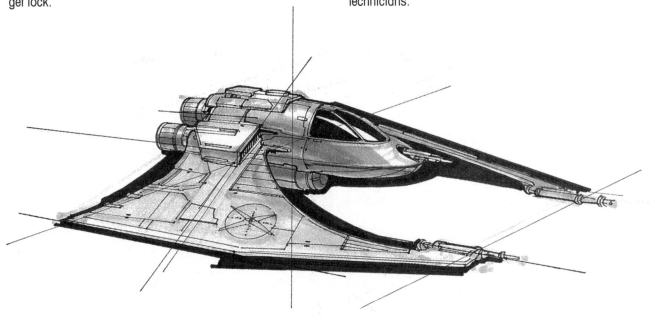

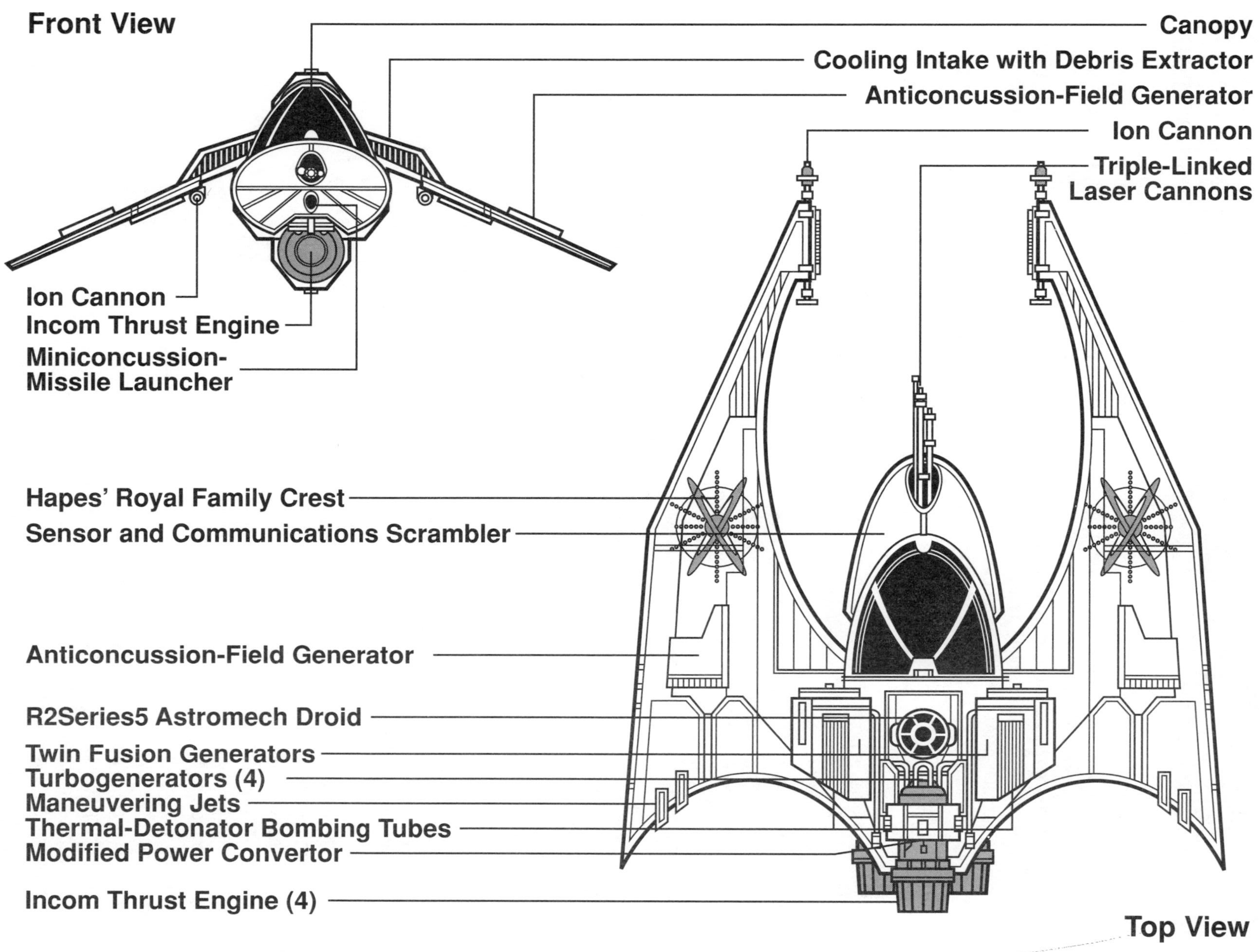

Canopy
Cooling Intake with Debris Extractor
Anticoncussion-Field Generator
Ion Cannon
Triple-Linked
Laser Cannons

Top View

Front View

Ion Cannon
Incom Thrust Engine
Miniconcussion-
Missile Launcher

Hapes' Royal Family Crest
Sensor and Communications Scrambler

Anticoncussion-Field Generator

R2Series5 Astromech Droid
Twin Fusion Generators
Turbogenerators (4)
Maneuvering Jets
Thermal-Detonator Bombing Tubes
Modified Power Convertor

Incom Thrust Engine (4)

SUN CRUSHER

IMPERIAL SUPERWEAPON PROTOTYPE

The Sun Crusher was an Imperial superweapon designed at the Maw Installation, an Imperial military think tank that had been secretly established by Grand Moff Tarkin. The Maw Installation was hidden in the heart of the Maw, a cluster of black holes near the infamous spice world of Kessel. The original Death Star superlaser was invented at the Maw Installation by Imperial Engineer Bevel Lemelisk and a top design team that included an Omwati female named Qui Xux. After Tarkin and Lemelisk departed to build the Death Star, Tarkin left Admiral Daala in command and ordered Qui Xux to create a new Imperial superweapon.

When Tarkin was killed at the Battle of Yavin, the Maw Installation was forgotten. Admiral Daala waited nearly ten years for word from the Grand Moff, and during that time Qui Xux and the design team made the many breakthroughs that led to the new superweapon, dubbed the Sun Crusher.

The Sun Crusher was only slightly larger than a fighter, yet its resonance torpedoes were powerful enough to destroy a star. The ship was a marvel of galactic technology that could not be bought at any price—its unique miniature systems, layered molecular armor, and resonance torpedoes each cost as much to develop as did the original Death Star superlaser.

The ship was a slender vessel that flew in an "upright" position: the cockpit was placed at the top of the ship, while a dish-shaped resonance projector hung from the bottom of the Sun Crusher. A number of rotating laser turrets were used to disable attacking enemy ships, although the shimmering quantum-crystalline armor made the Sun Crusher virtually impervious to damage.

The Sun Crusher carried eleven "resonance torpedoes" which were energized and launched through the resonance projector. The torpedoes could be launched into a star to trigger a chain reaction that would cause the star to go supernova, incinerating every world in its system.

The command cabin had room for six. Normally, the pilot handled navigation and control and the main gunner fired the resonance torpedoes, while the four other gunners handled the defensive laser cannons. All the controls could be linked through the central piloting station.

Han Solo was imprisoned in the Maw Installation, where he met the Sun Crusher's designer, Qui Xux, and convinced her of the evil the weapon presented. She, Solo, Chewbacca, and an escaped slave named Kyp Durron stole the Sun Crusher from the Empire. After they delivered the weapon to Coruscant, the New Republic Assembly voted to have the weapon cast down into the gas giant Yavin. However, Kyp retrieved the Sun Crusher and went on a rampage, destroying several Imperial worlds before surrendering the vessel. The Sun Crusher was destroyed at the Battle of the Maw, when it was caught in the gravity well of one of the Maw's black holes.

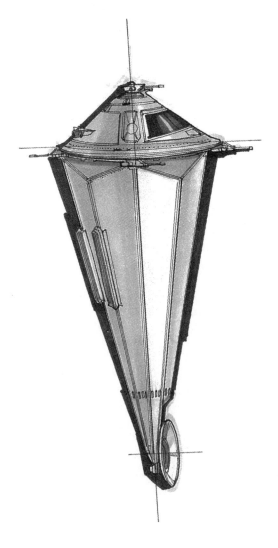

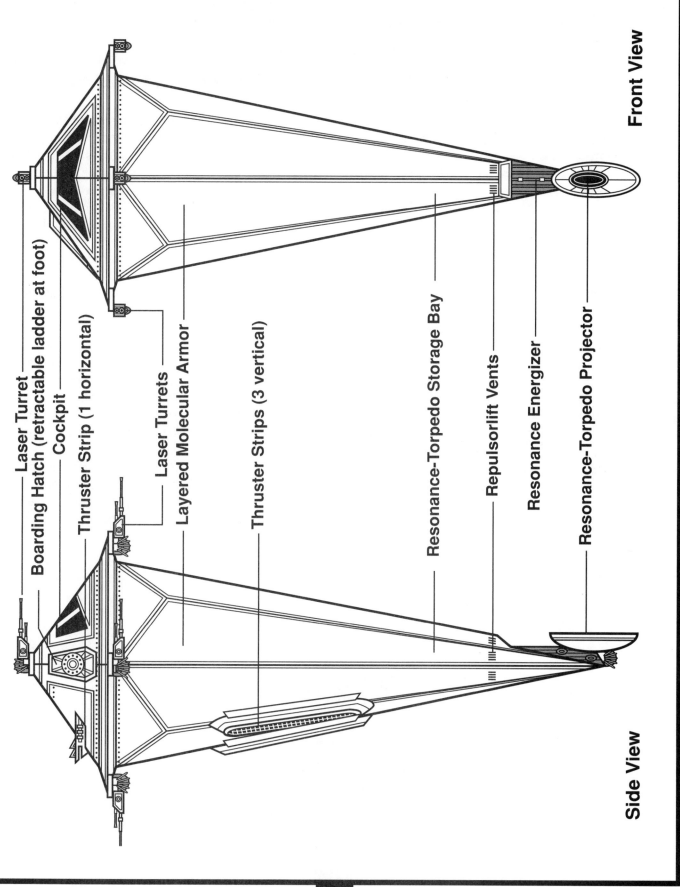

Front View

Side View

Laser Turret

Boarding Hatch (retractable ladder at foot)

Cockpit

Thruster Strip (1 horizontal)

Laser Turrets

Layered Molecular Armor

Thruster Strips (3 vertical)

Resonance-Torpedo Storage Bay

Repulsorlift Vents

Resonance Energizer

Resonance-Torpedo Projector

SWOOP

TaggeCo. Air-2 Swoop

Swoops are high-speed, lightweight speeder vehicles that are much faster than speeder bikes but are also far more difficult to control. These bare-bones vehicles are built around powerful ion and repulsorlift engines, with almost no amenities other than a seat and controls. The *only* safety feature is a seat belt to hold the rider in place.

Swoops are designed as one-being vehicles, although a few have a longer seat to accommodate a passenger. They achieve remarkable speeds because of their modified motors and are much lighter than most other repulsorlift vehicles, since some manufacturers use exotic composite alloys to further lighten their load. Top speed can exceed six hundred kilometers per hour; with an experienced pilot at the controls, a swoop can leave landspeeders and speeder bikes far behind. Unlike heavier repulsorlift vehicles, the shifting of the driver's weight significantly influences a swoop's handling. Maneuvering flaps and control vanes initiate turns, spins, and other complex maneuvers. While some swoops can fly several kilometers above a planetary surface, they generally are used for low-altitude flight.

Swoop racing is a popular sport throughout the galaxy. Formal events are held in immense stadiums, while "outlaw" racing is staged on temporary courses on many outlying worlds. Swoops often are used by criminal gangs both for their speed and for their "dangerous" image.

Han Solo has had plenty of experience with swoops: as a youth, he raced them professionally and acquired quite a reputation on the Corellian circuits. Solo's rivalry with the bounty hunter Dengar began when both of them were young racers. Solo bested him in a one-on-one swoop race through the crystal swamps of Agrilat. In that race Dengar was severely injured, although this was due to his own negligence. Upon recovering, Dengar blamed Solo for the accident and became a bounty hunter so he could exact revenge.

Han's swoop racing experience came in quite handy when he used a TaggeCo. Air-2 swoop to outmaneuver a group of slavers who tried to kill him on the planet Bonadan. Solo had a passenger, Fiolla of Lorrd, so he couldn't simply outrace the single-man vehicles. Instead, he attempted to evade the slavers by fleeing through a series of twisting canyons. He eventually led them through an automated weather-control station. The criminals couldn't match Solo's maneuvers, and all of them crashed, allowing Solo and Fiolla to escape.

The TaggeCo. Air-2 swoop is typical of the many swoop models. It has hand controls, with auxiliary controls in the knee and foot pegs. As with many other swoops, the pilot must shift his weight to enhance handling, and it has an optional transplast windscreen.

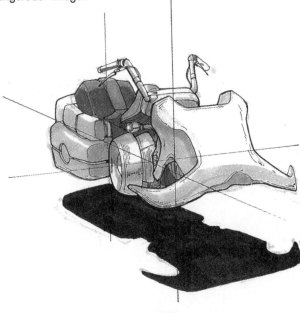

Front View

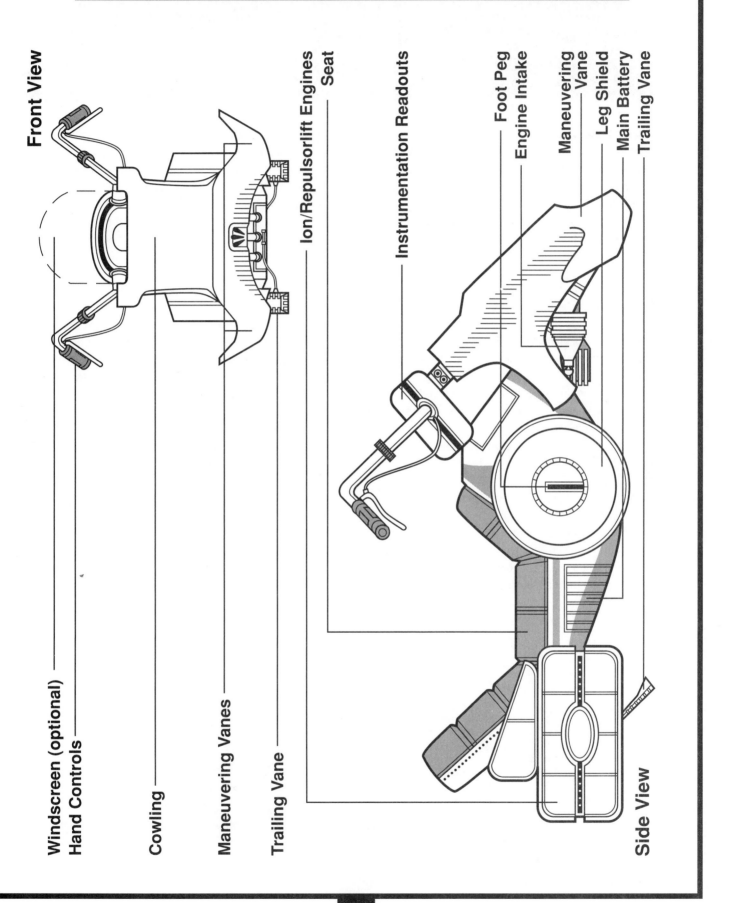

Windscreen (optional)
Hand Controls

Cowling

Maneuvering Vanes

Trailing Vane

Ion/Repulsorlift Engines

Seat

Instrumentation Readouts

Foot Peg

Engine Intake

Maneuvering Vane

Leg Shield

Main Battery

Trailing Vane

Side View

S-SWOOP

Mobquet Flare-S Swoop

Swoops are high-performance craft that offer exceptional speed but are demanding for even the most skilled pilots. They are not suited for the faint of heart . . . or the young and overconfident!

They are simple, crude vehicles best described as "engines with seats." They offer no protection to the rider or pilot and can easily spin out of control even at relatively low speeds; so the pilot is just a split-second mistake away from careening out of control.

Still, swoops offer the performance of airspeeders at a fraction of the cost. Some can exceed six hundred kilometers per hour—a frighteningly fast speed when one considers that they often are used to fly just a few meters above a planet's surface. They achieve this performance through a combination of repulsorlift and turbothrust engines. Maneuverability comes from atmospheric control vanes and repulsor balancers. Turns and maneuvers are accomplished by simultaneously angling turbothruster nozzles, adjusting the repulsorlift output, and angling maneuvering flaps.

All controls are typically tied into a handlebar controller, although some swoops may split controls between handlebars and foot pedals or run auxiliary controls into the foot pedals. The only safety features are simple restraint straps and the pilot's good luck and raw ability.

Learning how to fly a swoop is a mark of dedication and bravery. The best pilots awe even casual observers as they coax their vehicles through complex maneuvers commonly thought impossible; pilots who push themselves *beyond* their abilities end their careers abruptly.

Swoops are popular for advance military scouting, and have found their way into the hands of pirates and other criminals. Swoops are also popular sport vehicles, and swoop racing is a very popular (if deadly) activity in the Galactic Core.

Swoop pilots often wear fully sealed flight suits with independent oxygen supplies to counteract the effects of high-gee maneuvers and to supply oxygen and pressure when they are flying in a planet's upper atmosphere.

This particular swoop, the Mobquet Flare-S, is a hybrid that combines the best qualities of speeder bikes and standard swoops. While significantly heavier than most swoops, it has a reinforced chassis, reducing the chance of "chassis fracture" during high-gee turning maneuvers or incidental contact. Forward control vanes and longer stabilizer bars make the machine more forgiving of pilot error, and a central repulsor pod on the forward frame extension gives the pilot a greater chance of regaining control if the swoop begins to tumble. Intakes at the front of the engine force air through the turbothrusters, generating increased thrust, while directional thrust nozzles at the rear of the swoop allow increased fine maneuvering. However, this swoop is still tricky for even the most experienced pilot.

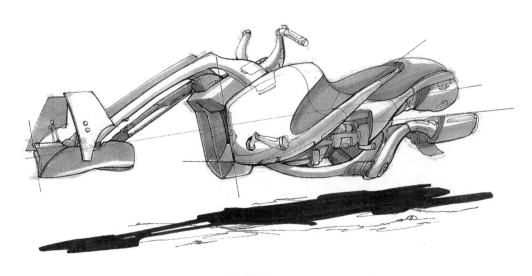

Top View

Side View

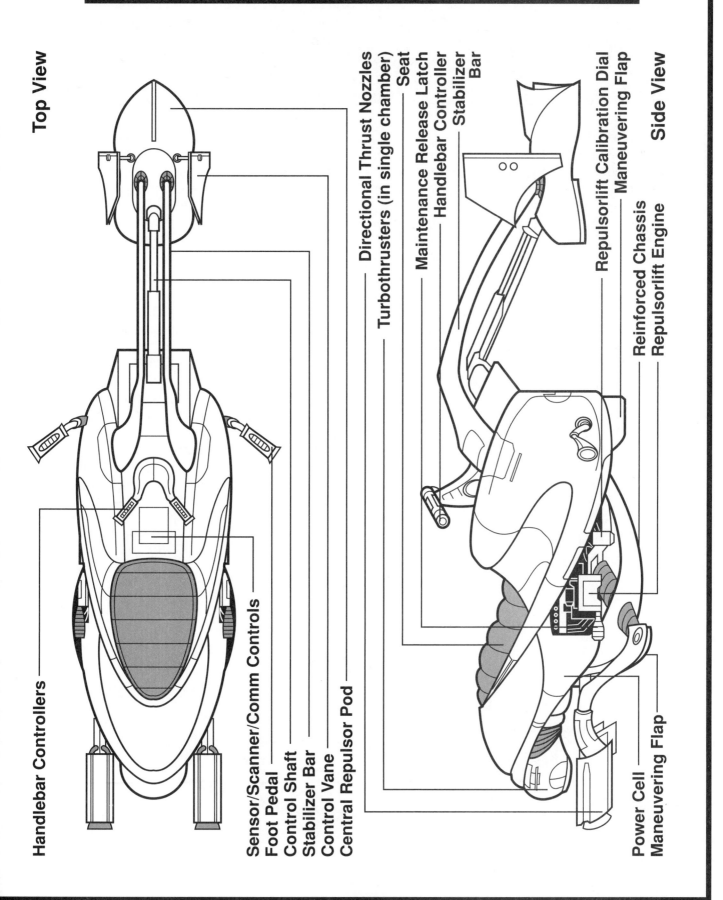

Handlebar Controllers

Sensor/Scanner/Comm Controls
Foot Pedal
Control Shaft
Stabilizer Bar
Control Vane
Central Repulsor Pod

Directional Thrust Nozzles
Turbothrusters (in single chamber)
Seat
Maintenance Release Latch
Handlebar Controller
Stabilizer Bar

Repulsorlift Calibration Dial
Maneuvering Flap

Reinforced Chassis
Repulsorlift Engine

Power Cell
Maneuvering Flap

TAFANDA BAY

ITHORIAN HERD SHIP

The Grand Herd Ship *Tafanda Bay* is an Ithorian vessel which soars above the jungles of lovely Ithor. The majestic eco-city is a popular destination for tourists and is a center of commerce in the Lesser Plooriod Cluster. Wedge Antilles and alien scientist Qui Xux ventured there when the New Republic tried to hide Qui from the forces of the Empire.

Ithorian herd ships are hundreds of meters tall and hover just above the surface of the planet. The Ithorians, often called "Hammerheads," consider the jungles sacred and will not allow themselves—or others—to set foot in them. The Ithorians have lived on these herd ships for thousands of years and point to them as examples of ways to integrate technology and nature harmoniously.

Unlike the gleaming towers preferred by humans, the *Tafanda Bay*'s exterior is covered by mosses, flowers, and immense trees. The *Tafanda Bay* has landing platforms for incoming starships and speeders, while dozens of gigantic repulsorlift engines propel it slowly over the jungle landscape.

The ship's interior environments reproduce virtually every terrain known to Ithor as well as many found on other worlds. The ship has several large halls where visitors can purchase goods from the shrewd Ithorian traders. A popular area to visit is the Great Atrium: it is nearly a kilometer across, with moss-covered walls leading to the open air above. Other popular destinations include the upper and lower observation decks, which offer stunning views of the jungle and Ithor's brilliant violet night sky. Adventurous visitors are allowed to rent speeders for guided sight-seeing tours above the jungle; because of Wedge's special standing with the New Republic government, he and Qui Xux were allowed to take a speeder unescorted.

Other Ithorian herds have built spacegoing herd ships such as the famed trading vessel *Bazaar*, which travels the starlanes of the galaxy. These traveling herd ships are self-contained communities with indoor environments populated by wild animals.

The *Tafanda Bay* and its keeper, Momaw Nadon, have had a troubled history. Imperial warships arrived in orbit around Ithor during the height of the Empire's power, and the Imperials demanded the cooperation of the Ithorian people. Momaw Nadon resisted, but the Imperial commander threatened to raze Ithor's jungles. When Momaw gave the Imperials the agricultural secrets they demanded, the Ithorian people banished him from their world. But when the Ithorians later joined the Rebel Alliance, Nadon was reinstated as herd leader aboard the *Tafanda Bay*.

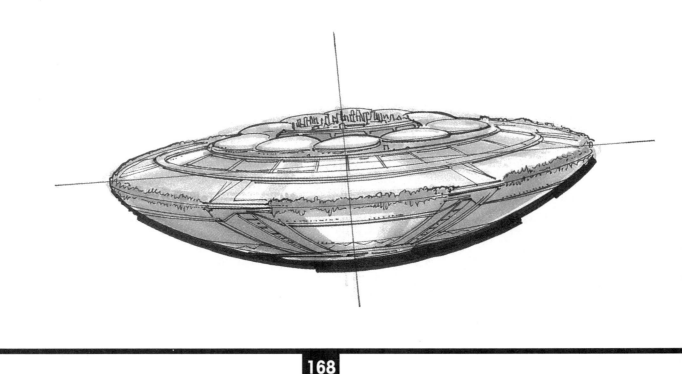

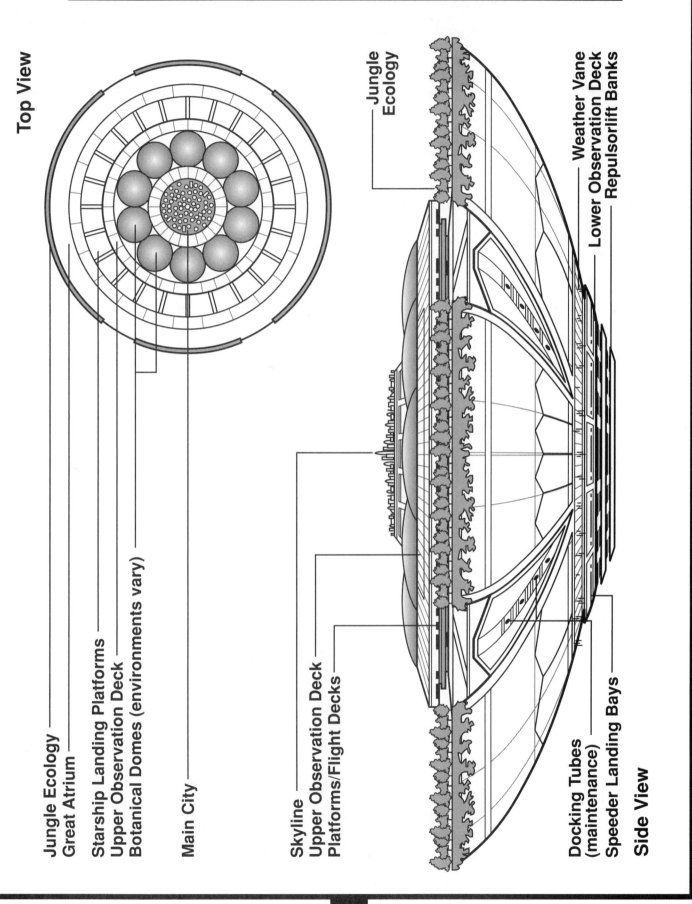

Top View

Jungle Ecology
Great Atrium

Starship Landing Platforms
Upper Observation Deck
Botanical Domes (environments vary)

Main City

Skyline
Upper Observation Deck
Platforms/Flight Decks

Jungle Ecology

Weather Vane
Lower Observation Deck
Repulsorlift Banks

Docking Tubes (maintenance)
Speeder Landing Bays

Side View

TANK DROID

ARAKYD XR-85 TANK DROID

During the galactic civil war, there has been a constant demand for new weapons. The Arakyd XR-85 tank droid is just one such weapon; the first prototypes were built before Grand Admiral Thrawn's campaign against the New Republic, but the experimental droid interface technology proved too expensive for mass production.

While Thrawn concentrated on the brilliant use of existing technology, Imperial designers went back to work and refined the XR-85. A year later, when the Empire managed to send the New Republic scurrying from Coruscant, tank droid technology had improved to the point of being practical for large-scale combat operations. Arakyd, famed for its Viper probots, was given the contract to manufacture XR-85 tank droids, and they played an important role in the battle for Imperial City.

The XR-85 was originally designed to deal with the widespread civil unrest that plagued Imperial worlds. The Empire's first priority was the offensive against the New Republic, and the best troops and vehicles were sent to the front lines. Imperial governors got the untested XR-85 units and discovered that they were brutally effective—so Imperial command promptly called them to the front lines.

The XR-85 tank droid is a fully automated combat machine driven by a droid brain. It is a tracked vehicle approximately thirty-two meters long and over thirty meters tall, making it double the size of an Imperial AT-AT walker.

The drive system gives the tank incredible traction, and internal seals allow it to travel in water up to fifteen meters deep. The XR-85 has a top speed of seventy kilometers per hour but is virtually unstoppable. It is particularly useful in urban assault operations, where independent treads allow turns in tight spots, and armor plating lets it plow through anything.

The droid's main weapon is a front-firing heavy particle cannon. It has an effective range of five kilometers and can level troop bunkers with a single shot. Backing up the particle cannon are a pair of front-firing turbolasers, which are typically used on secondary targets such as repulsor tanks or walkers. For dealing with light speeders and enemy troops, there are four twin heavy repeating blasters—two forward-mounted and two rear-mounted. The final weapon is a rear-mounted Golon Arms DF 0.9 antipersonnel cannon. Each weapon is fed by a separate power generator for virtually unlimited firepower.

The Arakyd tank droid is the most successful of the many droid-controlled combat vehicles currently in production. It uses a pirated Industrial Automaton R7 droid brain matrix, making it one of the few droids with sophisticated intuition programming. While combat performance consistently shows that there is no substitute for an organic pilot, these tank droids are far better at combat than are earlier generations of similar machines.

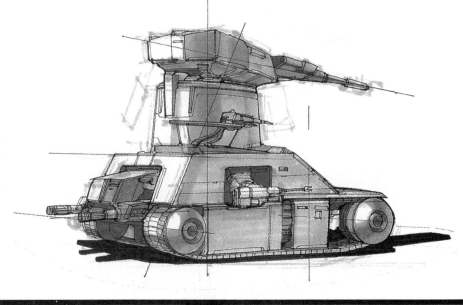

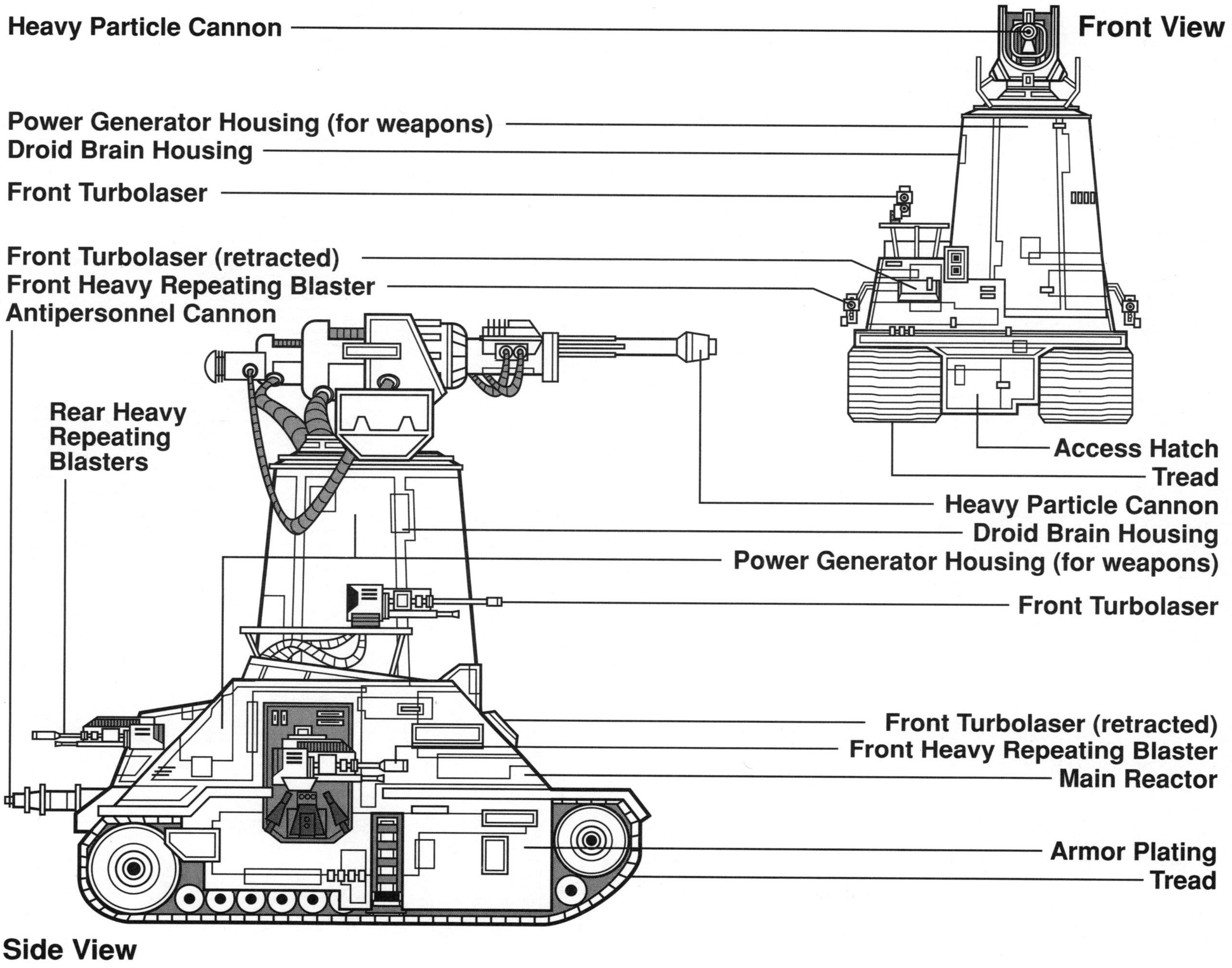

Front View

Heavy Particle Cannon

Power Generator Housing (for weapons)
Droid Brain Housing

Front Turbolaser

Front Turbolaser (retracted)
Front Heavy Repeating Blaster
Antipersonnel Cannon

Rear Heavy
Repeating
Blasters

Access Hatch
Tread

Heavy Particle Cannon
Droid Brain Housing

Power Generator Housing (for weapons)

Front Turbolaser

Front Turbolaser (retracted)
Front Heavy Repeating Blaster
Main Reactor

Armor Plating
Tread

Side View

TIE BOMBER

SIENAR FLEET SYSTEMS TIE BOMBER

The TIE bomber was the Empire's prime assault bomber. While slower and less maneuverable than standard starfighters, these bombers provided excellent "surgical strike" potential against ground and deep-space targets.

TIE bombers have double pods and elongated solar panels. The starboard pod holds the pilot's compartment (with ejection seat) as well as flight computers, communications, and life support. The port pod contains the forward and main ordnance bays as well as the targeting and delivery systems. The ship is powered by Sienar Fleet Systems P-s4 twin ion engines mounted as a single unit between the two pods.

The TIE bomber's weaponry includes high-yield proton bombs, guided concussion missiles, orbital mines, and free-falling thermal detonators. Depending on the mission configuration, TIE bombers can carry eight concussion missiles or four proton torpedoes in the forward ordnance bay. The main ordnance bay can carry eight more concussion missiles, four additional proton torpedoes, eight proton bombs, six orbital mines, or sixty-four thermal detonators. Two front-firing laser cannons provide protection from enemy ships.

The TIE bomber's targeting computers are mounted below the forward ordnance pod. Bombs are fed through the bombing chute behind the targeting computers, while missiles are launched through the missile port at the front of the port pod.

For space duty, the TIE bomber was used to deliver heavy ordnance against Rebel capital ships. Traditionally,

TIE fighters first softened up the target. Then the TIE bomber, in conjunction with assault gunboats and Skipray blastboats, used its precise targeting computers to disable vital areas such as the shield generators or engines. With the target crippled and unable to protect itself, Imperial boarding parties took control of the vessel and captured Rebel troops for interrogation.

TIE bombers were used to assault space stations and stardocks and to mine planetary orbits. TIE bombers normally had TIE fighters for protective escorts in hotly contested combat zones. The TIE bomber packed a high payload for its small size and could often slip through enemy defenses, which tended to be geared toward detecting capital ships. TIE bombers are preferable to large capital ships because of their pinpoint targeting—capital ship turbolasers are far less precise.

TIE bombers are also exceptional for ground bombing missions. Their targeting computers are precise enough to level specific buildings while leaving adjacent areas unscathed. They are maneuverable and fast enough for low-altitude bombing runs in cramped situations, such as canyons and cities.

A Star Destroyer typically carried one squadron of twelve TIE bombers. A rare, hollow-hulled version of the TIE bomber could carry small boarding parties when larger ships such as the *Gamma*-class assault shuttle were not appropriate to the task. Before the Emperor's death, the Empire began developing a more advanced bomber prototype, which eventually evolved into the Scimitar assault bomber.

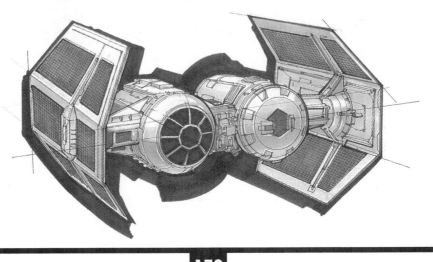

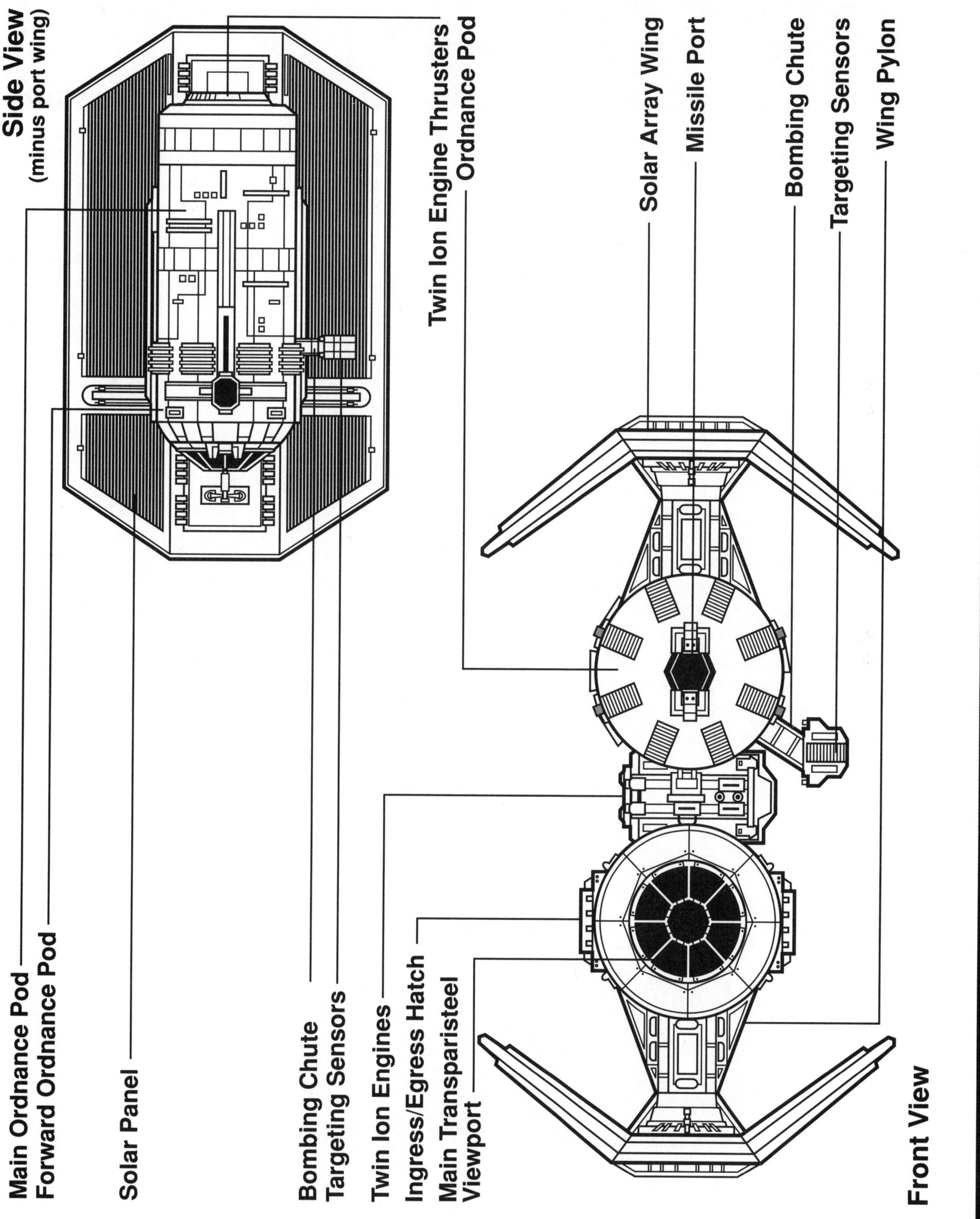

Side View
(minus port wing)

Twin Ion Engine Thrusters
Ordnance Pod

Solar Array Wing
Missile Port

Bombing Chute
Targeting Sensors
Wing Pylon

Main Ordnance Pod
Forward Ordnance Pod

Solar Panel

Bombing Chute
Targeting Sensors

Twin Ion Engines
Ingress/Egress Hatch
Main Transparisteel
Viewport

Front View

TIE CRAWLER

SANTHE/SIENAR TECHNOLOGIES CENTURY TANK

The century tank is a cheap mass-produced ground combat vehicle that became popular during the Imperial resurgence after the death of Grand Admiral Thrawn and the campaign to recapture the Imperial capital of Coruscant. While the proper name of the vehicle is the "century tank," Imperial soldiers took to calling the vehicle the TIE tank (or TIE crawler) because of the familiar command pod taken from the TIE fighter.

The vehicle is a simple combat machine with modular components and simple controls. It is the perfect light assault vehicle, with a light drive system and respectable weapons. It requires only a single crewman, who handles both piloting and gunnery.

The TIE tank has the same central pod used in the standard TIE fighter. It is manufactured by Santhe/Sienar Technologies, a sister corporation to Sienar Fleet Systems, manufacturers of the TIE fighter. The use of this pod, while awkward for old-line Imperial soldiers, cut the cost of the tank by thousands of credits per unit.

The twin Santhe SSct power generators are attached to each side of the pod and drive the tread wheels. The TIE tank has a top speed of only ninety kilometers per hour, but drive components are common and cheap. The drive sys-

tem is simple enough that many pilots can fix the tank themselves if it is damaged in the field, and it is not unusual to see damaged TIE tanks scavenged for parts.

The TIE tank can navigate most terrain and is substantially cheaper than comparable repulsorlift craft. The weapons are powered by a single power generator mounted in the rear of the command pod, and they include two medium blaster cannons that are forward-firing, while a retractable light turbolaser is mounted in the bottom of the command pod and can fire in any direction. The TIE tank has light armor plating on all surfaces, but the drive system and tread wheels are easily damaged by enemy fire.

Personnel enter through a top hatch. The pilot is strapped into an automatically adjusting grav-couch (slightly modified from the standard TIE fighter). Foot controls adjust the angle of steering and the speed, while the hand controls are tied into the weapons systems and the targeting computer. The TIE tank uses the familiar N-s6 fire-control module for weapon targeting and utilizes many of the same interfaces as the standard TIE fighter, requiring some retraining for ground vehicle troops but allowing Imperial commanders to place TIE fighter cadet washouts into the tanks.

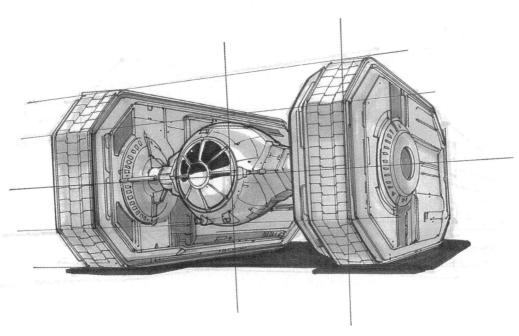

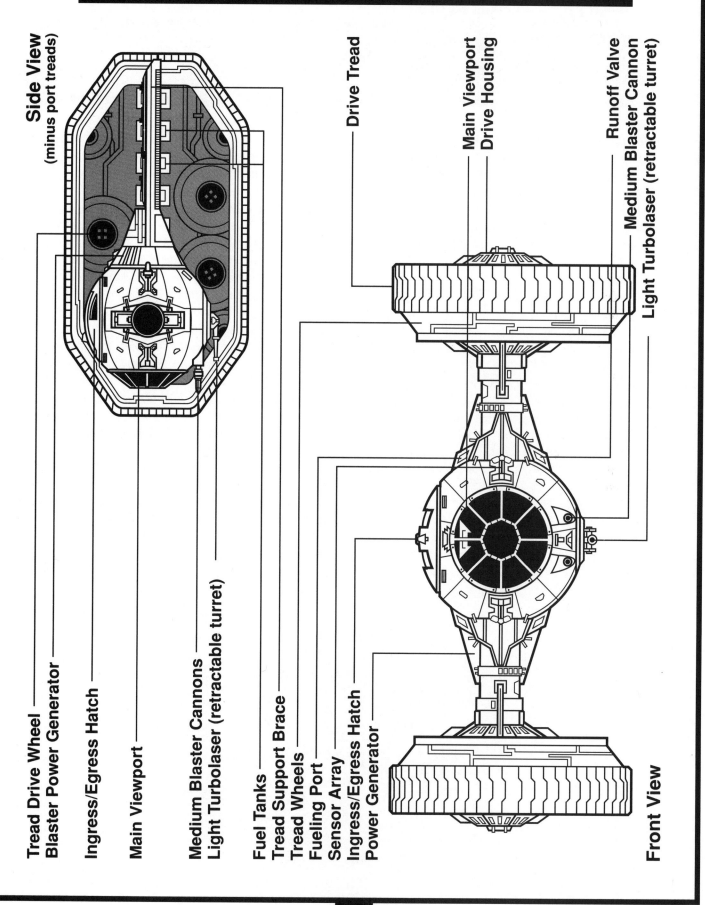

Side View
(minus port treads)

Drive Tread

Main Viewport
Drive Housing

Runoff Valve
Medium Blaster Cannon
Light Turbolaser (retractable turret)

Tread Drive Wheel
Blaster Power Generator

Ingress/Egress Hatch

Main Viewport

Medium Blaster Cannons
Light Turbolaser (retractable turret)

Fuel Tanks
Tread Support Brace
Tread Wheels
Fueling Port
Sensor Array
Ingress/Egress Hatch
Power Generator

Front View

TIE DEFENDER

Sienar Fleet Systems TIE Defender

The TIE defender was a prototype Imperial fighter that was developed shortly before the Battle of Endor. After initial testing, which was believed to be personally supervised by *top* Imperial Navy commanders, the TIE defender was deployed to a small number of elite TIE wings. Only a few key personnel in Navy command knew that the ship was used to defeat rogue Imperial Admiral Zaarin, who had planned to depose Emperor Palpatine.

The vessel represented a radical departure from conventional TIE designs and featured three sets of solar collection panels mounted at equilateral points around the fighter's cockpit. The TIE defender, while publicly touted as a "logical advance" for Imperial fighter design, was actually a quiet admission that the Alliance's fighter tactics had been successful. Following specific Navy directives, Sienar Fleet Systems developed a ship that was fast, heavily armed, and equipped with a hyperdrive—in other words, a ship just like the Alliance's fighters. At over 300,000 credits per unit, it was more than five times as expensive as a standard TIE/ln fighter.

The TIE defender's numerous weapons systems allow it to successfully engage multiple enemy fighters, while the hyperdrive permits the ship to operate independently of support carriers, giving the ship flexibility that was unmatched by any other Imperial starfighter. Standard Imperial doctrine called for the ships to be deployed in flights of four, although Imperial commanders took advantage of the ship's superior design by customizing mission forces on a case-by-case basis.

The TIE defender is one of the fastest production fighters ever used by the Empire: it's nearly 40 percent faster at sublight than the standard TIE/ln. The TIE defender still follows the basic twin ion engine model, but it uses the newer P-sz9.7 engines to generate added speed. Maneuverability has also been improved significantly through the addition of triple arrays of maneuvering jets on the triwing assembly, making the ship capable of dives and twists that would put even the remarkably agile TIE interceptor to shame.

The TIE defender features four laser cannons and two ion cannons, which can be fired independently for multiple targets or fire-linked for a concentrated assault. Rounding out the TIE defender's weaponry are two missile launchers which can be equipped with proton torpedoes *and* concussion missiles. For defense, the TIE Defender has a pair of Novaldex shield generators.

While the TIE defender is one of the most sophisticated fighters ever developed, its cost, combined with the upheaval that followed the death of the Emperor, prevented the fighter from ever coming into widespread use. A few of the ships were used by elite TIE fighter wings, but as a whole the TIE/ln and TIE interceptor continued to dominate the Imperial fleet even after Grand Admiral Thrawn reunited the Empire's forces against the New Republic.

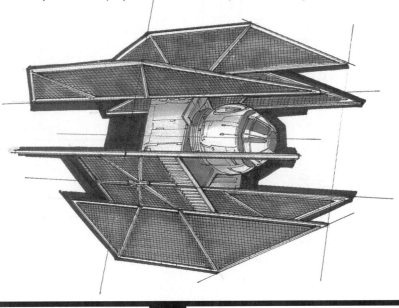

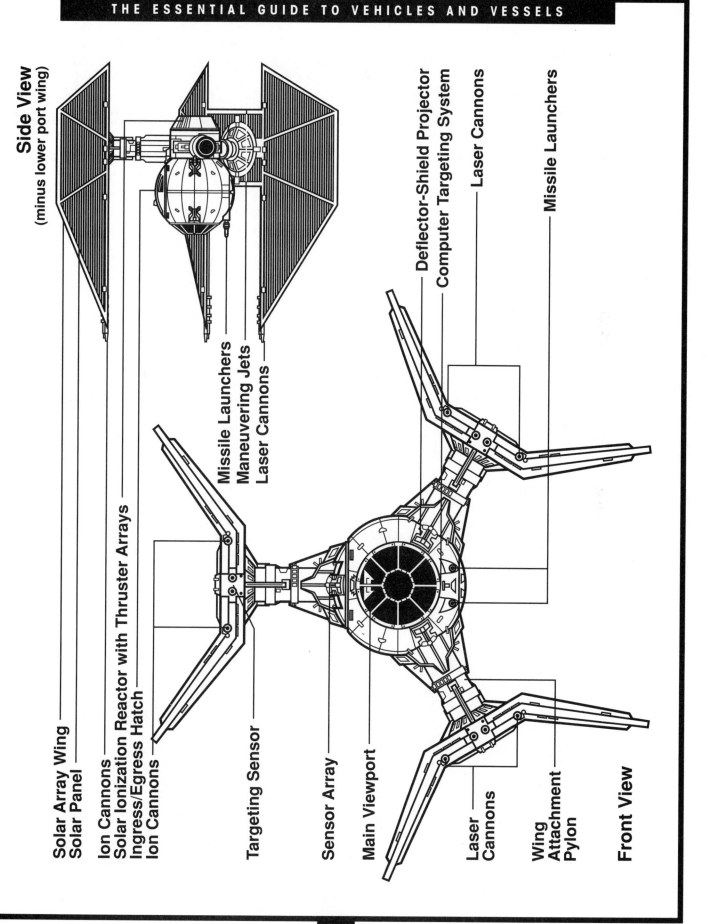

Side View
(minus lower port wing)

Solar Array Wing
Solar Panel
Ion Cannons
Solar Ionization Reactor with Thruster Arrays
Ingress/Egress Hatch
Ion Cannons

Missile Launchers
Maneuvering Jets
Laser Cannons

Targeting Sensor

Sensor Array

Main Viewport

Deflector-Shield Projector
Computer Targeting System

Laser Cannons

Missile Launchers

Laser
Cannons

Wing
Attachment
Pylon

Front View

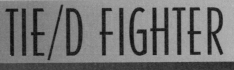

TIE/D FIGHTER

SIENAR FLEET SYSTEMS TIE/D FIGHTER

Imperial robotic starfighters called TIE/Ds (for TIE/droid unit) were introduced at the Battle of Calamari. These fully automated ships allowed Imperial admirals to field immense fleets of starfighters without sacrificing scores of qualified pilots.

TIE/Ds are essentially identical to the standard TIE/ln except for the onboard pilot station. The ship can be piloted by the droid brain or can be run from a remote piloting station aboard a capital ship.

The droid brains are advanced Cybot Galactica Ace-6 fighter units. Massing under ten kilograms, these brains are small enough to be installed into virtually any fighter with an appropriate computer interface. These droid brains have been equipped with advanced logic circuits that are supposed to allow them to achieve the same kind of performance as organic pilots, although actual combat results have shown that skilled living pilots are far superior to any pilot droid brain on the market.

The ship is built around the same standard TIE pod that is used in both the TIE/ln and the TIE interceptor. Like most Imperial designs, the TIE/D is modular, using weapon and drive components from both the TIE/ln and the later TIE interceptor. The ships have the same twin chin-mounted laser cannons found in TIE/lns, with an identical power generator and engine configuration.

TIE/Ds have rectangular solar array panels, with the extra energy being fed into the drive systems to improve maneuverability. Despite increased armor plating, the absence of a pilot gives the TIE/D virtually the same mass as the standard TIE/ln.

While each droid brain can easily be upgraded with new maneuvers and tactics, the brains are not as inventive and unpredictable as living pilots, and this gave the New Republic's pilots a decided advantage. However, the Empire's vast quantities of TIE/Ds at the Battle of Calamari overwhelmed the small number of New Republic fighters.

While initial tooling-up costs were high, the Emperor's strategists fully expected TIE/Ds to be inexpensive to produce once production lines got fully up to speed. However, most initial TIE/D factories were aboard the Empire's World Devastators, which were destroyed in the Battle of Calamari.

Engineers and programmers are constantly trying to improve the droid interface to give TIE/Ds better performance. Until they succeed, manufacturers will be more willing to devote their resources to traditional ships instead of to the robotic TIE/Ds.

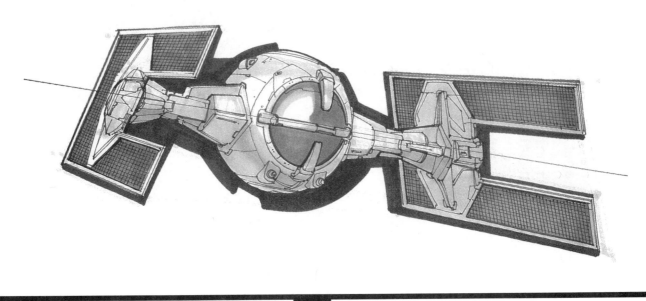

Side View
(minus port wing)

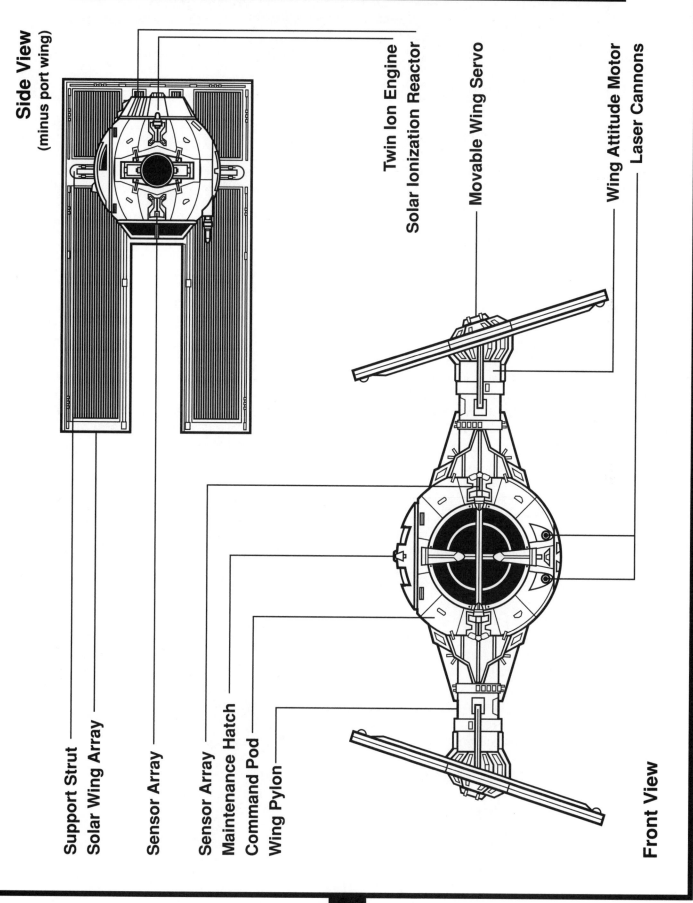

Support Strut

Solar Wing Array

Sensor Array

Sensor Array

Maintenance Hatch

Command Pod

Wing Pylon

Twin Ion Engine
Solar Ionization Reactor

Movable Wing Servo

Wing Attitude Motor

Laser Cannons

Front View

TIE FIGHTER

SIENAR FLEET SYSTEMS TIE/LN SPACE SUPERIORITY STARFIGHTER

Sienar Fleet Systems' TIE (Twin Ion Engine) fighter is the clearest symbol of the Imperial Navy's control of space. TIE fighters are present aboard even the smallest Imperial cruisers and are stationed at starports and garrison bases across the galaxy, an ever-present reminder of the Empire's might.

TIE fighters are short-range ships whose most distinguishing feature is the pair of dominant solar array wings mounted on either side of a small, spherical command pod. The TIE fighter presents a small target from the front and back, and its incredible maneuverability makes it difficult to hit in combat.

One TIE fighter may be vulnerable to attack and may be easily destroyed, but for every TIE that is defeated, thousands more will rise up. In battle, an Imperial cruiser can arrive near an enemy ship and launch all of its TIEs before Rebel gunners have a chance to respond. TIE fighters are used for planetary and cruiser defense as well as in assaults against Rebel, pirate, and alien vessels. A secondary TIE mission profile involves escorting heavily armed TIE bombers used in attacking planetary installations.

TIE fighters have only sublight drives. This saves weight and increases speed and maneuverability, but it makes TIEs dependent on a home base, such as a nearby planet or an Imperial cruiser. TIEs carry only two days' worth of supplies under optimal conditions; in actual combat, TIEs often must refuel after the first few hours.

The TIEs maneuverability and speed come at great practical cost to the pilot inside. TIE fighters have no shields, no secondary weapon or drive systems, minuscule fuel supplies, and no onboard life support system: pilots must wear fully sealed flight suits with self-contained atmosphere converters. By eliminating all these systems, the TIE saves mass and makes room for large power generators, engines, and weapons inside the compact hull.

With thousands of new TIE ships being manufactured each year and new pilots regularly graduating from Imperial military academies, casualties are deemed inconsequential as long as military objectives are achieved. Some military strategists claim that the TIE is *too* responsive to piloting adjustments: novice pilots may

attempt an advanced maneuver only to send the ship careening.

The pilot is strapped into a simple high-gee shock couch and is protected by crash webbing and a repulsorlift antigravity field. The pilot's feet slip into control yokes: pressing or pulling on the yokes controls speed and maneuvering. The hand-control yoke affects precise maneuvering, targeting, navigation, and fire control. Auxiliary speed and maneuver controls are also located in the hand-control yoke, but attempting both flight and fire control through the hand-control unit is very difficult.

The TIE has a pair of forward-mounted, fire-linked laser cannons. The laser generators are located in the undercarriage of the main pod and feed off the power generators and batteries. The TIE fighter draws much of its energy from solar radiation absorbed by the array wings.

The "common" TIE fighter is the TIE/ln, a successor to the earlier T.I.E. and TIE models, built by the company now called Sienar Fleet Systems.

Front View

Rear View

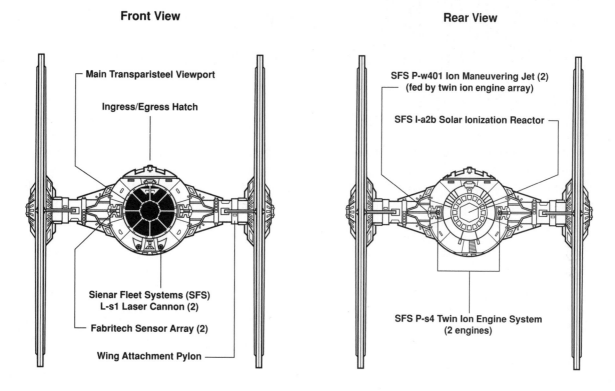

Main Transparisteel Viewport

Ingress/Egress Hatch

Sienar Fleet Systems (SFS)
L-s1 Laser Cannon (2)

Fabritech Sensor Array (2)

Wing Attachment Pylon

SFS P-w401 Ion Maneuvering Jet (2)
(fed by twin ion engine array)

SFS I-a2b Solar Ionization Reactor

SFS P-s4 Twin Ion Engine System
(2 engines)

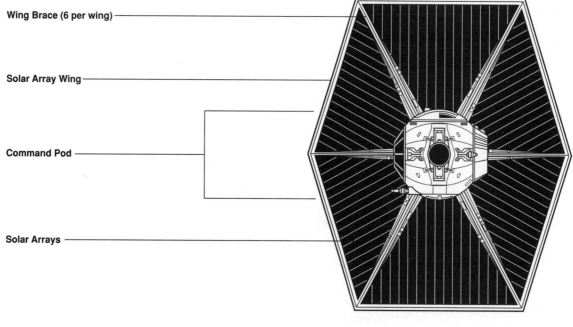

Wing Brace (6 per wing)

Solar Array Wing

Command Pod

Solar Arrays

Side View (minus port wing)

TIE INTERCEPTOR

SIENAR FLEET SYSTEMS TIE INTERCEPTOR

The TIE interceptor is the direct result of advancements developed for Darth Vader's TIE Advanced x1 Prototype. It is faster, more maneuverable, and far more lethal than the standard TIE/ln fighter.

This interceptor uses the standard TIE cockpit, drive pod, and wing braces. The solar collector panels have been elongated and bent, providing extra power while not limiting the pilot's field of vision. The solar panels appear to be "dagger-shaped," making the interceptor far more intimidating while giving it a smaller profile, making it harder for opposing gunners to target. The TIE interceptor has more powerful drives than does the TIE/ln and is almost as fast as the Alliance's A-wing fighter; it is faster than any other fighter in production.

The TIE interceptor uses an advanced type of ion-stream projector that allows pilots to execute tight turns and rolls. Twin-port deflectors can be manipulated individually for fine control and counterbalancing, making the TIE interceptor a superior choice for dogfights. With a skilled pilot behind the controls, the TIE interceptor can literally fly circles around X-wing starfighters.

For weaponry, the interceptor has four laser cannons, one at the end of each solar panel. Advanced targeting software gives the pilot greater fire accuracy even during complex maneuvers. While the interceptor does not have a pair of laser cannons below the pilot's compartment, the cannon hardpoint is still in place and additional cannons could be mounted there if technicians could find the room for additional power generators.

Like other TIE fighters, the TIE interceptor has little armor plating and no shield generators, and it is easily destroyed by enemy fire. Interceptor pilots rely on the ship's maneuverability and on superiority of numbers to survive engagements with better armed and armored fighters.

Every effort has been made to save weight on the TIE interceptor. There is no life support system, so pilots must still use fully sealed flight suits. The TIE interceptor has no hyperdrives and requires a large capital ship to serve as a base of operations. TIE interceptors are primarily deployed with Star Destroyers and at key star bases, such as the starship yards in Kuat and Fondor. Lesser capital ships, such as Victory Star Destroyers and Dreadnaughts, and more remote bases must make do with the older TIE/ln fighters.

The Empire intended the TIE interceptor to eventually replace the TIE/ln, but by the death of the Emperor only about 20 percent of the Imperial fighters in use were interceptors. As Grand Admiral Thrawn initiated his bid for power, he began arming TIE interceptors with shields, knowing that the Empire could no longer consider these exceptional ships to be disposable.

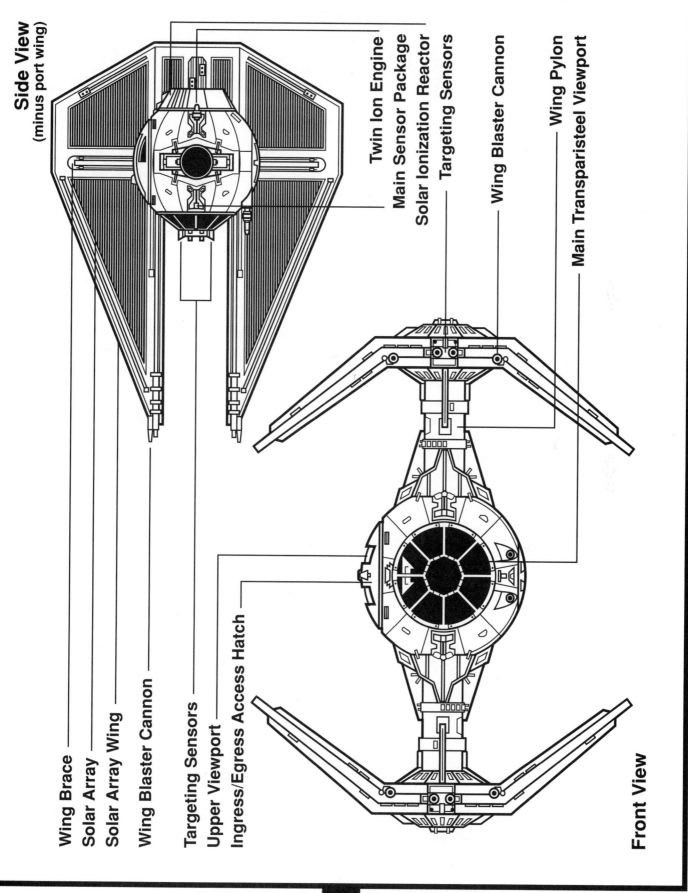

Side View
(minus port wing)

Twin Ion Engine

Main Sensor Package

Solar Ionization Reactor

Targeting Sensors

Wing Blaster Cannon

Wing Pylon

Main Transparisteel Viewport

Wing Brace

Solar Array

Solar Array Wing

Wing Blaster Cannon

Targeting Sensors

Upper Viewport

Ingress/Egress Access Hatch

Front View

TWIN POD CLOUD CAR

BESPIN MOTORS STORM IV TWIN POD CLOUD CAR

The famous cloud cars of Bespin are upper-atmosphere craft that are in common use across the galaxy. Cloud cars are a step up from traditional airspeeders, with top speeds of around 1,500 kilometers per hour and a flight ceiling that almost reaches low orbit. They are often used for patrol and reconnaissance duty, but civilians enjoy using them as pleasure craft for sight-seeing and travel.

Cloud cars are closer to starships than they are to airspeeders: ion engines provide their main propulsion, while repulsorlift drives merely enhance maneuvering. Cloud cars also have handling jets, flaps, control vanes, and rudders for intricate maneuvers. These vehicles require no life support system, although the pods are pressurized for high-altitude flight.

There are many models of cloud cars, ranging from small one- and two-passenger vehicles to immense pleasure craft and cargo barges. They can be used as personal transport, air taxis, or military patrol ships. They are ideal for planetary defense forces because they are tough enough to enter combat, but they are much cheaper than starfighters. While civilian models are a little on the fragile side, military cloud cars are quite sturdy. Many local police forces use cloud cars for patrols of starports and dense urban areas.

The largest cloud car manufacturer is Bespin Motors, which is based in the heart of Cloud City. Cloud City's Wing Guard pilots use Storm IV twin-pod cloud cars for patrol duty around the majestic floating city. The vehicles allow them to reach any exterior portion of the city quickly. The pilot sits in the port pod while the gunner handles the starboard pod. These cloud cars have been fitted with a blaster cannon on the outside of each pod. The single scaled-down Quadex Kyromaster ion engine, mounted on a connecting boom, is located midway between the two pods and is open to the air for cooling purposes.

The Wing Guard handles customs and entry clearances for Cloud City, ensuring that smugglers, Imperial informants, and other undesirables are turned away before they can cause trouble. For a modest "deal-making" fee, cloud car pilots can quietly arrange black market Tibanna gas deals, but only with the approval of the Baron Administrator.

The Storm IV is also particularly popular for military duty, both because it is sturdy and because modifications are a snap. The hull has several clearly indicated fixture points for extra armor plating, while the computer system is specifically designed to accept new weapons. The only drawback is the small Incom Corporation Tx-2 power generator, which has trouble powering the light laser cannons, let alone anything with some punch. Fortunately, the sensor suites in the forward section of each pod are bulky. If they are replaced with miniaturized Fabritech units, there is more than enough room for an additional power generator to supply each weapon.

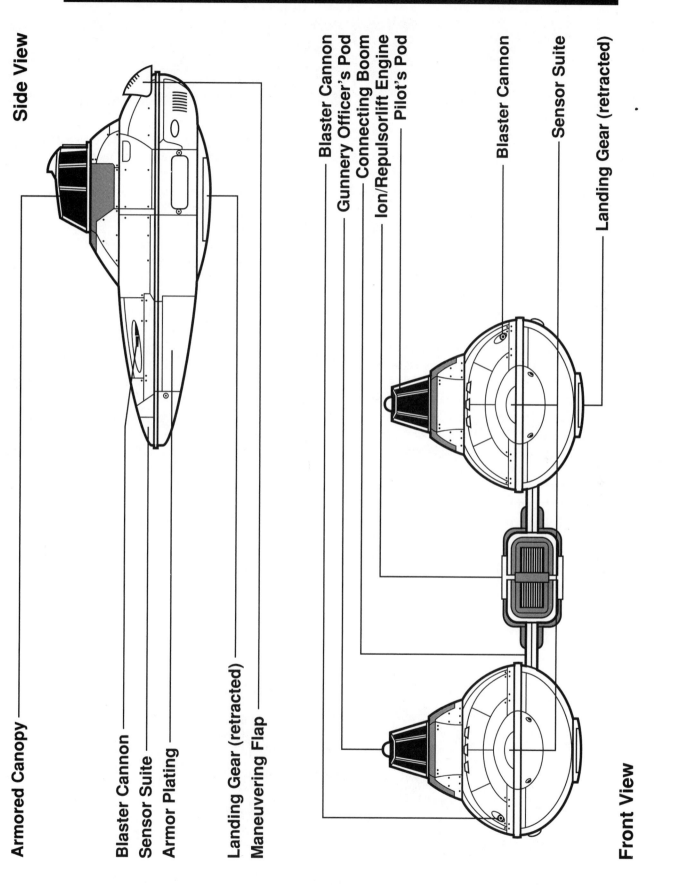

Side View

Armored Canopy

Blaster Cannon
Sensor Suite
Armor Plating

Landing Gear (retracted)
Maneuvering Flap

Blaster Cannon
Gunnery Officer's Pod
Connecting Boom
Ion/Repulsorlift Engine
Pilot's Pod

Blaster Cannon

Sensor Suite

Landing Gear (retracted)

Front View

STAR.WARS

V-WING AIRSPEEDER

SLAYN & KORPIL V-WING AIRSPEEDER

The New Republic's V-wing airspeeder fills the need for a true atmospheric fighter craft. These airspeeders played an important role in the New Republic's defense of the planet Mon Calamari. The airspeeder and transport system were devised by the Verpine Slayn and Korpil colonies, which designed the wildly successful B-wing starfighter. Since its introduction into the New Republic Navy, the V-wing has been successful in over a dozen battles.

V-wings are light-combat airspeeders, as fast as standard Rebel combat airspeeders, such as the famed T-47 "snowspeeder," but with a much higher flight ceiling, allowing a maximum altitude of one hundred kilometers. Using their normal ion afterburners and repulsorlift engines, they can reach 1,000 kilometers per hour. Then the speeder's streamlined surface forces air into a Chab-Ylwoum scramjet booster, which boosts the V-wing to a speed of 1,400 kilometers per hour. However, the scramjet is not practical for combat maneuvers, and a pilot attempting sudden maneuvers is more likely to rip his speeder apart than to pull off a turn. Rather, his best bet is to aim the speeder for clear sky, engage the scramjet, and hold on as his speeder outruns slower enemy craft.

The V-wing's only weapon is a double laser cannon with an effective range of two kilometers. The laser cannon is adequate for air combat but not powerful enough to damage heavily armored vehicles. Like most combat airspeeders, the V-wing may be fast and maneuverable, but it is vulnerable to fire from other speeders or walkers. The pilot has minimal protection, and pilot survivability is very low despite an ejection system: normally the pilot is killed in the first blast.

V-wings can be deployed to planetary bases or capital starships. They typically are used for combat against incoming enemy fighters or in surprise raids: the scramjet booster is exceptionally useful for a sudden assault. V-wings also are used to support New Republic artillery and ground troops. In the Battle of Calamari, V-wings proved to be devastating against the Empire's new TIE/D fighters and the water-based amphibions.

When aboard starships, they are brought into battle by Slayn & Korpil speeder transports, which can carry four or six V-wings. The transports are unarmed and require escort by starfighters in heavy-combat zones. The V-wings are carried outside the transport and are accessed through retractable docking tubes. Once in the upper atmosphere, the pilots climb down and strap into their airspeeders. After releasing the V-wings, the speeder transport can immediately return to the base ship to take on more V-wings. This makes the V-wing an economical speeder, allowing dozens of them to be deployed from space at a fraction of the cost of normal starfighters.

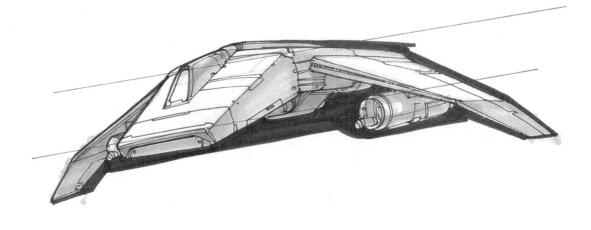

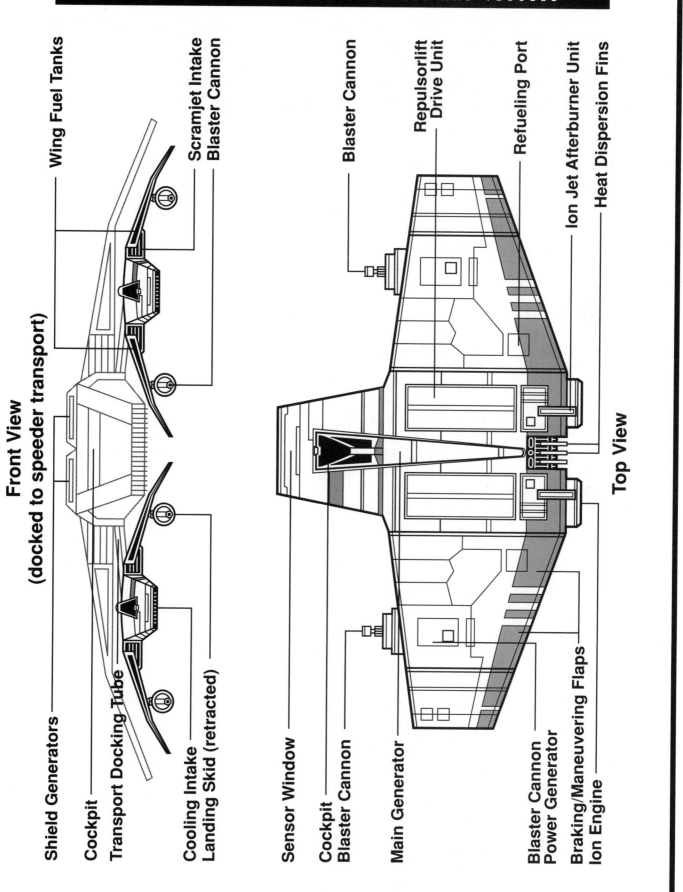

Front View
(docked to speeder transport)

Shield Generators

Cockpit

Transport Docking Tube

Cooling Intake

Landing Skid (retracted)

Wing Fuel Tanks

Scramjet Intake

Blaster Cannon

Sensor Window

Cockpit

Blaster Cannon

Main Generator

Blaster Cannon

Power Generator

Braking/Maneuvering Flaps

Ion Engine

Blaster Cannon

Repulsorlift

Drive Unit

Refueling Port

Ion Jet Afterburner Unit

Heat Dispersion Fins

Top View

VICTORY STAR DESTROYER

RENDILI STARDRIVE *VICTORY*-CLASS STAR DESTROYER

The Victory Star Destroyer is an older star cruiser that proved to be an important part of the Imperial space fleet even though it was over three decades old. When first launched, the *Victory*-class was considered the ultimate combat starship design, and even as the Empire waned it was overshadowed only by the Imperial Star Destroyer. The Victory was designed near the end of the Clone Wars, and these ships formed the core of the space fleet after that turbulent era.

Victory Star Destroyers are nine hundred meters long, carrying a crew of over 5,000 beings. Standard Imperial armament for a Victory Star Destroyer included ten quad turbolasers, forty double turbolasers, eighty concussion-missile launchers, and ten tractor-beam projectors. Victory Star Destroyers have sufficient space to carry two squadrons of TIE fighters, for a total of twenty-four support fighters. The Victory can carry 2,000 ground troops as well as planetary drop ships, troop transports, and a wide range of planetary assault vehicles, including AT-AT walkers, juggernauts, and Ubrikkian HAVr A9 Floating Fortresses.

As more Imperial Star Destroyers were built, Victory Star Destroyers found themselves reassigned to planetary defense roles or moved into reserve fleets deep in the Core. A number of Victory Star Destroyers were decommissioned and sold off to planetary defense forces. The Corporate Sector Authority purchased 250 of these ships.

Victory Star Destroyers were designed with three missions in mind: planetary defense, planetary assault and ground-troop support, and ship-to-ship combat. The ship is notably adequate for the first two missions, and its relatively fast hyperdrive (a Class One unit) allows it to reach galactic trouble spots in half the time needed by Imperial Star Destroyers.

The Victory's biggest weakness is found in ship-to-ship combat. The Victory's LF9 ion engines cannot produce sufficient speed for deep-space actions, and most modern combat starships can simply outrun them. To achieve success, Victory captains must first establish a superior position, for example, by pinning enemy ships in a planetary gravity well so they cannot escape into hyperspace. Victories can best surmount their shortcomings if they are assigned Interdictor cruisers, escort frigates, or light cruisers for support.

The usefulness of Victory Star Destroyers was renewed with the return of Grand Admiral Thrawn. The Imperial warlord found his forces lacking sufficient capital starships and began a systematic recommissioning and refitting of Victory Star Destroyers.

The Victory is an excellent ship for planetary actions because it is one of the largest capital starships that can operate effectively in a planetary atmosphere. While most modern combat starships are restricted to orbital bombardment, the Victory can bring the battle directly to an enemy on the surface, giving the ship both a tactical and a psychological advantage.

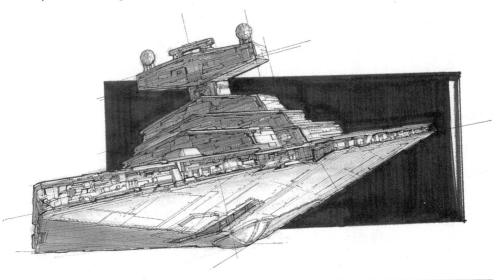

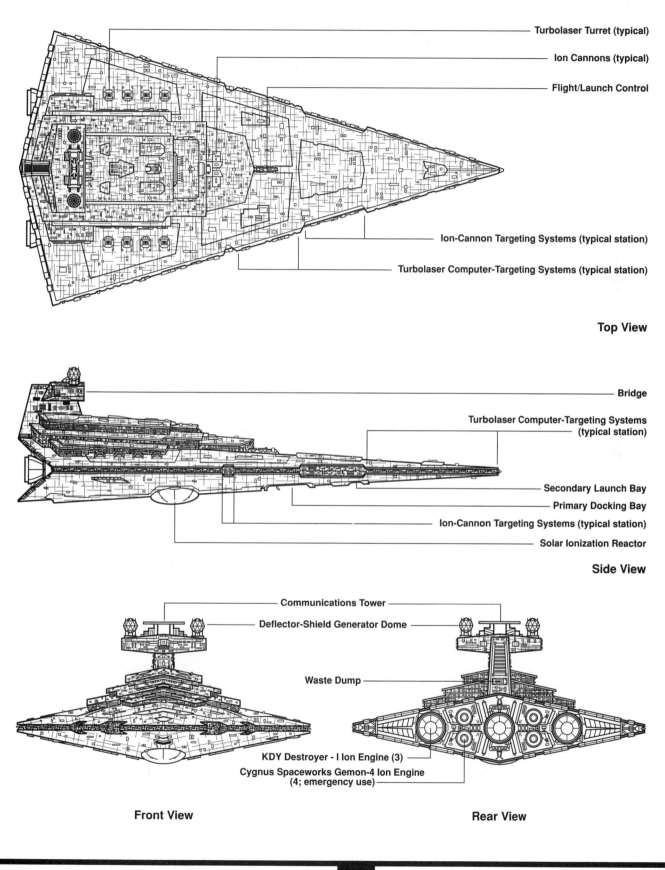

Turbolaser Turret (typical)

Ion Cannons (typical)

Flight/Launch Control

Ion-Cannon Targeting Systems (typical station)

Turbolaser Computer-Targeting Systems (typical station)

Top View

Bridge

Turbolaser Computer-Targeting Systems (typical station)

Secondary Launch Bay

Primary Docking Bay

Ion-Cannon Targeting Systems (typical station)

Solar Ionization Reactor

Side View

Communications Tower

Deflector-Shield Generator Dome

Waste Dump

KDY Destroyer - I Ion Engine (3)

Cygnus Spaceworks Gemon-4 Ion Engine (4; emergency use)

Front View   **Rear View**

WILD KARRDE

MODIFIED CORELLIAN ACTION VI TRANSPORT

The *Wild Karrde* is smuggling king Talon Karrde's personal freighter. A beat-up-looking Corellian Action VI bulk freighter, beneath the scarred hull plates hides a ship that serves as a mobile base of communications for perhaps the most well-informed person in the galactic fringe. Karrde maintains a large fleet, including at least two other bulk freighters, several Skipray blastboats, a Corellian corvette, and countless small freighters, but this particular ship is his favorite.

The Corellian Action VI is one of many common transport ships—lumbering, ungainly cargo craft. Stock Action VI transports are 125 meters long, with a cargo capacity of 90,000 metric tons—one bulk freighter can carry as much cargo as can nine hundred light freighters. These ships are slow, easily damaged in combat, and completely unarmed, so Imperial and New Republic cargo convoys often must deploy Nebulon-B escort frigates or corvettes to protect them.

The *Wild Karrde,* by contrast, is *far* from helpless. It has three turbolasers rated for combat against capital starships, with extra shielding and reinforced hull plating—the ship is as tough as an Imperial Lancer frigate.

Of course, the canny smuggler realizes that the best way to win a battle is to avoid it in the first place, and the *Wild Karrde* maintains an incredibly sophisticated sensor shroud system that rivals those found aboard Imperial spy ships. At long range, the *Wild Karrde*'s masking system can hide the ship from casual scans, while at close range this system makes the ship appear to be nothing more than an unarmed, helpless cargo vessel.

The transport's sublight and hyperdrive systems have been completely overhauled. At sublight, the ship is as fast as most Imperial warships, and while almost any fighter could overtake it, it is doubtful that any of them carries the weaponry needed to punch through the armor. The *Wild Karrde* has a Class One hyperdrive, making it as fast in hyperspace as most starfighters. Karrde's navigation computer is almost as detailed as those found aboard Imperial Star Destroyers.

The *Wild Karrde* contains a small docking bay, an air lock, and an extendable force tube for linking ships in deep space. Talon Karrde has converted much of the interior space: the rear holds have been fitted with a complete life support system, enabling the *Wild Karrde* to carry passengers or animals in addition to standard cargoes. The forward hold contains permanent living quarters and offices.

The sophisticated hyperradio communication array, which is normally found only on military or government vessels, allows Karrde to keep in touch with all of his smugglers and information gatherers, regardless of where his duties take him. With several basic medical bays, a droid bay, repulsorlift vehicles, and even a kennel for Karrde's vornskr guard animals, the *Wild Karrde* is prepared for almost any eventuality.

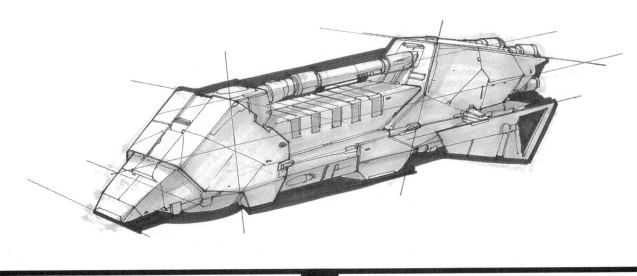

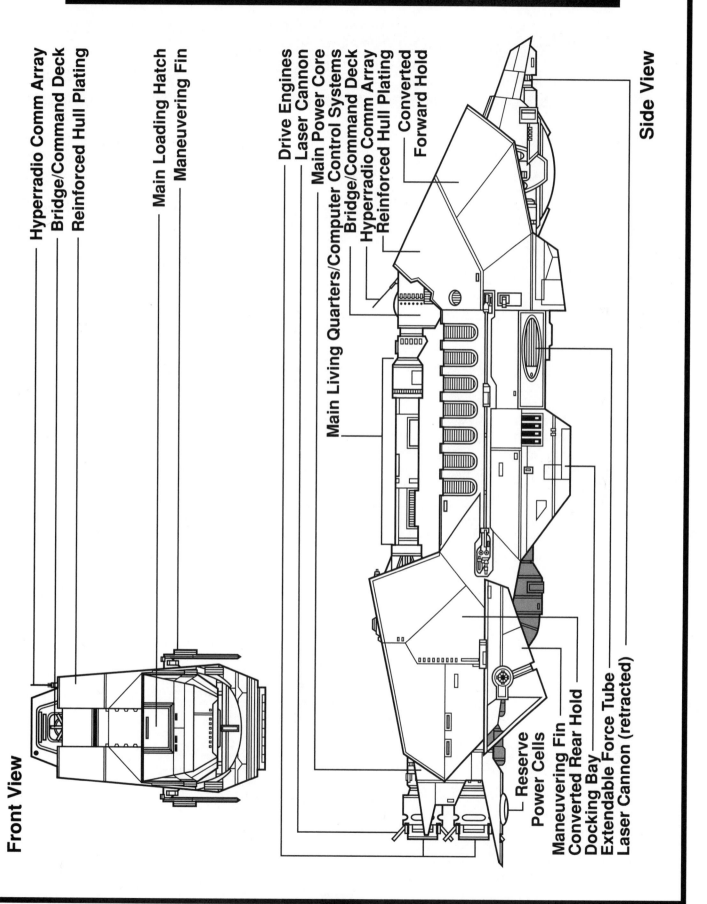

Front View

Side View

Hyperradio Comm Array
Bridge/Command Deck
Reinforced Hull Plating

Main Loading Hatch
Maneuvering Fin

Drive Engines
Laser Cannon
Main Power Core
Computer Control Systems
Bridge/Command Deck
Hyperradio Comm Array
Reinforced Hull Plating
Converted
Forward Hold

Main Living Quarters/

Reserve
Power Cells
Maneuvering Fin
Converted Rear Hold
Docking Bay
Extendable Force Tube
Laser Cannon (retracted)

WORLD DEVASTATORS

CUSTOM PLANETARY ASSAULT WEAPON

World Devastators were incredible planetary assault weapons that were used by the revived Emperor Palpatine when he attempted to retake control of the galaxy. World Devastators, like the Death Stars that preceded them, were more than weapons of mass destruction. They were symbols of the Empire's ability to utterly destroy any being or any world that would stand in its way.

World Devastators did not destroy planets. Instead, tractor beams drew a planet's surface into a molecular furnace, which broke the components down into raw materials. These materials were used in the World Devastator's droid-controlled factories. As the World Devastator chewed up a target world, that world's resources were used to create new weapons.

Designer Umak Leth was so proud of his creations that he called them "more lethal than the Death Star," though his claim proved to be a testament as much to his limitless ego as to the ships' abilities. Nonetheless, while World Devastators might take months to devour a world, the end result was profoundly terrifying.

World Devastators utilized hyperdrives and ion engines for transport in deep space, but their main role was to devour a planet's surface. A central droid brain controlled the onboard factories and stored plans for Imperial war vessels—a World Devastator could produce TIE fighters, battle cruisers, or even other World Devastators. During the Battle of Calamari, the World Devastators produced automated TIE/D fighters in large quantities.

The World Devastator "grew" by consuming planets and asteroids: some materials were devoted to building new additions and expansions for the Devastator itself. The Devastator's droid brain could create custom additions and alterations, so no two "mature" World Devastators were identical.

The *Silencer-7* was the largest World Devastator built and led the assault on Mon Calamari. At 3,200 meters long and 1,500 meters tall, it was larger than an Imperial Star Destroyer and had a crew of 25,000 beings. The *Silencer-7* could take on any target, with 125 heavy turbolasers, 200 blaster cannons, 80 proton missile tubes, 15 ion cannons, and 15 tractor-beam projectors.

The key to the defeat of the World Devastators was Palpatine's fear that these weapons could be turned against him. Palpatine created a command and control coding system that allowed him to seize control of them at any time. The New Republic was saved when Luke Skywalker provided these signals to R2-D2, who shut down the World Devastators on Mon Calamari, allowing the New Republic's forces to utterly destroy the helpless planet smashers.

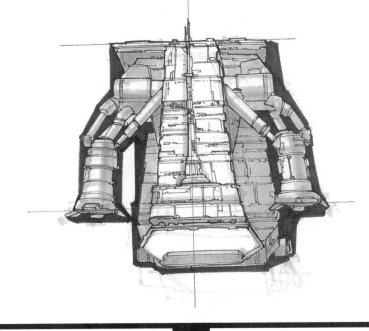

Front View

Side View

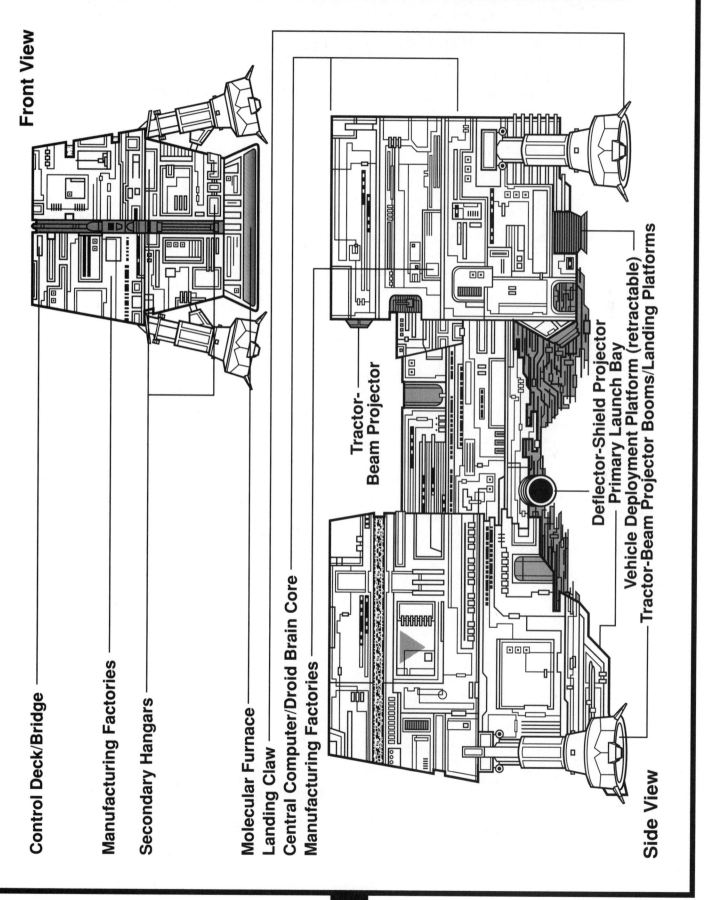

Control Deck/Bridge

Manufacturing Factories

Secondary Hangars

Molecular Furnace

Landing Claw

Central Computer/Droid Brain Core

Manufacturing Factories

Tractor-Beam Projector

Deflector-Shield Projector

Primary Launch Bay

Vehicle Deployment Platform (retractable)

Tractor-Beam Projector Booms/Landing Platforms

XP-38 LANDSPEEDER

SoroSuub XP-38 Sport Landspeeder

The XP-38 landspeeder, which is manufactured by the Sullustan company SoroSuub, is a popular landspeeder that can attain a top speed of over three hundred kilometers per hour. While they had been out for only a few months when Luke Skywalker left Tatooine, they had already become immensely popular even on that backwater desert planet. The XP-38's popularity decreased demand for older speeders, as Luke Skywalker discovered when he tried to sell his battered SoroSuub X-34 at a used speeder lot in Mos Eisley.

The XP-38 is a model that emphasizes smooth lines and sheer speed over practicality. As it has room for only a driver and passenger, it has been clearly aimed at the recreational market. Advertising has targeted younger customers, who often show a preference for style over value or durability.

The driver and passenger share a snug cockpit that features a retractable duraplex windscreen which opens to allow passengers to board. The optional sensor array is mounted on a swivel so that either the driver or the passenger can run the system, while displays can be viewed on the vidscreen or presented holographically. There is a small cargo compartment hidden behind the seats.

The XP-38 has a rear-mounted autopilot under the cowling, behind the pilot. The autopilot appears to be an Industrial Automaton R2 astromech droid, but this is a purely cosmetic effort designed to appeal to youngsters who seek the illusion that they are piloting a starfighter.

As with standard landspeeders, a repulsorlift generator produces lift and provides power to the turbine engines. The XP-38 sports a trio of rear-mounted turbine engines as well as twin maneuvering flaps and exhaust nacelles on the rear deck. The XP-38 has tight cornering ability and fantastic acceleration, making it a prize choice for those who engage in "neighborhood racing" against friends. It has a maximum hovering height of two meters, but drivers tend to set the speeder to hover at about one meter above the ground, following standard landspeeder repulsor altitudes. Engine noise is excessive, particularly by modern speeder standards, but that was considered a positive selling point with the target audience.

For all the hoopla about its performance, the XP-38 pulls many design features from earlier SoroSuub models such as the XP-38A and the Tx-37. A particular weakness it inherited is a very stiff repulsor generator setting. It's geared for performance but isn't durable enough for rough terrain, so the XP-38 is limited to extremely smooth surfaces. While the suspension can be recalibrated for rougher terrain, this can take up to three hours at a time. The control computer never seems to be able to properly reset suspension rates, either, so most owners just don't bother with the repulsor system.

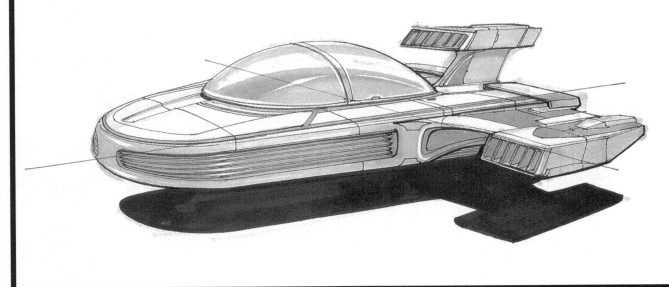

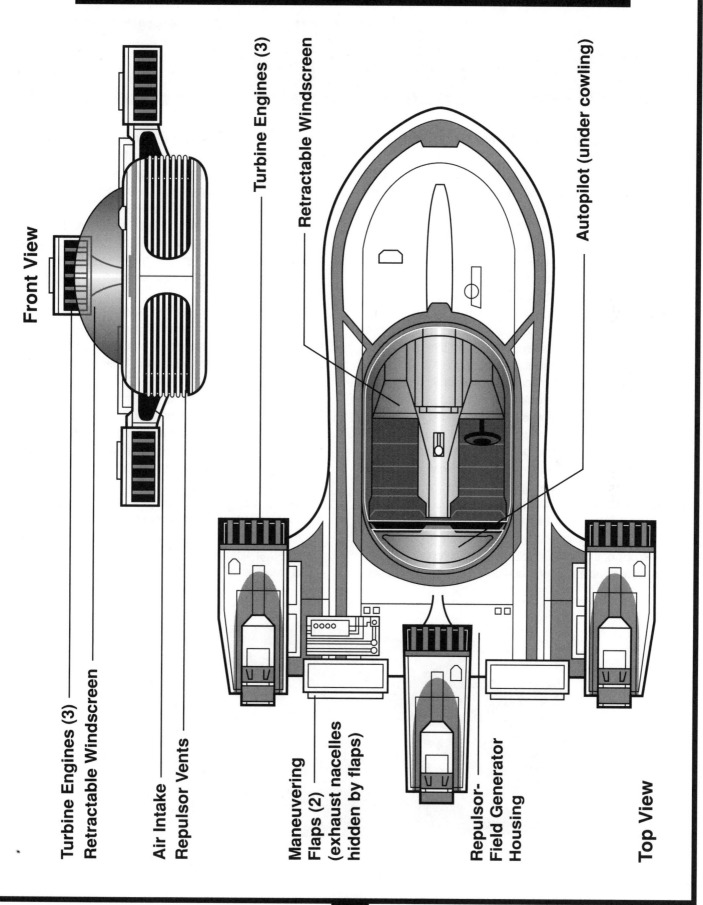

Front View

Turbine Engines (3)
Retractable Windscreen

Air Intake
Repulsor Vents

Turbine Engines (3)

Retractable Windscreen

Autopilot (under cowling)

Maneuvering
Flaps (2)
(exhaust nacelles
hidden by flaps)

Repulsor-
Field Generator
Housing

Top View

X-WING FIGHTER

Incom Corporation T-65 X-wing Space Superiority Fighter

The Rebel Alliance's X-wing starfighter was one of the most advanced fighters of its day when Luke Skywalker flew it into battle against the first Death Star. Many fighters have come along which are faster and more heavily armed, but the X-wing has been assured its place in history because of its role in that stunning Alliance victory.

Yet it's a miracle that the Alliance has the fighter at all. The T-65 X-wing was the last starfighter design produced by Incom Corporation before its seizure by the Empire. When the X-wing was in its final design stages, ISB (Imperial Security Bureau) agents began to suspect that members of Incom's design staff might have sympathies for the Rebel Alliance. A Rebel commando team helped Incom's senior design staff defect to the Alliance; the designers took with them all the plans and prototypes of the X-wing.

The X-wing takes its name from its pair of double-layered wings, deployed into the familiar X formation for combat. During normal sublight space flight, the double-layered wings are closed, giving the fighter the appearance of having only two wings. Each wingtip has a high-powered Taim & Bak KX9 laser cannon. The four cannons can be fired simultaneously, in sequence, or in pairs.

A pair of Krupx MG7 proton-torpedo launchers are located midway up the main spaceframe. Each carries a maga-zine of three torpedoes; those specialized weapons allowed the Alliance to destroy the Death Star. The battle station had thermal exhaust vents, unshielded against particle weapons such as proton torpedoes, meaning that a well-placed shot could cause a chain reaction to destroy the Death Star.

The X-wing is a small single-pilot fighter. An Industrial Automaton R2 astromech droid, housed in a snug droid socket behind the pilot, handles many in-flight operations, such as damage control, astrogation jumps, and flight performance adjustment.

The X-wing's controls are reminiscent of those of T-16 airspeeders and other common "sport" vehicles found on frontier worlds. Bush pilots train their reflexes on such vehicles and easily make the adjustment to the X-wing's familiar controls.

The X-wing is known for its durability, with a reinforced titanium-alloy hull and high-powered Chempat shield generators. It is a forgiving fighter and normally can take minor hits without a serious loss of performance. It has a full ejection system, and Alliance pilots have fully sealing suits and helmets.

Like the older Alliance Y-wing, X-wings have a hyperdrive for travel to other systems (the specific drive is an Incom GBk-585 unit). The R2 astromech unit can store up to ten sets of jump coordinates and handles all astrogation duties, because the X-wing lacks a navigation computer.

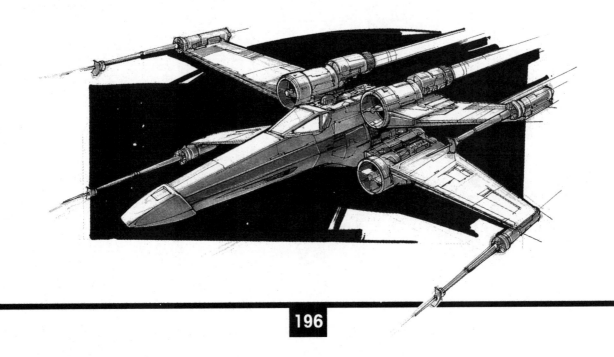

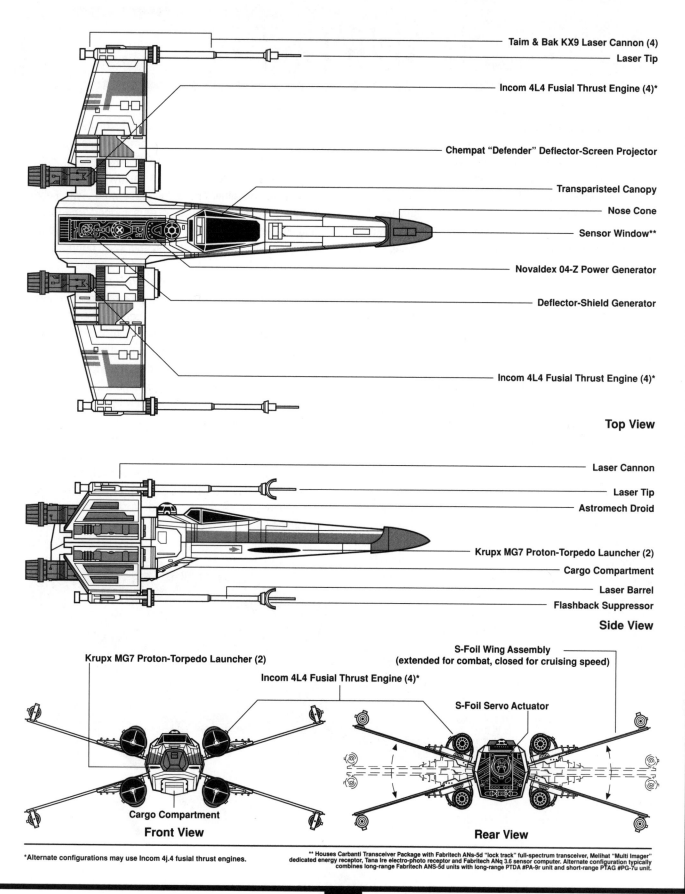

Taim & Bak KX9 Laser Cannon (4)

Laser Tip

Incom 4L4 Fusial Thrust Engine (4)*

Chempat "Defender" Deflector-Screen Projector

Transparisteel Canopy

Nose Cone

Sensor Window**

Novaldex 04-Z Power Generator

Deflector-Shield Generator

Incom 4L4 Fusial Thrust Engine (4)*

Top View

Laser Cannon

Laser Tip

Astromech Droid

Krupx MG7 Proton-Torpedo Launcher (2)

Cargo Compartment

Laser Barrel

Flashback Suppressor

Side View

Krupx MG7 Proton-Torpedo Launcher (2)

S-Foil Wing Assembly
(extended for combat, closed for cruising speed)

Incom 4L4 Fusial Thrust Engine (4)*

S-Foil Servo Actuator

Cargo Compartment

Front View

Rear View

*Alternate configurations may use Incom 4j.4 fusial thrust engines.

** Houses Carbanti Transceiver Package with Fabritech ANs-5d "lock track" full-spectrum transceiver, Melihat "Multi Imager"
dedicated energy receptor, Tana Ire electro-photo receptor and Fabritech ANq 3.6 sensor computer. Alternate configuration typically
combines long-range Fabritech ANS-5d units with long-range PTDA #PA-9r unit and short-range PTAG #PG-7u unit.

Y-WING FIGHTER

KOENSAYR BTL-S3 Y-WING ATTACK STARFIGHTER

The Y-wing is an older design, predating the X-wing and TIE/ln by several years. These fighters have a reputation for durability, and are in use at countless Rebel bases. Their limitations were made abundantly clear at the Battle of Yavin: only one fighter from Gold Squadron survived the battle. The Y-wing is easily recognized by its distinctive narrow central hull section and the two large engines set far away from the body.

Before the superior X-wing was introduced, Y-wings were the flagship fighters of the Rebel Alliance. They played a prominent role in the Battle of Vnas at Duro and the First Battle of Ord Biniir. Rebel Alliance Y-wings saved thousands of lives by holding off Imperial TIE bombers during the Siege of Ank Ki'Shor. Two squadrons of Y-wings were used at the Battle of Yavin, where the first Death Star was destroyed. As the Alliance gets more X-wings, Y-wing fighters are increasingly being shifted to outlying Rebel locations, and are more often being used for raids on Imperial convoys, rather than engagements with TIE fighters.

The Y-wing is a multipurpose vessel with a secondary mission profile as a light bomber. Y-wings are devastating in close-quarters combat, where their durability allows them to withstand several blasts.

It isn't uncommon for a Y-wing to be stripped down for assault runs against Imperial convoys, only to be refitted for a heavy bombing attack on an Imperial base just days later. Y-wings also are used on diplomatic escort missions, while the BTL-A4 Y-wing (LP), or *Longprobe*, has extra provisions and more powerful sensors for long-range patrol duty.

The Y-wing has three main components. The forward cockpit module is armored and houses the pilot's station and the weapons systems. A reinforced central spar stretches back from the cockpit mod-

ule; the Y-wing's Novaldex power generator and Koensayr R300-H hyperdrive unit are crammed into this narrow frame. A cross-wing houses the Thiodyne 03-R cryogenic power cells, with two powerful Koensayr R200 ion jet sublight drives on either end of the cross-wing. Twin Fabritech ANx-y long-range sensor arrays placed ahead of the engines feed data into the primary sensor array and targeting computer located between the laser cannons in the nose of the ship.

The pilot controls a pair of Taim & Bak IX4 laser cannons and twin Arakyd Flex Tube proton-torpedo launchers; a magazine of eight torpedoes can be fired from either launcher. In the BTL-S3, the most common Y-wing configuration, an ArMek SW-4 ion cannon turret sits directly behind the pilot and is normally handled by a weapons officer. The BTL-A4, an alternative Y-wing configuration, has only the pilot, with the ion cannon fixed directly fore or aft, to discourage close pursuit.

As in the X-wing, an R2 or R4 astromech droid fits snugly into the droid socket behind the cockpit and monitors all flight, navigation, and power systems. The droid also can handle fire control, perform in-flight maintenance, reroute power as needed, and stores hyperspace jump coordinates.

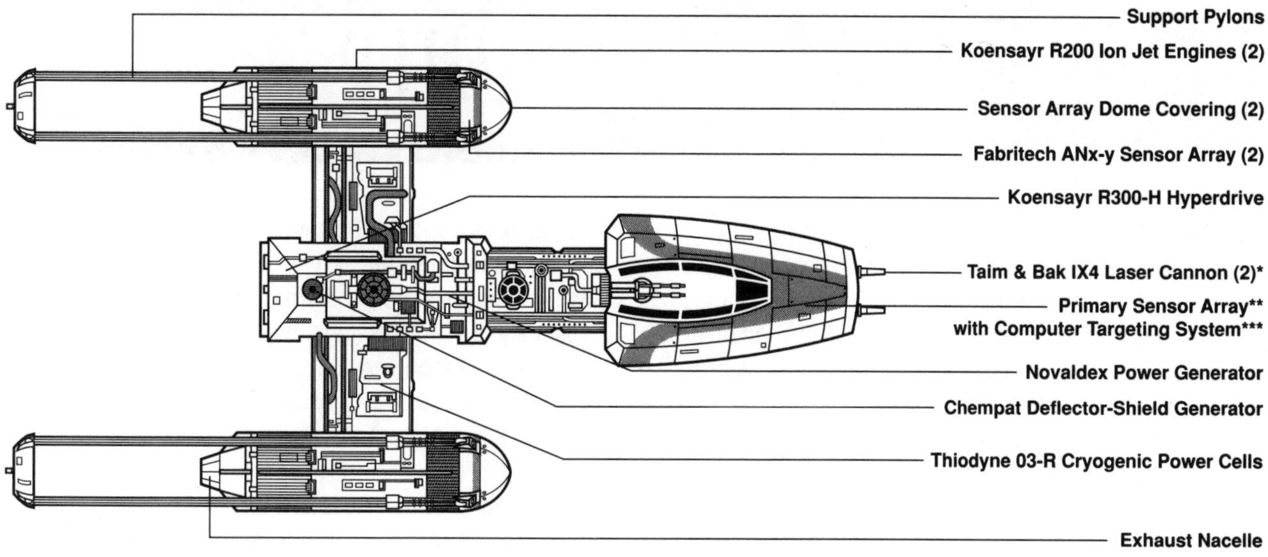

Support Pylons

Koensayr R200 Ion Jet Engines (2)

Sensor Array Dome Covering (2)

Fabritech ANx-y Sensor Array (2)

Koensayr R300-H Hyperdrive

Taim & Bak IX4 Laser Cannon (2)*

Primary Sensor Array**
with Computer Targeting System***

Novaldex Power Generator

Chempat Deflector-Shield Generator

Thiodyne 03-R Cryogenic Power Cells

Exhaust Nacelle

Top View

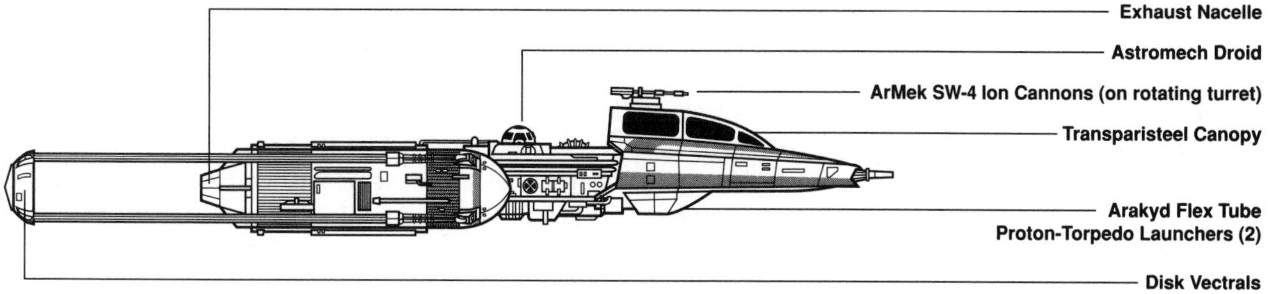

Exhaust Nacelle

Astromech Droid

ArMek SW-4 Ion Cannons (on rotating turret)

Transparisteel Canopy

Arakyd Flex Tube
Proton-Torpedo Launchers (2)

Disk Vectrals

Side View

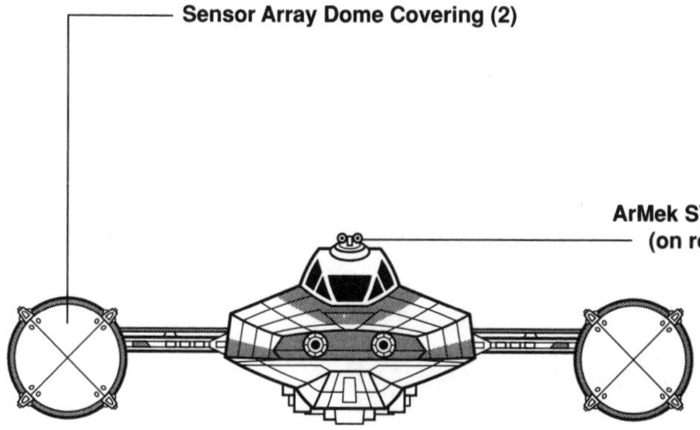

Sensor Array Dome Covering (2)

Steering Plates

Disk Vectrals

Engine Pylon

Astromech Droid

ArMek SW-4 Ion Cannons
(on rotating turret)

Thruster Control Jets

Front View

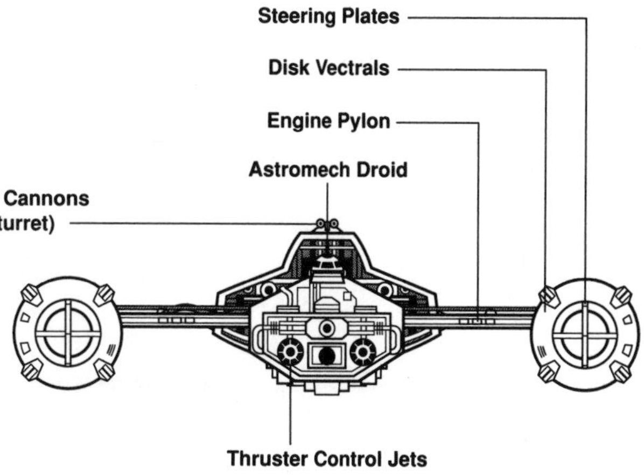

Rear View

*Alternate configurations may mount Taim & Bak
KX5 Laser Cannons

**Combines Fabritech ANs-5d unit with long-range
PTDA #PA-9r and short-range PTAG #PG-7u units.

***Combines Fabritech ANc-2.7 tracking computer
and SI 5g7 "Quickscan" vector-imaging system.

Z-95 HEADHUNTER

INCOM/SUBPRO Z-95 HEADHUNTER

The Z-95 Headhunter is one of the most common fighters in the galaxy despite the fact that the design is older than most starfighter pilots. The starfighter is maneuverable, and its durability is legendary. Headhunters often are found in planetary police forces, and many pirate and outlaw groups use these ships.

The original Z-95 Mark I Headhunter was designed as an atmospheric fighter craft that could be adapted to space travel. Mark I Headhunters are twin-engined swing-wing craft. The bubble cockpit gives the pilot a clear field of vision. Z-95s typically have a set of triple blasters on each wing. While Z-95 Mark Is aren't fast enough for space combat, their maneuverability gives them a clear advantage against starfighters that aren't streamlined for air combat.

Incom/Subpro designers made modest improvements with each model year, and the Z-95 fighters from the last production run are evenly matched against other fighters of that era. These later Headhunters are more likely to be found in operation today. The swing wings were replaced with fixed wings, although maneuverability was maintained by adding maneuvering jets. Another addition was a more heavily armored starfighter canopy much like the one used in the X-wing, while heads-up holographic tactical displays were improved. The last Z-95 models look like primitive X-wings, and with good reason—Incom's designers borrowed many Z-95 elements when designing the original X-wing fighter.

Countless variant Z-95 models have been built because the ship's technology is well understood, and starship mechanics have no problems modifying the ships. The most frequent modifications involve replacing the weapons systems or enhancing the motors for greater speed. For example, the Z-95-AF4 (Assault Fighter 4; pictured) has been refitted with Incom 2a fission engines and armed with two Taim & Bak KX5 laser cannons and a pair of Krupx MG5 concussion-missile launchers.

Z-95s are a good choice for defensive missions. Stripped-down Headhunters armed with concussion missiles can be used as assault ships. The Rebel Alliance used a number of Z-95 Headhunters for training missions because a pilot familiar with the controls of a Headhunter can quickly adapt to an X-wing or Y-wing. Remote Alliance bases also used Z-95s for defense to supplement Y-wing fighters.

Han Solo flew a Z-95 Mark I when he led the defense of an outlaw-tech base against Corporate Sector Authority fighters. Solo used the Z-95's superior atmospheric capabilities to good advantage against the Authority's sluggish IRD fighters.

Mara Jade uses a modified Z-95 Headhunter which has been equipped with a hyperdrive. That ship was nearly destroyed at the battle for the *Katana* fleet, but Talon Karrde's technicians were able to completely refurbish it, and Mara still uses it as her personal (and well-armed) courier ship.

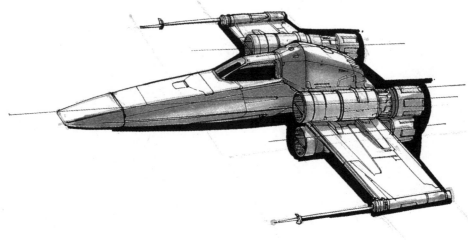

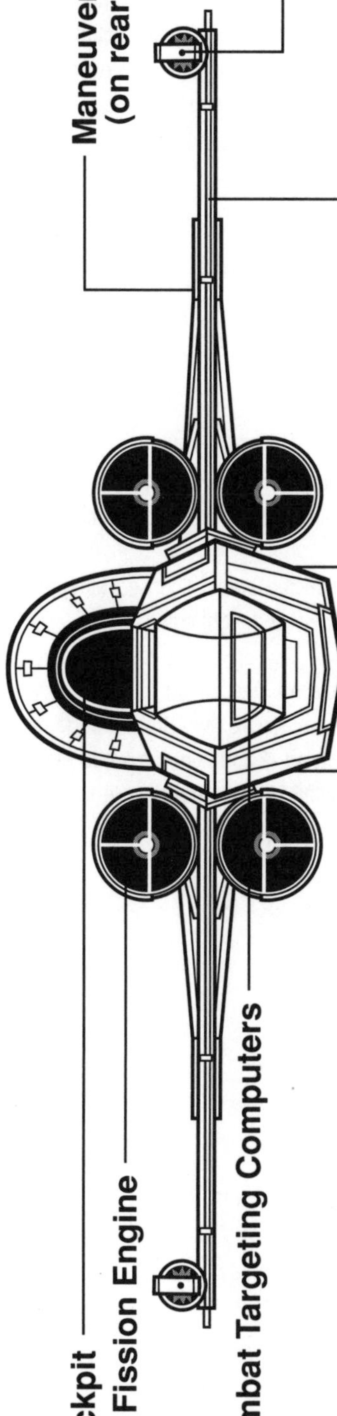

Front View

Maneuvering Jets (on rear of wing)

Laser Cannon

Wing

Cockpit

Ion Fission Engine

Combat Targeting Computers

Concussion-Missile Launchers

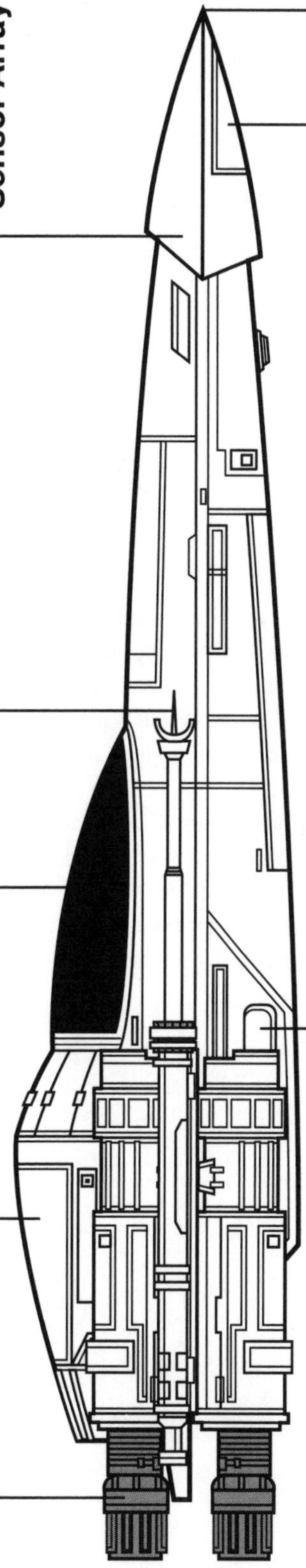

Ion Fission Engine

Cowling (protects main power generator)

Cockpit

Laser Cannon

Sensor Array

Concussion-Missile Launcher

Combat Targeting Computers

Nose Cone

Side View

About the Author

Bill Smith is the line editor for West End Games' popular *Star Wars* roleplaying game. Since joining the company in 1991, he has edited or designed over three dozen *Star Wars* games products, and his writing credits include the second edition of the roleplaying rules. He has also contributed to short-story anthologies and game supplements for the *Torg* and *Shatterzone* game lines. This is his first *Star Wars* work outside the roleplaying field. He lives in northeastern Pennsylvania.

About the Artists

Troy Vigil began drawing at age eight and cites the *Star Wars Trilogy* and its wondrous environments as the principle factors in his decision to pursue an art career. Each film chapter marked new directions in his personal life and current book/comic adventures continue to thrill and inspire him.

He began his professional career as a print production artist and has art directed studio licensed blueprint posters and portfolio sets. He lives in Venice Beach, California, with his partner, Stacey, and eight cats.

Doug Chiang has worked at Industrial Light & Magic since 1989 as Visual Effects Art Director on films such as *Terminator 2, Death Becomes Her,* and *Forrest Gump.* Chiang has earned an Academy Award, two British Academy Awards, and a Clio Award for his work. After serving as Creative Director for the ILM art department, he left to head up the art department for the next Star Wars. He is currently the Concept Art Director for the prequels. He lives in Northern California with his wife, Liz.